The
Cynical
Americans

Living and Working
in an Age
of Discontent
and Disillusion

Donald L. Kanter
Philip H. Mirvis

The Cynical Americans

Living and Working
in an Age
of Discontent
and Disillusion

 Jossey-Bass Publishers

San Francisco • London • 1989

THE CYNICAL AMERICANS
Living and Working in an Age of Discontent and Disillusion
by Donald L. Kanter and Philip H. Mirvis

Copyright © 1989 by: Jossey-Bass Inc., Publishers
350 Sansome Street
San Francisco, California 94104

&

Jossey-Bass Limited
28 Banner Street
London EC1Y 8QE

Library of Congress Cataloging-in-Publication Data

Kanter, Donald L. (Donald Lucky), date.
  The cynical Americans : living and working in an age of discontent
and disillusion / Donald L. Kanter, Philip H. Mirvis.
      p.   cm. — (Jossey-Bass management series)
  Bibliography: p.
  Includes index.
  ISBN 1-55542-150-4
  1. Industrial management—United States.   2. Work environment—
United States.   3. Work ethic—United States. 4. Cynicism.
I. Mirvis, Philip H., date. II. Title. III. Series.
HD70.U5K36   1989
306'.36'0973   88-46087
                                                            CIP

Manufactured in the United States of America

The paper in this book meets the guidelines for
permanence and durability of the Committee on
Production Guidelines for Book Longevity of the
Council on Library Resources.

JACKET DESIGN BY WILLI BAUM

FIRST EDITION

Code 8925

The Jossey-Bass
Management Series

Contents

Contents

to

Peggie Kanter

Harold Mirvis

Preface

If you read the management texts and journals, listen to the stories of older executives and union leaders, or reflect on the experiences of your parents and grandparents (and maybe your own experiences), you can come to believe there was *once* a time when people knew how to work and American business got the job done. Real old-timers hark back to the first decades of this century, when the great corporations were taking shape and wave upon wave of immigrants was coming to our golden land of opportunity. It is more common, however, to hear the *recent* past romanticized. Many look back on the 1950s and early 1960s as the "good old days."

During that era, there were plenty of opportunities to get a good job, to get ahead, to make something of oneself—or so the story goes. Industrial productivity was rising, and so were wages. Craftsmanship was alive and well, and people lived by their belief in a fair day's work for a fair day's recompense. Moreover, new systems and procedures were being introduced that made work easier and people more efficient.

Make no mistake—life in the factory was hard. But people got along: Corporate offices hummed with energy and esprit de corps. The bosses bossed and the workers worked. And people took pride in their labor, respected their superiors, and were loyal to their organizations. On the social front, the men brought home the bacon; the women worked for pin money; and the wives reared the kids and stayed at home.

That is *one* story of American industry in this period. It is corporate life seen through rose-colored glasses. There is, of course, quite another way to recollect our industrial history. Ask old-timers about working conditions in the early 1900s and the Great Depression in the 1930s. Likely as not, you will get a painful earful. Ask the average working man or woman about his or her job in the 1950s: We have found that the rosy depiction just mentioned hardly matches everyday reality.

Yes, there were plenty of opportunities, but the veterans of World War II had to scratch for them. The most motivated and lucky ones found jobs as engineers, accountants, middle managers, top salespeople (white-collar work) in growing corporations. Blue-collar workers who had the training and connections to get a job in a unionized factory were lucky, too. But many were not so fortunate.

Businesses were forming conglomerates and reducing their ranks. Consequently, a great many older, dedicated workers and managers were given early retirement. The men who did not go to a university or learn a skilled trade could get jobs only as pencil pushers in an office or as the muscle in a factory. Their pay was low and their prospects were dim. Furthermore, there were few opportunities open to women or members of minorities who wanted to get ahead.

Certainly there were gains in American productivity and efficiency in this period, but not because of good management; rather, many say, this progress occurred in spite of management. The ranks of business were being swollen by corporate staff men—quintessential bureaucrats who added no direct value to products and services and who instituted rules and procedures that only got in the way. Managers surrounded themselves with other managers—adding much to their budget, entourage, and seeming importance but little to the bottom line. Corporations were peopled by organization men—clones who would play it safe and, ultimately, put American business at risk in the face of global competition in the next decades.

Some of the harmony in business was just a mirage. Top managers got the big money, the fancy offices, and the handsome perks. They could afford to be the workers' friends. But down the line the managers and supervisors could boss any way they pleased. And plenty of them were petty tyrants, heel grinders, and yes-men.

People worked, but mostly to earn a living and, in many instances, mainly because the boss was watching. Ordinary work was numbing, and many "clocked out" their intelligence and ideas, not to mention their identities, as they "clocked in" at work. Furthermore, rigid role definitions, at work and at home, were setting the stage for future strife—when people would break out of those roles in the next decade and corporations would misunderstand and resist them.

This is, of course, the jaundiced view of work—the story as seen through the lens of cynicism. It is the *other* way of looking at life in the 1950s and early 1960s. Some readers may hold a more upbeat image of this and earlier eras. No doubt many will find grains of truth in both the upbeat and the jaundiced way of looking at the workplace. Our point is that the lens people use to see the world—in society or in their work—colors their sense of the past and certainly their views of the present. However one chooses to look at the work force and workplace, there are ample signs today of disaffection and discontent that we read as earmarks of cynicism.

Overview of the Contents

We introduce this volume with a look at how cynical tendencies in America are growing into a consensus worldview with implications for society, business, and the workplace. In the introduction, we describe the cynical mind-set and signs of cynicism in everyday life. We show why cynicism is on the increase in America and illustrate how hyped-up hopes lead to disillusionment when leaders and institutions fail to deliver. Readers are invited to complete a survey on cynicism and see how their ratings compare with national trends.

Part One examines various cynical "types" in the work force and describes how cynicism is cultivated in companies and in modern society. In Chapter One, we diagnose several cynical types, including Command Cynics at the top of company hierarchies and Hard-Bitten Cynics at the bottom. We also describe Articulate Players and Squeezed Cynics; the young, up-and-coming hustlers and the downbeat, downwardly mobile types; as well as ruthless, rule-conscious Administrative Sideliners and Obstinate Stoics. We consider how cynicism helps these individuals adapt to their environments and maintain their self-pictures.

In Chapter Two, we describe the characteristics and values of the cynical organization. Brief case studies highlight the mismanagement of expectations in an R&D lab, dead-end disillusionment in retail operations, unbridled ambition in a marketing department, and sources of suspicion and mistrust in a manufacturing makeover. These illustrate how "vision-killing" managers promote greed over ideals and how shoddy goods and services can be traced to cynical company cultures.

In Chapter Three, we show how cynicism has spiraled up and down in twentieth-century American life to the point that it has become an endemic part of the psyche in the 1980s. This chapter examines how America's recovery from the Great Depression and victory in World War II gave way to a letdown in the 1950s, the constraining life-style of the organization man, and the cold war cynicism of McCarthyism. We show how high hopes were renewed in the 1960s and then dashed by political assassinations, the Vietnam War, and Watergate. We conclude the chapter with an analysis of the cynical decade of the 1980s and the trend toward the "Europeanizing" of America, which has led to lowered standards and heightened self-interest.

Part Two focuses on the roots of cynicism in America's industrial history and its growth in modern organizations. In Chapter Four, we show how the transition from the Moral

Reform movement in early American industry to an era of exploitation provided fertile soil for cynicism. We look at how the hopes engendered by scientific management were dashed by guileful industrialists and how human relations–style management was undermined by the many inhuman characteristics of bureaucracies.

In Chapter Five, we compare the rising expectations of the new work force with management's failure to meet them. The chapter illustrates the growing gap between what people want and what they get from their jobs, the folly of humanistic management theory, and the failings of human resource management.

In Chapter Six, we contrast the search for excellence with industrial realities today. In this chapter, we look at the emergence of the Articulate Player and the Squeezed Cynic—winners and losers in the 1980s—and at the contradictions inherent between expanding psyches and a constraining economy.

Part Three reports on the prevalence of cynicism in major segments of the population and examines how the cynical outlook colors people's dealings with their bosses and peers and their views of their jobs and organizations. In Chapter Seven, we present data, drawn from a national survey, on the prevalence of cynicism in the population today. We compare cynicism across age groups and among men versus women and whites versus minorities, and we examine its prevalence among distinct socioeconomic groups and across different life-styles and regions of the country.

Chapter Eight compares cynicism across occupations and industries. This chapter examines attitudes of cynical versus upbeat workers on trust in management and in co-workers, as well as on fairness, management communication, and company life. The chapter highlights the corrosive impact of cynicism on work attitudes.

In Chapter Nine, we present data on Americans' work ethic, self-reliance, and ambition. We compare the strength of cynicism with that of traditional values as ingredients in work attitudes. The results of this comparison show the importance of reinforcing traditional values while taking steps to counter cynicism at work.

Part Four considers how organizations can counteract cynicism and regain trust and confidence. In Chapter Ten, we contrast company cultures founded on cynical realism with those based on realistic idealism, and we list the values of the upbeat company. We look at the importance of company credos and risks of violating them and how to counteract fatalism and instill a sense of community. A case study of Ben & Jerry's Ice Cream shows how to cultivate a positive culture, and a look at the merger of Burroughs and Sperry into Unisys shows how to recreate an upbeat outlook and restore people's confidence in the organization.

Chapter Eleven discusses how to instill realistic expectations and channel ambition toward desirable ends. We explore why people are cynical about their pay, management's trustworthiness, their company's *modus operandi,* and who controls their time—and what to do about that. A case study of Caterpillar Tractor illustrates how to formulate a new psychological contract between employees and management. In addition, we examine Graphic Controls's audit of its human organization to show how people can proactively make their company more effective and a better place to work.

In Chapter Twelve, we show how, specifically, to communicate to a cynical workplace by planning message delivery. Lessons that managers need to learn about anticipating and relating to the cynical mind-set are derived from communications and marketing theory.

In the epilogue, we show how more upbeat and salutary developments in society and the workplace provide a basis for realistic hope and for counteracting cynical tendencies in the populace and the work force. The epilogue concludes with a description of the key intrinsic values that need to be resurrected and reinforced by leaders, managers, unionists, and everyday working people to give idealism its voice and its proper place in American and company life.

Given that cynicism is actively at work in Washington and on Wall Street and being passively bred into disillusioned Middle America, there is a need for a book that sheds light on the current managerial mind-set and public mood. No publication to date has highlighted the corrosive spread and implications of cynicism in the work force. Nor has any shown, through survey data and case studies, how cynicism impedes commitment, cooperation, communication, and contribution in companies today. This book talks to real problems and presents viable actions to be taken by management, unions, government, executives, and workers who are interested in people and concerned about the future.

It will be easy to read this volume and conclude that we are crape-hangers. Gloom and doom tend to permeate our analyses of cynicism in American life. So let us acknowledge that people *adapt* to their environments in many ways in order to sustain their personal equilibrium and maintain their self-picture and self-esteem. Cynicism is but one means of adapting to life's vicissitudes. We acknowledge that, for some, cynicism is a viable adaptive mechanism. But in our view, skepticism is as functional, less restrictive, and more generous. We are neither determinists nor pessimists. This is only to say that personal cynicism may be leavened and, in the best of circumstances, transformed into a more generous view of humankind. We also believe that cynical forces in society can be managed or, at minimum, offset by high-minded political and corporate leadership and by credible and humanly responsive public and private institutions. That, in essence, is where we stand and why we have written this book.

Acknowledgments

This book has a long history—as do most books that try to take a series of disparate facts and observations and from them define a central socioeconomic and moral problem. It has perforce had many benefactors and contributors, none of whom bears responsibility for the final outcome.

To the Interpublic Group of Companies, and to Lester A. Delano in particular, go our initial thanks for subsidizing a study of European attitudes that provided a starting point for our investigation of national character. Gregory Wood and Mark Agostini, principals of Diagnostic Research, Inc., provided funds and facilities for the national survey of life and work attitudes reported in this book. In this they were joined by Stephen A. Greyser of the Harvard Business School, who contributed generously both money and mind. Fred Foulkes, head of the Human Resource Policy Institute at Boston University, who partially funded the statistical analysis, was also a valued supporter.

For analytic counsel throughout this project, from its inception as a study of national character to its reconception as a book on cynicism, our gratitude goes to members of the Committee on Research Development. Richard Dunnington contributed significantly to the study's design; Edward Hackett and Harold Salzman helped us through successive stages of statistical analysis; and Dennis Perkins gave us valuable commentary on early drafts.

Ann Rawson Kanter helped synthesize early differences between our two points of view, and Katherine Farquhar, Alexa, and Lucy kept us from devolving further into the cynical mindset, as did Sarah, James, and Liz. Maureen Mahoney provided early research assistance. Jennifer Bump, Rachel Kligerman, and Charity Quinn assisted importantly in preparing the manuscript. We extend our special thanks to Scott Hutchison, who incisively and fortunately put his editorial talents to work on the text.

Donald Kanter wishes to extend personal appreciation to David Chambers of the London Business School for hosting his lectures on cynicism. Comments from students helped us distill our thinking. Lastly, during a time of trial in London, some English friends—Dean Barry, Jules Goddard, and Elizabeth Nelson—stiffened a sagging upper lip by focusing attention on the incipient manuscript. Kanter expresses special gratitude to Professor John Goodwin, whose example of science and humanity helped write this book. Lastly, to the neighbors in Belton-in-Rutland, who endured the trials of authorship: hearty cheers.

Boston, Massachusetts	Donald L. Kanter
February 1989	Philip H. Mirvis

The Authors

Donald L. Kanter is chair of the Department of Marketing of the School of Management, Boston University. He received his B.S. degree (1948) from Northwestern University in psychology, his M.A. degree (1950) from the University of Nebraska in psychology, and his Ph.D. degree (1953) from the University of Connecticut in social psychology.

Previously, Kanter was chair of the Department of Marketing at the University of Southern California. Prior to beginning his academic career, Kanter was vice-president of marketing services in advertising agencies in London, New York, Chicago, and Los Angeles. He has been a visiting professor at the London Business School (where his studies in cynicism originated). He is active in international consulting in America and in Europe.

Philip H. Mirvis is a private researcher and consultant. He received his B.A. degree (1973) from Yale University in administrative science and his Ph.D. degree (1980) from the University of Michigan in psychology. He has been with the Center for Applied Social Science, Boston University, and the Survey Research Center, Institute for Social Research, University of Michigan.

Mirvis's research concerns human behavior in organizations and focuses on the changing character of the work force and workplace. He has published widely for academic and professional audiences; edited, authored, or coauthored several books, including *Failures in Organization Development and Change* (1977, with D. Berg); and created a "map" and guidebook to *Work in the 20th Century* (1984).

Mirvis has lectured in China, India, and Japan and to faculties at leading universities in the United States and Canada.

The
Cynical
Americans

Living and Working
in an Age
of Discontent
and Disillusion

Introduction:
Cynicism
in American Life

Ours is not the best of all possible worlds, and cockeyed optimism is not the smart way to look at things. Threat is the operative perception: threat to survival, savings, status, and self-esteem. Self-interest and opportunism mark today's clued-up person. Suspicion is on the rise. Trust is on the wane.

It will take time, and leadership, to regain the middle ground between untempered idealism and gothic misanthropy. Surely this is skepticism, a tendency to disbelieve but a willingness to be convinced.[1] At our best we are a nation of skeptics: hard-nosed but open-minded, realistic in real time but ever mindful of timeless ideals. By contrast, cynics are close-minded and disillusioned. They cast aspersions upon those they deal with and believe that people are self-centered and self-serving. America is sliding into widespread cynicism today.

Some 43 percent of the American populace fit the profile of the cynic, who sees selfishness and fakery at the core of human

1

nature. We base this conclusion on the results of a national survey we conducted whose findings we report here. The survey shows that cynics mistrust politicians and most authority figures, regard the average person as false-faced and uncaring, and conclude that you should basically look out for yourself. Cynical tendencies are growing into a consensus worldview with implications for society, commerce, and the workplace. Cynics at work deeply doubt the truth of what their managements tell them and believe that their companies, given a chance, will take advantage of them.

Much has been said about the momentous decline in people's work attitudes the past three decades, the loss of loyalty and the rise in self-dealing, and the growing cleavages between the haves and have-nots, the well educated and the lesser skilled, the high-tech operators and the sour service deliverers. In all of this are to be found earmarks of cynicism at work. Here we will see how widespread the cynical outlook is in the American work force, what a lack of trust and probity means in the modern workplace, and what might be done to redress wrongs and regain credibility—American style.

American organizations today are restructuring and reshaping themselves, with an emphasis on improving quality, reducing costs, and regaining competitive vitality. At best, cynics adopt a chary "wait and see" attitude to these initiatives. At worst, their negativism produces a self-fulfilling prophecy that foredooms any management message, customer promotion, or proposed improvement. Overall, this corrosive attitude diminishes country and community and, in business, shrinks the fabric of organization life.

Our reasons for studying cynics in the workplace revolve around their mistrust of management, their readiness to disparage fellow workers, their predilections for rumor-mongering and backstabbing, and in many cases their ingrained resistance to change.[2] These workers and managers are hard to reach and harder still to enlist. They mistrust the motives of those in charge and look out for number one when called to action. But we believe that they can be reached and won over to better serve customers, companies, and the commonweal. A starting point is to understand the cynical outlook and its ingredients.

There are three key ingredients in the development of the cynical outlook. One is the formulation of unrealistically high expectations, of oneself and/or of other people, which generalize to expectations of society, institutions, authorities, and the future. A second is the experience of disappointment, in oneself and in others, and consequent feelings of frustration and defeat. Finally, there is disillusion, the sense of being let down or of letting oneself down, and, more darkly, the sense of being deceived, betrayed, or used by others. Turning their disillusion inward, cynics fear they might be seen as naive or be taken for suckers.

Clinical experience suggests that people's expectations and hopes, as well as their disappointments and disillusionment, are shaped by basic biological and social aspects of their development. Certainly cynicism is conditioned by early parenting, youthful socialization, and patterns of reinforcement throughout life. In a psychological sense, then, cynicism is simply one way that people cope with life, not only with certain personal experiences or the broadest of social trends influencing them, but also with everyday life transactions. Like any worldview, it is functional and adaptive: It guides the way that some people acclimate to culture, society, and workplace and relate to their peers, subordinates, and superiors.[3]

It should be apparent, too, that cynicism is a reaction to and barrier against culturally induced and socially reinforced hopes that have been dashed. We live in an imperfect and, some would say, hopelessly materialistic and shamelessly manipulative society that bears false witness to our ideals. Cynicism does not begin or end with everyday people and their psyches. It is, so to speak, part of everyday life around us.

Cynicism and Everyday Life

Daily events continue to reflect and reinforce national mistrust and the cynical outlook. To cite a few of the feature news stories of the past few years is to show just how the reservoirs of cynicism are kept filled:

- Lawbreaking in the Iran arms deal and the opportunistic diversion of funds to the contras
- Insider trading on Wall Street (the Ivan Boesky scandal), followed by the Pentagon arms procurement indictments
- Drug dealing by the head of state in Panama, with seeming U.S. complicity
- Philandering and fraud by pious electronic preachers
- Coverup in the Challenger tragedy by the parts manufacturer and NASA
- A national debt and trade deficit threatening the American standard of living
- Negativism and distortion characterizing an "issueless" 1988 presidential campaign, which had the lowest voter turnout in modern times.

To the extent that these past few years represent the tenor of the times, one may get some flavor of the media's contributions to an already cynical society from the news alone. This flavor tastes of duplicity and deceit by politicians and their handlers and of larceny and greed by brokers and "Beltway bandits." Unresolved questions linger in the case of the Iran arms deal, the Panamanian drug scandal, and the Challenger tragedy that undermine standards of truth and justice. Meanwhile, rampant drug abuse, street crime, and gang warfare, along with the AIDS crisis, threaten the "American way." In all, this is a dispiriting and disillusioning picture.

But this is hardly the only contribution to cynicism that the media environment makes daily or weekly by legitimately telling a democratic society what is happening in and around it. In addition to the national news, the local TV news emphasizes crime and disaster, albeit lessened by "happy talk" and leavened by the occasional inspirational story. Furthermore, advertising, pop music, and films, as well as programming, feed the cynical mind-set. Advertising, for example, which is omnipresent, hawks possessions and celebrity routinely, as if they were cultural imperatives. This makes it necessary, psychologically and economically, for a substantial minority to disbelieve ads. If people cannot trust television and advertisers, whom can they trust? Packaged politicians? Packaged preachers? Or even packaged goods?

At the same time, radio and tapes reach younger people with lyrics that are cynical about time-honored institutions and preach world-weary messages about the phoniness of family life, school, work, and citizenship. Films and TV programs do their share by portraying contemporary society as a jungle where street smarts, save for an occasional mawkish lapse, are the only thing that helps one survive in a violent, dishonest world.

But the inputs of the media environment do not in themselves constitute the raw materials of society; they are simply delivery systems. The media reflect the substance of society at least as much as they shape it, and changes in our political, economic, and religious institutions, our values and attitudes, all seem to embody signs of a more cynical citizenry and public.

Signs of Cynicism in a Changed America

On this point, Daniel Yankelovich, a noted social analyst, reported in 1978: "We have seen a steady rise of mistrust in our national institutions. . . . Trust in government declined dramatically from almost 80% in the late '50s to about 33% in 1976. More than 61% of the electorate believe that there is something morally wrong in the country. More than 80% of voters say they do not trust those in positions of leadership as much as they used to."[4] The statistics are even more depressing today. Harris polls show that confidence in the Supreme Court, Congress, and the executive branch, in state and local government, and in organized religion and the press declined precipitously from 1966 to 1974 to 1986. We have the lowest rate of voter participation of all industrialized nations. To many eyes, the system simply doesn't work anymore.

Nowhere have the decline in confidence and rise in mistrust been more evident than in people's attitudes about business and its leadership. Confidence in business and business leadership has fallen from approximately a 70 percent level in the late 1960s to about 15 percent today. Many fewer people today than eight years ago believe that business is doing a good job of investing its money or providing steady work for employees. Fewer think that business is hiring, developing, or retaining the best management. Paeans to free enterprise notwithstanding, business gets even lower marks than government in ratings of public approbation.

This is a sign of more than a letdown. People are worried. Only one in four Americans believes that we can compete with foreign businesses. The attitude seems to be shared by top business officials: A majority believes that the Japanese produce higher-quality products and services than we do, and 75 percent say Japanese workers are more productive than Americans. People are angry. Nearly 80 percent say that business doesn't pay its fair share of taxes, and 70 percent say it doesn't see to it that its executives behave ethically. And people feel ripped off. Most Americans think they get "poor value" from the products and services they purchase. This perception applies, too, to evaluations of doctor, dentist, and lawyer fees, to used cars, auto repairs, and auto insurance, to movies and children's toys, to almost everything we buy, save foodstuffs and ice cream. All these are earmarks of disillusionment.

Harris polls have measured alienation almost every year since 1966. The number of people who say, "What I think doesn't count anymore," "The people running the country don't really care what happens to me," "The rich get richer and the poor get poorer," and "Most people with power try to take advantage of people such as myself" has doubled over the last two decades. The average figure for those expressing disaffection on a combination of these items increased from 29 percent in 1966 to over 60 percent today.

There are further signs of cynicism in 1980s American life: Church attendance has fallen; divorce rates remain high; and there is more income tax evasion than ever before.[5] At the same time, the polarization of the rich and the poor has been exacerbated; America has become a debtor nation as both the national debt and the trade deficit have risen astronomically; national priorities emphasize a military buildup at the expense of a broad federal health plan; there is not nearly enough adequate child care for working parents; and aid to education has been reduced. The Catholic church has been in turmoil over birth control while the moral influence of all religions has declined, except among evangelicals and those born again (who themselves are now experiencing disenchantment).

In our view, cynical people make for cynical societies (and, as we shall see, cynical companies, too). But the question of whether individual cynicism is cause or consequence of the national malaise, the loss of confidence, and the many other signs of discontent and distrust in America today is moot: Cynical individuals are being encased in a cynical environment.

Of course, the human condition has always faced some threat to its equilibrium, and the pendulum has always, sooner or later, swung back to the point where goodwill and generosity seem to predominate in American society. But these current threats are especially ominous because our political supports have been weakened while the support of the extended family has waned. Moreover, the tendency to behave cynically is being reinforced to an unprecedented degree by a social environment that seems to have abandoned idealism and increasingly celebrates the virtue of being "realistic" in an impersonal, acquisitive, tough-guy world. In citizen and country alike, there seems to be a loss of faith in people and in the very concept of community. Upbeat aspirations for togetherness seem hollow in the selfish 1980s. Cynicism is not a new phenomenon, but today it is especially pronounced.

National Survey of Workers

Surprisingly, the makeup of the cynic and the attitudes that define the cynical personality have not been specifically studied by behavioral and social scientists or by clinical psychologists and psychiatrists. There are, however, several instruments that measure personality traits characteristic of cynicism. Wrightsman's measures of people's "philosophies of human nature" assess attitudes about trustworthiness and altruism. Rosenberg created an index of "faith in people" that measures attitudes about people's honesty, goodness, and generosity.[6] Furthermore, there are various instruments to measure misanthropy, selfishness, and Machiavellian inclinations. Our research draws on these studies and aims to provide a sharper picture of the cynic's outlook and profile in the American work force.

We questioned a cross section of Americans about their attitudes toward people and toward their work through a tele-

phone survey. The survey was administered by Diagnostic
Research, Inc., a marketing and public opinion research company. It began with a pilot study, completed in June 1983, and
the data to be reported here were collected in July and August
of that year. The phone interview began with an introduction
of the interviewer and a request that respondents express their
"opinions about the life-styles and attitudes in the country today." Each interview lasted between twenty and thirty minutes.

Interviewers collected basic demographic data on the
respondents, such as their sex, race, age, marital status, and
the like, as well as information on their education and income.
The national probability sample consisted of 850 persons in total.
Students and retired people were not sampled. Eliminating non-
working spouses, the analyses concentrate on the 649 who were
employed at the time of the survey. The contours of the employed sample closely match those of the American work force.
Respondents ranged in age from eighteen to seventy and represented proportionately all the major occupational groups and
employment sectors in the country. (A description of the sample
is reported in Appendix A.)

In the body of the interview, we asked respondents a
number of questions about their attitudes toward people and
about their jobs and work situations. These questions were
phrased in the form of a statement, and respondents were asked
to rate how much they agreed or disagreed with the statement
on a four- or five-point scale ranging from "strongly agree"
to "strongly disagree." (The indexes created from individual
questions appear in Appendixes B and C.)

How Much Cynicism Is There?

To help the reader assess our findings on how much cynicism
there is in America, we provide a self-assessment instrument
in Exhibit 1, which contains the statements that make up the
index of cynicism used here. Do you believe that most people
will tell a lie if they can gain by it? That most people claim to
have standards of honesty and morality, but few stick to them
when money is at stake? That people pretend to care about one

Exhibit 1. A Survey of Cynicism.

Here are some statements about how you may or may not feel about other people. Please check the box to the right of each statement to show how much you agree or disagree with the statement. A "1" means that you *strongly agree* with the statement and a "4" means that you *strongly disagree* with it. You may check any number from 1 to 4.

	Strongly Agree	Slightly Agree	Slightly Disagree	Strongly Disagree
How much do you agree that . . . ?				
Most people will tell a lie if they can gain by it.	(1)	(2)	(3)	(4)
People claim to have ethical standards regarding honesty and morality, but few stick to them when money is at stake.	(1)	(2)	(3)	(4)
People pretend to care more about one another than they really do.	(1)	(2)	(3)	(4)
It's pathetic to see an unselfish person in today's world because so many people take advantage of him or her.	(1)	(2)	(3)	(4)
Most people are just out for themselves.	(1)	(2)	(3)	(4)
Most people inwardly dislike putting themselves out to help other people.	(1)	(2)	(3)	(4)
Most people are not really honest by nature.	(1)	(2)	(3)	(4)

another more than they really do? We urge you to complete this survey before turning to the results for the national probability sample.

What do American workers say about their attitudes toward other people? Some 60 percent agree (either strongly or slightly) that people will tell a lie if they can gain by it. As many agree that people pretend to care more than they really do (58 percent) and that people claim to be honest and moral but fall short when money is at stake (62 percent). A smaller proportion believe that people are just out for themselves (46 percent) and that most people are not really honest by nature (34 percent). (A full profile of responses appears in Appendix D.) On the basis of answers to these questions, we divided the sample into three categories—the cynics, the wary, and the upbeat—reflecting people's degree of cynicism (see Figure 1).

Figure 1. Profile of the Work Force.

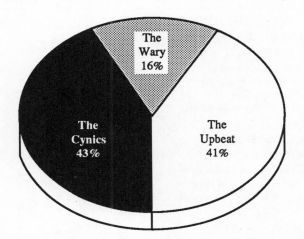

The group we call cynics strongly agree with the majority of the statements making up the index. We find that 43 percent of the American working population fit the profile of the cynic, who, to put it simply, believes that lying, putting on a false face, and doing whatever it takes to make a buck are all part of our basic human nature. Many no doubt justify their sour outlook by seeing themselves as "realists." Indeed, Ambrose Bierce defined the cynic as "a blackguard whose faulty vision sees things as they are, not as they ought to be."[7] Yet a substantial segment are unvarnished cynics who see selfishness as fundamental to people's character and believe that people inwardly dislike putting themselves out for others. They also believe that the unselfish are taken advantage of in today's world and think that people are simply dishonest by nature.

A second group, 16 percent of the population, we characterize as the wary. The wary tend to slightly agree or slightly disagree with the statements making up the cynicism index. Thus they believe that people are motivated primarily, but not solely, by self-interest and have a less suspicious, more circumspect opinion of the honesty and intentions of their fellowman.

Finally, in the third group, we find 41 percent of the working population to be basically upbeat about people. They have a sunnier view of human nature and ascribe a measure of idealism and fellow feeling to other people. While this group no doubt includes some Pollyannas, it is also populated by many who simply delight in others' humanity. Sam Walter Foss depicted their life orientation in his poem *The House by the Side of the Road:*

Let me live in my house by the side of the road
Where the race of men go by;
They are good, they are bad, they are weak, they are strong,
Wise, foolish—so am I.
Then why should I sit in the scorner's seat,
Or hurl the cynic's ban?
Let me live in my house by the side of the road
And be a friend to man.[8]

The Cynical Cycle

Our thesis is that cynicism permeates a society whenever the high hopes of many are raised and frustrated and their deep disappointment gives way to disillusion. While the signs of cynicism in American society are apparent enough, there are indications that the cynical cycle has come full circle in the 1980s. The Reagan administration promised lower taxes, more effective national leadership, a balanced budget, and the chance for America to feel good about itself again, all wrapped in the "Morning in America" theme. It worked during President Reagan's first term. Historian Alan Brinkley wrote, "America's upbeat mood . . . is not, as some have charged, a media creation, but a significant change in public perception." In the last years of the administration, however, public approval ratings (not likability) of the president plummeted, and critics suggested that it was "the morning after." Barbara Lipsett writes that the climate was "cynical as hell."[9]

This sea change in public opinion contrasts with the wave of cynicism that washed over the country during the Great Depression. It was a quarter-century in the making and took years to fully grip the American psyche. The next wave, the disillusionment of the baby boomers, was fifteen years in coming and was fully realized only with the reelection of Richard Nixon and the Watergate affair. The current wave of disillusion, by contrast, has been comparatively compact and rapid-fire. What can account for this?

Certainly media coverage of politicians' promises and failings has become more widespread and instantaneous. Public polling may, in its fashion, not only be documenting but also creating faster-paced changes in the outlook of the American public. Influences on public attitudes go well beyond the thirty-minute newscast, however, and the public's mood runs deeper than is accounted for by political pollsters. To understand what is behind the emotional booms and busts that produce widespread cynicism, we need to look, first, at our hopes and how they are inflated to unreal and unrealizable levels, which in turn leads to their inevitable disappointment.

Hopes and Hype. In a sense, Americans are great "marks" for a con job. Polls show that most people have a relatively high opinion of themselves and an optimistic outlook on the future.[10] This makes depictions of the good life especially alluring because "having it all" seems possible and "going for the gusto" fits our self-picture. It also sets us up for disappointment.

Every society whose members are so susceptible to temptation depends upon personal inhibitions and cultural restraints to maintain itself. To the extent that religion has traditionally restrained people from the occasions of sin, values cultivated in the home and at the hearth have also kept us from being carried away by hedonistic fads and taken advantage of spiritually and financially. There was, for example, not too long ago in this country an ethic of sacrificing for one's offspring and for the sake of the future. Life seemed to be more measured and slower paced. People were urged to have patience, to be wary of false prophets, and to save for a rainy day.

By contrast, many observers have made the point that we live in an "instantaneous society" today, where time is com-

pressed and patience is at a minimum.[11] Ours is an age of instant friendships and intimacy, instant commitment to causes
and movements, and instant access to information, analysis,
money, and all sorts of products and services. This point can
be generalized with reference to people's hopes and how they
are manipulated. On the matter of heightened hopes, for example, many people today are unable to delay their gratification and, in effect, are urged not to try. The anthem is do it
now and get it now. This is more than a yuppie phenomenon.
On the material front, polls show that eight of ten people agree
that making a lot of money is not only desirable, it is the "in"
thing to do. Two-thirds of the population are concerned about
looking trimmer, stronger, and better.[12] We also seem to be a
nation of emotional junkies gravitating to instant highs and
responsive to easy and painless solutions to our problems. Certainly the TV generation is used to seeing matters resolved in
no more than one hour.

On a broader scale, events appear to happen more quickly
and fortuitously today, emanating from all parts of our tech-
nologically accessible world. Americans give these events a
"quick take," whether through television, radio, weekly magazines, or daily newspapers. Instant analysts look for an angle
on them, and countless tipsters advise people on how to make
a quick financial or experiential killing. Plainly, media technology is now geared to play to instant needs: *Time* magazine
compresses the news for those who want to "keep up" at parties while the *Wall Street Journal* is sold to those who must "keep
ahead" every business day.

Disappointment and Disillusionment. Although highs are
experienced more rapidly and immediately in the high-tech
1980s, they are quickly undermined by people's alertness to
disappointment and betrayal. People and events, for example,
seem to disappear as fast as they arrive in this instantaneous
age. There is more to this than the average American's attention span or Andy Warhol's adage that everyone is a celebrity
for fifteen minutes. There is the suspicion that the media mold
the news as much as they report it. In any case, the news media
do seem to play up the hottest stories and then drop them because
the audience tunes out quickly. People simply don't trust tele-

vision anymore, or what they read or hear (save for negative missives, as the 1988 election showed). It seems commercialized and hyped and thus is to be discounted and discredited. Why has this come about?

We are, in the words of Marshall McLuhan, literally in a "wired up" society.[13] The reach and depth of mass communications in the last forty years is unprecedented. Television, cable, VCRs, portable radios, satellite, and national newspapers have been added to local newspapers, magazines, radio, the films, and recordings. As a result, society has experienced a barrage of hype and hope orchestrated by advertising, programming, preaching, politicking, and self-help enterprises never before experienced in such concentrated doses and with such graphic delivery systems. Thus the media environment, particularly television, has had a profound influence upon our worldviews.

We contend that one effect of all this pitching of the good life is to have made people climb into a shell of cynicism as a matter of self-preservation. Constant images of a wealthier, wiser, healthier, and holier you are tantalizing. Lacking cultural restraints, people turn to other time-honored mechanisms to resist the temptation and avoid being suckered. Cynicism enables people to discount the message and the medium. It operates inwardly to ensure that they will not let themselves be carried away. This media-induced mind-set may partly account for the prevalence of the suspicious outlooks of many in American society, even among the comparatively favored members.

Among the less favored members of society, such as black teenagers and single-parent women, the constant media presence of images of affluence and the free life has to some degree raised questions of self-worth, fairness, and opportunity that can only contrast invidiously with their present circumscribed lives. Here cynicism leads people to conclude that everyone is "hustling." Turned inward, sadly, this cynical set leaves them estranged and powerless.

There are, of course, differences in individual coping strategies, but the broad public is beginning to conclude that behind much of what they see, hear, buy, and read is hypocrisy.

The profligate promises of politicians, the easy answers of preachers, the glittering generalities propounded by countless self-helpers—all are leading to a cooling down of expectations and shedding of ideals. People simply expect less honesty and fairness from media messengers. They set their sights lower. In that way, they suffer less disillusionment and keep their emotional temperatures at a bearable degree.

Stories about insider trading and public sector profiteering are unsurprising. The majority of Americans seem to agree with inside trader Dennis Levine that "everybody is doing it." News of widespread repression and corruption, as well as everyday acts of malfeasance and various misdoings, is compartmentalized by viewers, listeners, and readers with confirmatory statements like "It just goes to show you." As a consequence, overheated stories and coverage cool down quickly.

The point we are making is that both the media and their audience are interconnected parts of today's cynical cycle. People today *expect* to have their hopes inflated; hence, there is a greater receptivity to negative stories. They have also been conditioned to expect disappointment. Those whose emotions have been repeatedly raised to the heights have a reinforcing mechanism to cushion their fall. In this way, cynicism has become an accepted, even commonplace, means of coping with modern American life. Wised up to hype, people today exchange winks and knowing glances, trade in double entendres and put-downs, scoff at what they see and hear, and in other ways cope with the disappointing world around them. This is their cynicism at work.

Patterns of Coping. One indication of this cooled-out coping pattern is to be found in the ways people now relate to the once hallowed and seemingly wholesome world of sports. Sport has been celebrated as a vicarious way through which people can taste the "fruits of victory" and experience the "agony of defeat." Today, however, the attentions of the sports-minded are drawn to the political and financial side of the sporting life. The news concerns greed of players and owners, duplicity of sports agents and promoters, and collusion, legal maneuverings, drug abuse, and other unsavory parts of the "game." Meanwhile, fans wonder if their favorite stars will move, if the local franchise will skip town, or whether this is all a smokescreen to raise ticket prices, secure a new stadium, or in some other way take advantage of their loyalty.

Fans may still cheer the winners and applaud achievements in the stadiums and playing fields. But they are no longer surprised by greed, duplicity, and the dark side of sports, whether it is found among professionals or collegiates. On the contrary, they expect to be disappointed and have scaled down their hopes and shed their ideals.

Quite another way of coping with disillusionment is to fight back or even the score. Much as some use cynicism to protect their dignity and self-interest, others use it to advance their own agendas and gain advantage. Stockbrokers involved in insider trading are more than products of permissive parents and an affluent upbringing. They are self-promoters and self-seekers who will do whatever it takes to make a buck or even millions of them.

Selfish stockbrokers are only one kind of self-serving cynic. Many managers and professionals, seemingly emulating their sports counterparts, have become "free agents" in the business world, selling their services to the highest bidder. Headhunters are having a hard time keeping up with demand. These cynics believe that only saps and suckers are loyal to their companies today. Savvy climbers have learned how to make their mark and then leave before they are found out to have exploited their subordinates and backstabbed their peers. Who can blame them? "Everybody does it."

Media-Induced Misanthropy. It is hard to know how much the omnipresence of the media reinforces cynicism. What is certain is that all media—not only news, but also music, television programs, and film—influence generations of Americans. Garry Wills, in his book *Reagan's America: Innocents at Home,* talks about the role of film-induced fantasy in shaping the president's image of the world.[14] In the case of Ronald Reagan, he argues, the president's worldview was molded by a simple, romantic, sentimental view of life; hence, he is both a maker of and believer in the film fantasies of a more innocent generation. We share Wills's belief in the powerful influence of film, either in the theater or on television, but must add that the cinema's influence on today's generation is unlike that on Reagan's generation. Today's film fare, like that of the news, is not "innocent"; on the contrary, it is in large measure menacing and morally ambiguous.

The consequences of mass media are far-reaching. The influence of advertising is purported to be so intense that some products are not advertised on television at all, including strong alcohol and tobacco. There is also a powerful movement, led by Action for Children's Television, which argues that children are being unduly influenced by television that intertwines toys, toy advertising, and programs in ways that influence children in both aggressive and materialistic directions. This is a moot point but one that cannot be lightly waved away. There are, for example, enough imitators of Charles Bronson's *Death Wish* and one too many imitators of the *Taxi Driver* to raise concern. And, on Saturday mornings, when space-age violence is the norm and products are intermingled with programs, it is a wonder to many that children ever exhibit equanimity and generosity.

As much as life may imitate art, art also imitates life. The media are today reflecting and recycling the cynical outlook in their own self-scrutinizing fare. The cynical overlay has made its way into movies, such as *Network,* and has appeared on television and in advertisements starring "Max Headroom." None of this is, of course, to be equated with serious self-scrutiny in the industry. It simply puts people in the seats, or yields share points and advertising money.

Although many have commented on the contributions of film, music, and TV programming to the public's cynicism, the role that advertising can play in reinforcing cynical dispositions is sometimes overlooked. Advertising, the sustaining economic force of mass media, both in amount and content, has something to do with the perception that the world is full of phonies. When an institution like television (a societal surrogate) shows so much patent advertising overstatement, it is not surprising that many viewers come to feel that other cultural values are suspect, too.

In a sense, advertising presents the kind of white-picket-fence America that the Andy Hardy pictures did in the 1940s: a slumless, clean, prosperous environment in which most problems are trivial enough to be solved by the purchase of products that are touted by wise grandmothers, honest garage owners, or understanding pharmacists. It is a world that emphasizes possessions, easy solutions, superficial good looks, and narcissistic self-preoccupation—a world in which everyone wins through buying the right stuff. The "Barbie and Ken" world of advertising, which deals with surface and not substance and legitimizes phoniness, surely must have an effect on reinforcing cynicism.

At this point, of course, many people are wise to advertising pitches and inured to the appeals of celebrity product-promoters. It seems to us, though, that a society which has its main communication channels filled with easy-to-see-through ads must begin to imitate to some degree the interpersonal superficiality, self-preoccupation, and materialism endemic to much but not all of American advertising.

We concede the case is not conclusively proved and the extent of social learning in advertising is not known; but we believe that the data on violence indicate that television reinforces attitudes and, hence, that advertising, like other portions of the media, must leave its mark on the cynical outlook.

Cynicism and Human Character

Many conceptions of human nature have been proposed since the beginning of recorded history. These range from Dale Carnegie's what-me-worry optimism to Freud's impulse-ridden pessimism, from Adam Smith's rationalism to Shakespeare's tragicomic characterizations of humanity. The cynics have made distrust of human nature the central feature of their view of life.

Antisthenes, the founder of the Cynic school in the fifth century B.C., "barked" at the follies of society and thus demarked cynics as having "doglike" contempt for their fellow man. His followers, Diogenes among them, were idealists disappointed with the turn of Greek society. They harked back to the "natural" values prominent during the Golden Age in Greece and disparaged the pursuit of wealth, reputation, and conventionality.

There is a positive side to classical definitions of cynicism.[15] In ancient times, the Cynics held to virtuous ideals and, according to one observer, "sought to shock a deluded humanity into awareness of its foolishness." In its modern formulation, however, cynicism argues that idealism and involvement have few payoffs and that social distance and emotional detachment are superior ways of life. In contemporary definitions, cynics believe that human conduct is motivated solely by self-interest and have a sneering disbelief in the more high-minded motivations of their fellowman.

One does not have to be a clinician to define this jaundiced view about life. The blues, as sung by two masters of the idiom, Bessie Smith and Billie Holiday, are evocative of the mood and sound. Woody Allen's films capture cynicism in character. The list of writers, playwrights, and musicians who have voiced the cynic's view, as well as of artists who have expressed it, is endless. Our purpose here is to show that the signs of cynicism, including deep suspicion and mistrust, as well as cold detachment and selfishness, are common themes in the arts and popular culture, much as they are in philosophical and psychological discourse.

The Expressions of Cynicism

It would be a mistake, however, to view cynicism as though it were the product of a single mind-set or one-dimensional view of the world. The manifestations of cynicism are as varied as there are types of people and personalities. Contrast, for example, the open, outspoken, articulate cynic versus the stubborn, negativistic, close-mouthed variety. Vocal cynics stir the pot, often regaling peers with dark suspicions and inside dope. Such types scrupulously catalogue their own histories of betrayal and have a ready—and bloody-minded—reason for belittling any proposal that might be advanced. Writer William Burroughs described this type as "a man who knows a little of what's going on.''[16] Open cynics trade in conspiracy theories. They see collusion or back-room politics in any orchestrated effort to win them over, and they callously calibrate what involvement will cost and gain them. Oscar Wilde was likely thinking of this type when he defined a cynic as ''a man who knows the price of everything, and the value of nothing.''[17]

By contrast, the quiet cynic's attitude may come from feeling powerless to counter the guile of sales and service personnel and helpless in the face of large-scale manipulation by politicians or executives. The negative cynics can be envious, often feeling that the goings-on of the rich and famous invidiously provide a contrast to their own hard-won rectitude. Furthermore, they can be harshly judgmental, always waiting to pounce when their time comes.

How cynicism is expressed also varies by situation. The cynic's relative status, role, and relationship to the object of suspicion are all of significance. A leader, for example, may engage in flattery, tell half-truths, and be guileful, all in service of building alliances and motivating subordinates. Such stratagems have been passed down throughout recorded history and are well documented in modern times in Anthony Jay's book *Management and Machiavelli*. [18] Surely many leaders justify their manipulation as realistic, pragmatic, even essential to their role. It is also cynical. However they may justify their methods, Machiavellian managers act primarily out of self-interest and harbor a dark and suspicious view of those they lead. Followers who in turn guard their dignity and protect their flanks may see themselves as being equally realistic and pragmatic. Scoffing and putting down the boss also serve them well with their peers. The point is that subordinates have just as many self-serving strategies to foil their bosses and, sometimes, outmanipulate them.

Cynicism can be more or less pronounced among various socioeconomic or demographic groups. Many at lower income and education levels have much to be cynical about in their daily lives. Landon Jones, in his book *Great Expectations*, emphasizes that baby boomers, the children of high hopes in the 1960s, had their ideals dashed by the Vietnam War, political assassinations, and Watergate, and they too have their reasons to be cynical.[19]

On this same point, Yankelovich reports that many baby boomers have been infused with the "psychology of entitlement." Born and raised in relative affluence, they have come to expect material security and comfort and, freed from such mundane worries, came to search for self-fulfillment. Certainly their sense of entitlement was dampened by inflation in the 1970s and recession in the 1980s. Many are now disillusioned by the downsizing of corporate hierarchies and the meager incomes provided by employers in the service economy. Yankelovich writes: "Our culture and economy are on opposite courses: while the culture calls for more freedom, the economy calls for constraint."[20] To the many infused with the psychology of entitlement, this contradiction has been painful and unjust. Some have adjusted their expectations and made peace with their circumstances. Others feel "ripped off" and have turned into opportunists. It is worth noting that more than half of the yuppies who prepare their own taxes admit that this makes it easier for them to cheat.

Finally, the expression of cynicism varies from culture to culture.[21] An anecdote from our experience will illustrate. In measuring the degree of cynicism of managers in Great Britain and France, we found the French managers to be far more cynical than their British counterparts. When these data were reported back to them, the French managers prided themselves on their realism. Some said that the British were hypocrites, unable to admit their distrust of people and unwilling to face grim realities—accounting for their decline as a nation. The British in turn said the data confirmed that the French were congenitally dishonest—accounting for their convoluted and exasperating ways of negotiating and doing business, not to mention their decline as a nation. They added that the French lacked real humanity, which made France such an inhospitable place for strangers. This exchange illustrates how cynicism has different faces and rationalizations in different lands.

Our point is that the manifestations of cynicism are many and varied. Hypocrisy, lying, scoffing, negativism, sophistry, disparaging, mistrusting, manipulating, rumormongering, goldbricking, featherbedding, politicking, bootlicking, and the like—all are examples of the ways that people put their cynical views into action. We all engage in such cynical acts some of the time. Cynics engage in them more often, in more situations, and in more problematic and pernicious ways than any culture, even a society that celebrates gritty realism, can comfortably sustain.

Cynicism in Society

One need only read the writings of Karl Marx to obtain one monolithic perspective on how cynicism plays out in society. Other political philosophers have given ample attention to the expressions of cynicism in matters of commerce and the state. Certainly an essentially jaundiced picture of society was expressed by Thomas Hobbes when he characterized human life as "short, nasty, and brutish."[22] Modern-day believers think it essential to control people's inherent selfishness in order to prevent the outbreak of social chaos. Their political system is predicated upon a perverse view of human nature which dictates that a strong central authority is needed to keep the rabble in place.

Niccolò Machiavelli, in his pragmatic fashion, expressed cynical contempt for the human character.[23] His stratagems for advancing the self-interest of the Prince incorporate duplicity, cunning, and deceit in service of the acquisition and retention of power. Machiavellians view political (and commercial) life as amoral and pursue any means, however regrettably unscrupulous, to achieve their ends.

The point is that models of governance, political and corporate, and certainly modes of organization and management, are premised upon assumptions about human nature and reflect certain understandings about the world and how it works. Cynicism is one lens people use to see other people and the world about them. It informs their philosophy of life and governs their pattern of relating to other people and going about their own work. The cynical outlook is necessarily represented in a society's governance, organization, and management and in its culture. Through the lens of cynicism, then, we may see the cynical society.

Cynics' Perceptions of Life

Do cynics see the world around them differently from other people? Our survey included a number of questions that enable us to assess how the lens of cynicism colors people's perceptions of life and the world around them.

Figure 2. The Cynic's Philosophy of Life.

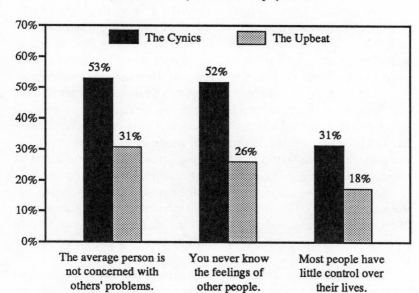

Philosophy About Life. A larger proportion of cynics than upbeat respondents believe that the average person is unconcerned with the problems of other people, as Figure 2 reveals. This attitude attests to the cynic's preoccupation with self-interest at the expense of the commonweal. These data show that cynics simply see less goodwill in the world around them.

The second finding is that many more cynics also believe that it is not possible really to understand the feelings of other people. We have suggested that cynics are more apt to compartmentalize their views and see the world through the lens of gritty realism. These data show that cynics see others as more complex and less understandable than do upbeat respondents. Cynics have a self-sealing and self-reinforcing view of the world.[24] Although they may develop diverse explanations for disappointments, a common attribution is to the manipulation and self-seeking of other people. Cynics ingeniously twist the meaning of events to fit their subjective outlook—especially when it comes to their dealings with other people. In this sense, then, cynicism proves adaptive by protecting the cynic's mental and emotional construction of the world. Suffice it to say that as much as the cynic's outlook makes other people more complex, it also prevents the cynic from seeing them and their motivations clearly.

On the third indicator of people's philosophies about life, our data show that a somewhat larger proportion of cynics than upbeat respondents believes people have little control over their lives. Here we see that cynics are more likely to believe that people are manipulated by their environment—an indicator of their frustrations in negotiating the world around them.

These three measurements of the philosophy of life provide only the barest data on the cynic's construction of the world. Nevertheless, they add evidence to the claim that cynics have a more jaundiced view of human nature than upbeat respondents do.

Experiences with Life. As Figure 3 shows, a larger proportion of cynics than upbeat respondents believe public officials are uninterested in the problems of the average citizen. Interestingly, the data show that the majority of the population, whether cynical or not, comes to this conclusion. Many no doubt feel powerless and disenfranchised in the political process. What marks the cynic is the perception that politicians themselves don't care about them and are only out for themselves.

On this point, we found that a much smaller proportion of cynics votes in presidential elections. While this is a self-report of voting behavior, it shows how cynics translate their outlook into apathy. Many have speculated on the reasons behind low voter turnout in this country. Cynicism has to rank high on the list. What is discouraging is that all the proposals to ease voter

Figure 3. The Cynic's Experience with Life.

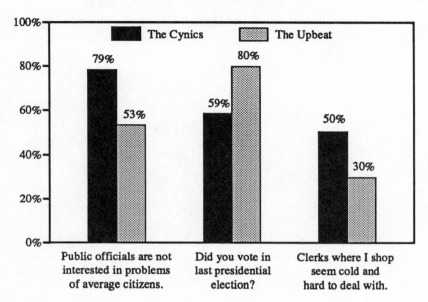

registration and reduce inconveniences at polling places are not likely to get the cynics out to vote.

Finally, as one might expect, a higher proportion of cynics finds the clerks in stores where they shop to be colder and harder to deal with. Later we shall see that store clerks, salespersons, service and repair people, as well as police officers, taxi drivers, and other private and public servants, are themselves strong adherents of the cynical outlook on life. In a very real sense, then, those in the service sector are colder and harder to deal with. Even so, we suspect that clerks and the like find a cynical customer base harder to deal with as well. Cynical consumers constantly badger and criticize retail help, are hypervigilant to signs of manipulation by service and repair people, and can further sour the workdays of already sour employees. There are many reasons why the quality of service in this country has declined. One may be cynicism at work.

1

The
Cynical
People

The character traits of people at work are as conspicuous to the observant as various types of criminal *modus operandi* are to detectives. In every office or plant there are people who fall into broad commonsensical categories of behavior. It is easy to spot cynics at work. Simply listen to conversations at the water cooler, on the sales floor, in the service shop. The message is the same: "They [the managers, union heads, customers, even co-workers] are not to be trusted and are only out for themselves."

Cynics come in all shapes, sizes, and styles. Many are doubting Thomases who have lost their faith in people and institutions. Some are scoffers and put-down artists. Others are manipulators and schemers—always looking for an angle. Still others are insatiable gossips who feed on inside dope to advance their own interests. More than a few are malcontents.

As a function of their personality and life experiences, their position, power, and status, and their opportunities to advance their self-interest, cynics can be classified as certain types. Everyone is familiar with characterizations of working people as, say, either blue-collar or white-collar types. In the same way, we have also characterized the variety of cynical types as wearing, so to speak, different kinds of collars. To introduce these cynical types consider:

If they wear:	They might be:
Custom-tailored collars	Command Cynics
Tight Collars	Administrative Sideliners
Button-down collars	Articulate Players
Fraying collars	Squeezed Cynics
Open collars	Obstinate Stoics
Dark collars	Hard-Bitten Cynics

Command Cynics

On a senior level of management, wearing custom-tailored collars, are Command Cynics and their advisers.[1] Classically, Iago (evil) and Machiavelli (pragmatic) represent the mind-set of these manipulators and schemers; today it is embodied in J. R. Ewing of the "Dallas" TV episodes. Count Metternich, who was studied by Henry Kissinger, is another historic example; more recent ones include Mayor Daley and Presidents Nixon and Johnson. Hustlers like Uncle Duke of the comic strip "Doonesbury" fit here as well.

Without meaning to caricature these complex men, and without passing any moral judgments upon them (although it is difficult not to do so), we cite them as examples of Command Cynics. We believe that this category embraces certain CEOs of mid-size and small companies, politicians, big-time fixers and salesmen, and more than a few media advertising and PR kingpins.

Some of the characteristics of this group appear to be single-minded opportunism and an unrivaled capacity for sophistry (making the better argument appear the worse). They have the ability to put a face on things and to play on emotions and weaknesses of others. They are skilled in controlling information and with apparent ease can disparage others when they feel it will help to advance their own cause.

The fixer, schemer, and manipulator may be found on many levels of an organization. Command Cynics, though, run corporations, are high-level advisers, or else have powerful supervisory positions where they play the politics of everyday living that many of them consider their particular art of leadership. These cynics consider company politics an end in itself, rather than a means; it is their power trip.

Of course, many national leaders, including Franklin Roosevelt and John Kennedy, sometimes confused the ends and the means; they were surely expeditious and certainly cynical at times; like everyone in command, they could manipulate and play power games. But these exercises of power were tactical components in the achievement of broader goals. Command Cynics have a different motivation. They play power games for their own satisfaction and to protect their flanks from people like themselves.

In their putative command posts, they formulate long-range plans, manage with a short leash, and define the enemies. Studies of top executives show that most do have strong needs for power, but the power drives of Command Cynics seem exaggerated. They tend to fragment the big picture and delegate responsibility, often with little authority. They shorten everyone else's time horizons and look for a scapegoat when problems arise. Finally, they search out and exploit the vulnerabilities of those who report to them.

What distinguishes Command Cynics from Machiavellians, egoists, and other self-interested schemers in an organization is their utter contempt for people who are not in power positions or whom they wish to use. They subscribe to the Darwinian logic that they "made it," so everyone else must be weak, naive, inept, or just plain dumb. In Michael Maccoby's study of organizational types, Command Cynics come closest to being Jungle Fighters. Renoir's film *The Rules of the Game* is a close approximation of their outlook.

Often they surround themselves with yes-men and clones. Embodiments of more paternalistic and less aggressive management are cast aside as deadwood wimps and excess baggage in their organization. The Command Cynic's sour, uncaring, manipulative view of people inevitably is carried through other levels of management to employees, thence through sales and service personnel to the customer base. Command Cynics, as we shall see, are linchpins in the cynical company.

We are not talking here about visionary corporate leaders who try to build companies in their own image. "New age" executives, like Donald Burr of People Express, and high-tech charismatics like Apple's founder, Steven Jobs, may have their faults but they build camaraderie in their companies and exude a thoroughly upbeat outlook on people. Nor are we talking about Lee Iacocca and other turnaround artists, who insist on calling their shots and in doing so extract some pain from their organizations. They have a clear sense of their companies' goals and openly win people over to their point of view. We do, however, include undisguised authoritarians and countless other imperturbably arrogant top executives under the umbrella of Command Cynics. The Command Cynics we refer to have certain other characteristics in common:

- They tend to use hatchet men to do their dirty work, generally people who will excuse the commander in the eyes of his subordinates by rationalizing what the "poor guy is forced to do." They want to be seen as sinned against more than sinning.
- They have a low opinion of human nature (probably a projection of their own impulses), feeling that everyone has a price and can be bought or has a weakness that can be manipulated.
- They are vigilant and suspecting of any disloyalty.
- They are highly expeditious and responsive to shifts in circumstances; they are prepared to "survive" regardless of former alliances. They are more opportunistic than loyal.
- Psychologically, they are able to play the raw opportunist because they can compartmentalize and hence not experience as much conflict or dissonance as other people. They don't

agonize over the people they hurt to advance themselves, because that is the way they believe life plays out.

For these commanders, then, cynicism appears to overrule conscience in favor of expediency and self-aggrandizement.

Administrative Sideliners

Administrative Sideliners are rule-conscious, righteous, and sometimes ruthless.[2] They tend to have less charisma than Command Cynics and less personal magnetism than on-the-go manipulators and schemers. Instead, they are quiet and bloodless bureaucrats and technocrats—rulers over office and paperwork and masters of PERT charts and plans. Staff vice-presidents, comptrollers, personnel representatives, countless consultants, and many academic administrators seem to wear this tight collar as well.

Administrative Sideliners control others' destiny, but on a less comprehensive scale than the Command Cynics. They check expense accounts and trip reports, update the policy manual and personnel records, maintain schedules and billings, oversee security and company facilities. They tend to be in staff rather than line positions. The rules for staying clean and above blame are paramount to them. They put virtually everything on the record or through a process and use the memo as a shield of personal probity. Drafting and overseeing rules and regulations is their base of power in an organization. They gain emotional rewards from small victories—often from catching an adversary ignoring procedures or taking unauthorized initiatives.

What makes Administrative Sideliners cynical is their view that people are like machines—really cogs in a larger machine—who can be engineered. They will ''bend, fold, and mutilate'' people to ensure that policies are implemented and orders carried out, no matter how nonsensical or exploitative. This is their power trip. Cynical Sideliners have no real concern for people, save as instruments or objects of policy, or for the current goals of the enterprise, except when they relate to their own perks, pensions, or job security.

Their view of human nature is predominantly cold; the organization is made up of rules and processes rather than people. They tend to be literal. They are "spoilers" of new ideas because they have "seen it all before." Quintessential bureaucrats who simply follow orders from above embody the type. Many of these cynics feel most comfortable in the armed forces and militarylike organizations: Ambiguity is at a minimum and there is a rule for every situation.

To a degree, aspects of the Administrative Sideliner's *modus operandi* fit Maccoby's characterization of the modern-day Company Man. This is not to suggest that all managers are risk-averse and self-protective or that staff bureaucrats are all cynics. We are talking about those in administrative positions who tend to depersonalize human capital and subordinate it to turf protection or to rules for their own sake. These cynics know the price of everything and the value of nothing. Their horizons are short, but their memories are long and precise. The Administrative Sideliners have some other things in common:

- They tend to be industrious retailers of gossip, particularly about those who are currently in or out of favor with superiors. Of course, the grapevine is used by most people in every organization. But for the Sideliner, gossip and leaks are weapons of survival and revenge, and their cynical use is crucial in the Sideliner's power struggle.
- They are highly security-conscious. They seem to operate best in very structured, unambiguous situations where orders come from the top and the culture emphasizes implementation, rather than creativity, risk, or initiative. They follow the party line without much personal conflict.
- They appear to be tough guys in executing what they are sure their bosses want but tend to lose confidence when directions from above are unclear. They are the backbone of corporate culture and fear change as a threat to their clear understanding of what is expected of them. While this is true of most organization men, the Sideliner is more resistant to change than others.
- They are risk-averse and least like entrepreneurs.

- They often play favorites, particularly with subordinates who fawn over them.
- Psychologically, they seem to feel that the world is a mortal coil, and the people with whom they get on best are those who feel the same way. This type resents people who seem to do things the easy way. When they pass a like-minded soul in the hall, it is usually with a sigh and a dolorous shake of the head to signify that ''life is hard, but duty calls us good soldiers.''

The cynicism of Administrative Sideliners really resides in their dehumanizing attitude toward others, in their lack of personal convictions and values, and in their ruthless use of corporate apparatus to preserve themselves. It is the wise manager who understands the mind-set and behavioral limitations of these cynical Sideliners. They require constant review, management by a short lead, and careful communication, for what few confidences they gain they are sure to peddle.

Articulate Players

Articulate Players are open and vocal about how the game is played.[3] They are essentially inside-dopesters who pride themselves on their ability to see through what is going on and why it is going on. They populate television shows, currently ''Moonlighting'' and ''L.A. Law.'' In companies, they can be found wherever the action is—say, in project management posts or in myriad so-called intrapreneurial roles. They can also be seen scrambling up the corporate ladder or making the entrepreneurial killing.

While many of them may be strivers and status seekers, all of them are status- and trend-aware. They fancy themselves as students of human nature and seem to be prodigious consumers of how-to books of all kinds. They read magazines such as *New York* and probably are interested in *People* as a source of inside information and role modeling. They have the real story, or so they like to think.

Media celebrities such as Johnny Carson and Joan Rivers

are exemplars of this trendy, mugging, winking inside knowledge of what is going on in society. W. C. Fields, the outspoken cynic who would "never give a sucker an even break" and was never surprised at the venal side of humankind, represented this point of view in his movies. Today, it seems true to say that many journalists, lawyers, salespeople, union activists, and gossip columnists are part of this cynical ménage.

The "young urban professional" belongs to this same variety of cynicism. The crass materialism of yuppies and their willingness to play selfish games to get what they want have the essential components of cynicism. Their personal goals seem to be paramount; ethical considerations are often put aside in favor of what they consider achievement. They are acutely conscious of winners and losers; loserhood is an object of derision to them. It is here that one sees the grindingly cold behavior that says, in effect: "I will do anything to get ahead and not be left behind."

Young Articulate Players openly manifest their self-interest and plainly put their cynicism into style. They are fad-conscious because their values reside largely in the eyes of their peers. Individualism or eccentricity is acceptable on the periphery (like hobbies), but having it all means holding one's own in the mainstream of current definitions of what the successful person has or does. They not only dress for success and have power breakfasts but also take physical care of themselves because they feel better and want to be able to stay in the chase for success.

Their sense of humor is topical more than it is ironic, insightful, or witty. They are serious about having fun. But genuine humor has elements of self-mockery, and Articulate Players feel that they cannot afford too much self-mockery; they must stop before they expose their vulnerabilities. They are also actors better at faking expected emotions than allowing themselves real feeling, beyond self-pity. The moral of the recent movie *Down and Out in Beverly Hills* is found in the bum's secret of his success: tell people what they want to hear. Bogus indignation and fawning admiration are important tools in the Articulate Players' networking game.

The essential Articulate Player could be characterized by Shrike, the editor in Nathaniel West's novel *Miss Lonelyhearts*, or by P. T. Barnum, who openly believed that a sucker is born every minute. Articulate Players have elements of Maccoby's "Gamesman" and live in the self-oriented world that Christopher Lasch described as the "culture of narcissism."[4] What these cynics have in common is a willingness to do whatever has to be done to others in order to advance. Many are quite vocal about this strategy, perhaps as a ploy to scare their peers. This requires, of course, some dissembling, some style, and a good deal of energy. Above all, it requires the assumption that most people are only out for themselves and that you are better off zapping them before they do it to you.

Other common traits of Articulate Players include the following:

- They are cool; nothing must appear to faze them. To show hurt is to reveal vulnerabilities or commitment. Vulnerabilities can dull a person's competitive edge, while commitment, they feel, requires loyalty and shows needs. This, they feel, is dangerous in an untrusting, selfish world.
- Success, they believe, is not happiness (which is unattainable). Success is power, independence, and manifest acquisition. Who can quarrel with the power of appearances in the age of cynicism? Most Articulate Players feel: "It's not what you are, it's what you appear to be."
- They are materialistic because possessions are palpable and countable, unlike trust or feelings of well-being. It is a feeling akin to David Reisman's "hardness of the material," in which the concrete and specific take the place of the spiritual and the emotional.
- Metaphorically, they are porcupines whose quills are at the ready, prepared to attack whenever attack is anticipated. Attack often takes the form of confidential put-downs rather than direct confrontation. The key is anticipation—alertness to being attacked, or taking the opportunity to attack peers-cum-competitors.
- The psychological function of cynicism in the case of these

relatively young Articulate Players is to reduce their moral conflicts about their single-minded materialism and its associated predatory behavior and wiseacre sensibilities.

While Command Cynics operate from positions of comparative power and Administrative Sideliners operate as "gray eminences," Articulate Players are openly striving and in the game. As such, appearances and networking are vital, and "don't tread on me" messages are conspicuously disseminated. The Articulate Players are difficult to manage. Plainly, they need running room, require affirmation, and want to set their own rules and terms. In loose corporate cultures, however, there is a risk of cynical Players running wild, backbiting peers, breaking legal rules, hurting feelings, and harming the company's long-term interests. Command Cynics are the worst role models for the Articulate Players. Instead, the latter require thoughtful grooming by corporate executives of unquestioned probity who can offer them guidance as to what is acceptable in corporate life and what is not.

Squeezed Cynics

In their fraying collars, the Squeezed Cynics are the mirror opposites of the Articulate Players. They are the victims, rather than the masters, in the information age.[5] In a sense, they have been swamped by the "third wave" that Articulate Players surf with ease. We regard them as squeezed and made cynical by changing socioeconomic forces, to a degree beyond their comprehension and surely beyond their control. Many of them are the sons and daughters of skilled workers or lower-middle-class clericals, who at one time had aspirations of climbing the social ladder through education and work status. Some attended college, usually by living at home and taking odd jobs to finance their studies at local institutions, and many more attended technical schools in preparation for skilled jobs that would top their parents' income and status.

These earlier aspirations have faded along with the decline of heavy industry. The jobs they expected have been automated, eliminated, or sent overseas. As a result, they have been forced to lower their hopes and take whatever is being offered. This usually means lesser jobs in service industries, working alongside relatively unskilled people, at salaries that are commensurate. Their futures are not bright, at least compared with the material and social options they expected. These are young people who are downwardly mobile and for whom the American dream is a chimera.

While many of those squeezed by a changing economy are adjusting and accommodating to new circumstances, the Fraying Collars are alienated and cynical. The system has let them down, they feel, and they have concluded that life isn't fair. Many blame political and economic institutions for their sorry plight. With detached coolness, Squeezed Cynics cope in public moments but feel desperately estranged in their private thoughts.

The cynicism of many of these Squeezed Cynics is manifest in their anthems: ''Where's mine?'' and ''what's in it for me?'' They exhibit the dead-ender's self-interest when it comes to new assignments and responsibilities: They are ready to gold-brick when it comes to putting in what they regard as a fair day's work. More than any other cynical type, they practice what Thorstein Veblen called the ''politics of envy.''[6] They scoff at the effort and energy of successful types and chalk up others' accomplishments to their connections, their blind ambition, or just plain luck.

These are workers who, brought up on high hopes, are now faced with the ordinary and consequently have little loyalty to their employers. Not for them the cocky optimism of past American generations and corresponding materialistic dreams— these people are disappointed. Their best compromise with life's rewards is to trade off long-term acquisitions and concrete status symbols for short-term pleasures and freedom from job pressures. This approach often leaves a residue of bitterness and generalized cynicism concerning politics, economics, and corporate America.

These Squeezed Cynics have certain attitudes in common:

• They see themselves as economically stagnant. This bothers the more educated and skilled among them more than it does the lesser educated and unskilled.

- The less cynical see life as a series of trade-offs, such as time for money and ease for pressure; others resent their economic gridlock.
- They share an instinctive suspicion of the system, the company, and the bosses and do not easily relate to these authorities.
- They put in their hours on the job but withhold their involvement.
- Psychologically, the better educated of these cynics feel disenfranchised; their perspectives are limited to the here and now. They tend to be more scornful about the system—which has disenfranchised them—than cynics who know how to work it. They show manifest disillusionment with a system that promises a lot and probably will not deliver.

As the service economy grows at the expense of the smokestack industries, these Squeezed Cynics will present increasing problems of motivation to their employers. Plainly, gaining their loyalty and commitment is high on the corporate agenda, as it is on the political one. They are being joined, however, by larger numbers of older middle managers and staff personnel who have reached a plateau in their careers and anticipate shrinking responsibilities, influence, and income in a downsized corporate America. Many, of course, have already been victimized by the current wave of megamergers and corporate restructurings, given early retirement, laid off, and even dismissed. More seem to feel that they are at risk.

Obstinate Stoics

In metropolitan areas, the Obstinate Stoics wear open collars. They are disproportionately found in the blue-collar classes. These are the silent Archie Bunkers of the world. In contrast to the savvy Articulate Players and seething Squeezed Cynics, these obstinate types generally keep to themselves. They are uncommunicative and confine their socializing to family and a few outsiders. They tend to have a strong work ethic and get on with their jobs. Many regard the world as composed of two kinds of people: us and them. They do not trust establishment types, especially lawyers, and feel basically that if more people were like them—hardworking and independent—the country would be in better shape.

In rural areas, these Obstinate Stoics tend to be non-gregarious and almost survivalist (not necessarily politicized) in their thinking. They do not trust people, outside of close family members, and feel hostile toward bankers, businessmen, foreigners, media people, and all politicians. Many are vigilant about their rights, their property, and their daughters and are suspicious about social movements (save religious ones), welfare, and other income-redistribution efforts (save farm subsidies). Obstinate Stoics seem to feel more strongly than most that expecting anyone to help you makes you a damn fool.

In many respects, stoical cynics are what David Reisman calls "inner-directed" persons.[7] They operate, metaphorically speaking, as if they were gyroscopes—that is to say, once started, they run in a steady, regular manner whithin predictable parameters, without requiring inputs from other sources. In a similar way, the stoical cynics do their jobs, guided gyroscopically by their strong work ethic but quite independent of others, both emotionally and stylistically.

In many respects, they live their lives in the same way: They are hostile to outsiders, change, and authority. They tend to find a niche, stay in it, and guard it from intrusion. Obstinate Stoics are not exploratory in their life-style; they are rigid in their child-rearing practices and basically nonempathetic to others and are creatures of habit.

In common with all cynics, Obstinate Stoics are ever vigilant against what they fear may be incursions against them. This is what often makes these particular cynics potentially difficult employees. With their strong work ethic, they are most capable of being solid producers in a stable environment. When the environment changes, as it inevitably must, the Obstinate Stoics, running on their gyroscopes (not on their antennae or radar, unlike the Sideliners or Articulate Players), have the most difficulty. It is as if the winds of change blow them away.

Change is more of a threat to them than to other cynics and certainly more than to upbeat personalities. They tend to be obstinate because they feel the malevolent "powers that be" are interfering with them for their own selfish reasons. They are not corporate-oriented, and so getting these stoical cynics on board is not easy, no matter what management offers. The strong work ethic of the stoical cynics is best channeled when the firm is in equilibrium (as they see it); when change occurs, it takes somewhat longer to convince them that things will get sorted out, largely because they have a hard time imagining a benign future or a changed routine. Their time perspective is unusually clouded with mistrust and foreboding. The Obstinate Stoics are characterized by these additional traits:

- They tend to be introverted, pursuing their own promptings rather than being tuned in to others.
- They have strong habit patterns and are not flexible in their responses to others; this makes them stubborn and even bloody-minded.
- They tend to be holier-than-thou because of their own strongly felt work ethic and believe that hard work is the solution to most problems (and laziness is their cause).
- Psychologically, they are down-to-earth thinkers who are cognitively more at home with the here and now than with the future. They appreciate simple answers to complex questions more than the average person does. They are happiest in a restricted life-style where lines of authority are clear and long established. On the other hand, they are skillful miniaturists (often able hobbyists). When they focus their attention on specific problems related to their jobs or family dwellings, they are at their best.

In short, Obstinate Stoics want to be left alone to pursue the work ethic and gain the respectability so important to them and their families.

Hard-Bitten Cynics

One of the best ways to understand the outlook of the Hard-Bitten Cynic is to listen to country-and-western singer Johnny

Paycheck's anthem: "Take This Job and Shove It." It demarks the outlook of the type who lives on the razor's edge between independent respectability and antisocial aggression. Many Hard-Bitten Cynics today are like the sympathetic characters from the prison pictures that Warner Brothers made in the 1940s; in movies, they are depicted by George Raft, Yves Montand, and Jean Gabin as competent but unlucky, world-weary loners.

Some Hard-Bitten Cynics are shop-floor workers and relatively unskilled laborers.[8] Older ones have felt the burden, for years, of "working for the man." They can be clannish with their own kind, manfully sociable, always ready to sneer at young tyros with big plans who fawn their way to success. On the job, they will go about their business, but always at their own pace or at one regulated by their peers. Some of these Hard-Bitten Cynics adopt the worldview that management is the enemy and cannot be trusted, so the smart ones look out for themselves.

We also see Hard-Bitten types in the lower middle class— perhaps underpaid schoolteachers, social or government workers, and secretaries whose status and salaries are disappointing given the former respectability of their jobs. They have become burn-outs on their jobs and, to a degree, in life. Moreover, many of these Hard-Bitten Cynics are police officers and firefighters. They are people who have seen life in the raw and feel they know firsthand the seamier sides of human nature; it is, so to speak, the "Hill Street Blues" syndrome.

Some members of disadvantaged minority groups belong in this category as well. They have felt racist discrimination, with all the frustrations it can bring. There is, in addition, a smaller group of cynics who are older and feel that life has given them a raw deal. Surely many of these older people take a calmer view of what they may or may not have achieved. But others appear to be bitter and regretful and seem to collect injustices past and present and hold them out to view. At any rate, the unskilled, the disadvantaged, the minority groups, the people who live respectable, hardworking, but somehow unrewarded and unappreciated lives are some of those who fall into this estranged cynical category.

These are the people in the work force who can be best motivated by more attention to the "fixable" aspects of their job situations (including benefits, work hours, and working conditions), by more thoughtful and genuine management attention, and by a warmer company atmosphere and more two-way communication. As their environment changes, this breed of cynic can become more amenable to doubt and skepticism rather than out-and-out cynicism—for, often, their environments have indeed given them much to be cynical about.

There are Hard-Bitten Cynics on all levels of the occupational scale. Most of them, however, have certain attributes in common that distinguish them from other cynics:

- These are people who have a clear if simplistic philosophy of life, often in the form of maxims ("Never give money to anyone who needs it"). They do not sham; they conspicuously play cynical roles whenever their opinions are solicited.
- On the higher reaches of the socioeconomic scale, these people are eager to display their lack of gullibility to spectators. Many, for example, wink behind the backs of people to whom they speak and proclaim their bitter experiences. This is the way they manage their impressions.
- On the lower reaches of the socioeconomic scale, they tend to be know-it-alls and obstructionists. Their watchword is "What's the catch?"

In short, the Hard-Bittens are the most suspicious of all the cynics we will examine. It is worth saying, though, that many of these cynics have come by their bitterness through hard experience.

We have not included extremists in our pantheon of cynics. We have only touched on those who might be considered transient cynics, people who sometimes obscure the ends and means, who tend to put their interests ahead of others', who scheme and scoff only on occasion and sometimes with good reason. Essentially, we have tried to sketch some types of frequently observed cynics to whom we will be referring as the book unfolds. In the course of these profiles, we have only hinted at some of the things that might be done to neutralize the corrosive effects of cynicism in the work force. The next step is to see how cynicism functions in the lives of people at work.

The Functions of Cynicism—Sword and Shield

Cynicism has distinct functions for the character types just introduced. Broadly speaking, cynicism can advance one's self-interest and serve, so to speak, as a sword for dealing with other people in the world. In turn, it can also be used as a shield to protect one's self-interest, to ensure that one's hopes are not inflated, and to cushion any disappointment. Specifically, cynicism is used to attain or retain power, to signal or sustain personae, to protect oneself from manipulation and exploitation, and to seal oneself off from contradictory information and preserve one's worldview and sense of self-esteem.[9]

Custom-Tailored Collars. The self-propelled and highly ambitious Command Cynic has many uses for cynicism; a primary function is to exert power and inspire fear in subordinates. Command Cynics follow Machiavelli's dictum that it is better to be feared than loved. They also know how to extract loyalty from their "ministers," as Machiavelli put it, by "bestowing honors and riches" on them, and how to gain their subservience by sharing "distinctions and offices." Machiavelli cautions such "princes" to avoid flatterers, fawners, and yes-men and at all costs to avoid being despised. Many Command Cynics fail on these counts. Although they may win some loyalty, they lose needed and loyal dissent; and although they may acquire a following, they also engender conspiracy and risk upheaval.

Command Cynics also use their cynicism to signal their personae: "The guy is ruthless, he doesn't give a damn for anyone." "Don't step out of line or he'll kill you." These are ways that people characterize the private personae of tough and cynical bosses. The more adroit Command Cynics know how to cultivate a prestigious public persona. Many are patrons of the arts, members of civic boards, facile speakers on public issues, and ostensibly concerned with the moral imperatives of

country, community, and corporation. Behind all of this, however, the fulsome cynics are advancing their own personal causes
and interests—transparently so to those who know "what the
guy is really like."

Command Cynics create organizational structures and
cultures that embody their cynical outlook on life. They are the
architects of authoritarian corporate environments, where communication and influence are one-way, where nobody dares
speak his or her mind, and where everyone makes sure that the
boss hears only good news.

In the same way, these cynics use their contempt for people
as a personal boost. If others are weak, they are strong; if others
are naive, they are crafty; if others are crippled by conscience,
they are bold; if others are unwilling to, say, backbite or issue
disinformation, they are not. To do many of these things requires
cynicism, and knowing they are capable of doing easily what
others find hard gives them confidence in their political acumen
and therefore confidence in themselves and their command.

In this respect, cynicism prescribes the world of the Command Cynic; it avoids a troubled conscience by justifying ruthless acts. Among other things, a cynical life view casts knowing
contempt upon most employees, thereby reducing the cognitive
dissonance that might arise by having to be tough in dealings
with them. An extreme analogy seems to be the view of the South
African government toward its nonwhite citizens: as inferiors,
they, according to the government line, ought to accept inferior
status, thereby justifying apartheid and hard-nosed arbitrary
measure to maintain it.

What we see in the Command type, then, is cynicism
largely as a mechanism for wielding power, for signaling a contemptuous and powerful persona, for building Machiavellian
monarchies and cultures, and for salving conscience and preserv-
ing self-confidence.

Tight Collars. Rule-oriented and cautiously ambitious Administrative Sideliners have something in common with the
Command Cynics: a contempt for people. But they wield power
and express a persona in a far less visible and much more en-
capsulated fashion. For Administrative Sideliners, procedural

means become ends, and people become faceless pawns. These cynics seem to make few genuine friends (at least on the job) and are prepared to use devious politics to stay clean themselves, to entrap anyone who may fall from grace, or to ingratiate themselves with anyone who may be of influence. To play such self-aggrandizing politics almost requires a cynical life view and a sense of estrangement from one's fellow employees, with a concomitant desire to advance one's own standing. It is the cynical toady's way of becoming a small winner.

The Administrative Sideliners' cynicism also helps them to cope with doing the many cold-blooded personnel acts they are asked to perform. Their emotional distance from people is an enabling mechanism and their cynicism a rational analogue of their affective removal. To hire, fire, transfer, reward, and punish by implementing transitory corporate needs demands, for conscience' sake, a view of human nature that essentially sees people as interchangeable parts. The Administrative Sideliner is, so to speak, a holdover from the days of Frederick Taylor's "Scientific Management," where jobs were engineered by simplifying, dividing, and supervising and where people could be moved expeditiously to accommodate management's needs or wishes.[10]

So the function of cynicism in the mind-set of the Administrative Sideliner is to advance oneself quietly, to protect one's turf and security vigilantly, and to distance oneself emotionally from fellow workers. These cynics can survive, even build smallish empires, so long as they stay above the battle and administer the bosses' wishes, whatever they may be, to whomever they may affect.

Button-Down Collars. Self-oriented and loudly ambitious Articulate Players are found chiefly among the baby boomers (age twenty-five to forty). Cynicism is a major weapon in their psychological arsenal. For a start, they believe they have acquired their jaundiced view of human nature rightly. As the book *Hopes and Ashes* clearly articulates, they have seen their high ideals of the 1960s and 1970s turn more or less to ashes.[11] Out of this, we estimate, have come unbridled self-interest and unyielding disillusionment, making way for the twin specters of materialism and cynicism.

Indeed, these articulate and assertive cynics have come to believe that their idealism was foolish and that high-mindedness is inconsequential. The idealism of "Bright College Years" has given way to the lessons of "The Big Chill": Most people cannot be trusted in this Darwinian world; hence, materialism is the only philosophy, in the long run, that will keep one safe from selfish people. Most of them have not reached the status and power of Command Cynics, but neither do they aspire to the security and encapsulation sought by Administrative Sideliners. Thus Articulate Players gravitate to the game of achievement; they savor the thrill of victory and will do whatever it takes to avoid the agony of defeat. Money is their scorecard, and power comes from accomplishment.

Surely, too, cynicism is part of the persona of Articulate Players. It is evident in what they read and eat, how they dress and seek recreation, how they comport themselves—on the job, in restaurants and nightclubs, and, we fear, in their own homes. More than this, they signal their street-fighting skills. They want prospective rivals to be wary of them. And they want all of their peers, and anyone else who might be interested, to know that they are in the know. This type is somewhat different from the others insofar as cynicism is a badge of honor.

As much as cynicism advances the self-interest of young Articulate Players and tells the world who they are, it also protects them in a hypocritical society where honesty is a myth and shortcuts are the name of the game. The reaction to the 1987 wave of insider trading on Wall Street is illustrative: Most traders felt it was just the tip of the iceberg.

Finally, cynicism is a coping mechanism that enables Articulate Players to get along and get ahead in a world that they postulate is as greedy and narcissistic as they are themselves. They project, as it were, their own feelings of cynicism upon the world and, by doing so, reduce the dissonance and anxiety they might otherwise feel for having such a nakedly opportunistic outlook on life.

Cynicism serves several other functions, as we will see in the case of Squeezed Cynics, Obstinate Stoics, and Hard-Bittens (by far the majority of cynical Americans). Cynicism especially enables these types to cope with a sometimes capricious and often seemingly malevolent environment. They lack the status and leverage to wield their cynicism to great effect or to personal advantage. In many respects, too, they are less ambitious and self-confident and are more estranged and self-deprecating than the Commanders, Administrators, and Players. This means that their cynicism helps them avoid the pain of disappointment. Still, there are noteworthy differences in the use of cynicism among the Squeezed, Stoical, and Hard-Bitten types.

Fraying Collars. Cynicism plays a different role in the personality of Squeezed Cynics than in the Articulate Players. Whereas the Players use it to advance their self-interest and to signal their formidability, the Squeezed Cynics use it to preserve what little power they have and to retain a measure of dignity in a job and life-style far below their expectations. Cynicism serves a protective function for them: It protects them from being manipulated by bosses, politicians, and other influentials, who ask so much but give so little in return.

Squeezed Cynics turn their aggression toward the system, the politicians, and generalized others when their frustrations take over. The cynical worldview helps them to attribute blame to political and economic institutions. It also protects their egos from acknowledging any personal shortcomings (rightly or not). The Squeezed Cynics' suspicion and disparagement are as manifest as those of the other cynical types, but the objects of their doubt and scorn are less personal and more abstract.

Certainly cynicism helps to prescribe the world of the squeezed worker. For the young, it rationalizes any lack of ambition and justifies a less straitlaced life-style. Thus, while their cynicism is aimed at a system that makes social and economic mobility difficult, at the same time it excuses a casual value system.[12] For more mature people, squeezed by corporate downsizing and threatening economic developments, cynicism is an accommodation to a new set of corporate and social expectations and conditions. As such, it helps to defuse their bitterness and ground their sense of betrayal.

Open Collars. The cynical outlook of Obstinate Stoics helps them to keep things on an even keel; it gives them the

power to avoid temptation and the self-confidence to stick to
what they know to be trustworthy. Cynicism, by its disparagement of the new and exciting, sets them gyroscopically on course
and keeps them there. For these cynics, change is threatening;
and their defense against it is as straightforward as it is
unyielding.

In the workplace, their cynicism treats change agents as
objects of derision and communication from management as
self-serving rubbish. Their kind has seen it all before. In their
narrow home lives, their suspicion of newcomers (like their
daughters' boyfriends or most of their spouses' recent friends)
keeps life under control and predictable. In their case, too,
cynicism is a protection against getting involved or getting into
trouble by making dumb mistakes. Cynicism keeps a clamp on
their lives and eliminates the risk of taking chances.

One basis for their cynicism, as we have seen, is their
righteousness about their strong work ethic.[13] They seem to
believe that few people work as hard as they do or as well.
Talkers are suspect but work is not; longevity is good but ambition is dangerous. Their cynicism is a self-fulfilling prophecy
and, on the job, makes them unusually resistant to new ideas
or ways of working. Cynicism simply keeps them obstinate.

Dark Collars. Cynicism is primarily protection and pre-
scription for the Hard-Bitten Cynics. Manifestations of the twin
pillars of cynicism—mistrust and suspicion—give the Hard-
Bittens their power and persona. Certainly some of the most
vocal, sneering, and ambitious of the Hard-Bittens gain status
as peer leaders—at least until co-workers have had enough of
their negativism. Others act out their cynicism and extract their
revenge on the job, by bullying naifs and weaklings or through
vandalism, thievery, and such, even to the point of punishing
the company by absenteeism or slowdowns.

Many of the Hard-Bittens have in fact much to be cynical
about. A high proportion come from the less advantaged classes
and have come up the hard way. Still, there are many others
from equally disadvantaged backgrounds who are not so cynical.
Moreover, even among those (such as the police) who see the
dark side of human nature every day, there are those who seem

to have a more tolerant and open-minded view of human nature.

Many of the Hard-Bittens, as we shall see, have stayed on the comparatively lower rungs of the socioeconomic ladder, and cynicism serves them well (if not their employers) on the job. For instance, there are innumerable ways to goldbrick. In the same fashion, there are countless ways to skim on the job in the many layers of public and private organizations and in retail trade. We hasten to add that everybody goofs off once in a while and that jobs on all levels have their perks. But for the Hard-Bitten cynic, goofing off is equated with getting even, and ripping off is a way of getting back.

Certainly there are signs of cynicism in today's working world. Command Cynics and Articulate Players such as Frank Lorenzo and Ivan Boesky, who manipulate people and assets largely for their own ends, seem larger than life. Yet self-interested scheming and manipulation are on the rise at every level of corporate America. Employee theft costs businesses today $75 billion annually. This compares with $16 billion just fifteen years ago. Surveys indicate that more than half the workers in the country take supplies, materials, and equipment from their employers.[14] It appears then, that the Hard-Bittens and Squeezed Cynics have their own ways of putting self-interest ahead of the common good. The question at hand is: How did we get to this point?

2

The
Cynical
Organization

One need only scan the want ads in the daily newspaper, read company promotional material, or listen to the sales talk of recruiters to see how quickly employees' expectations can be "hyped" in the world of work. Many seemingly forward-looking, aggressive companies promise managers a fast track to success and tantalize everyday workers with pledges of outstanding pay, generous benefits, and bright opportunities. Cynical companies especially give their recruits the come-on in much the same way that they hustle their customers and deceive the public. What are the realities?

Consider this message about company promises posted by betrayed employees on the bulletin board of a plant experiencing widespread layoffs following a merger:

> We can't promise you how long we'll be in business.
> We can't promise you that we won't be bought by
> another company.

We can't promise that there'll be room for promotion.
We can't promise that your job will exist until you
reach retirement age.
We can't promise that the money will be available
for your pension.
We can't expect your undying loyalty and we aren't
sure we want it.

Another way that corporations inflate hopes is by hiring
overqualified job candidates with the expectation of getting more
work out of them. Many people with whom we have talked noted
that their employment interviews were usually accompanied by
vague promises of early salary reviews and new job openings.
Seldom did these promises come to fruition in cynical companies.
On the contrary, many interviewees, particularly women and
minorities, reported that their companies seemed to prey upon
their relatively low job mobility.

Our overarching thesis throughout this book is that unmet
job expectations lead to disillusionment and then to cynicism.
This recipe can be applied to Squeezed Cynics, many of whom
are overeducated for jobs that promised them more. Broadly,
we see American companies in the midst of a vicious cycle,
wherein high expectations are setting people up for disappointment; yet, in so many instances, managers contribute by playing on those expectations and then failing to deliver.

As an example, the short-term orientation in many companies often leads to expedient overpromising by management
and consequent false expectations on the part of employees. Thus
promises or hints made in the heat of meeting a looming crisis
or bottom-line crunch often lead to behavior that employees see
as exploitative and cynical.

A study comparing the expectations of British and American workers illustrates the larger point. As the study showed,
American workers have more favorable attitudes toward their
pay and working conditions than have the British. But the Americans have less favorable attitudes toward management. The
researchers interpreted the findings in this fashion:

The [American] company spent a great deal of effort in "selling" itself to the workers, explaining what a good company it was and how much it did for its employees. This was often commented upon in interviews—"They try to brainwash you," "There's too much propaganda—it builds up people's hopes too much."

[Americans said that] while promotion opportunities might be good, they should have been better; while the company preached participation, it did not really practice it; even its admitted efficiency was a source of discontent: it was said that they were "ruthlessly efficient," that "all they care for is production"; and it was claimed that there were too many petty rules adhered to rigidly and that there was no flexibility, no "come and go" in management.

In short, [their management] did not meet their expectations. The U.S. company had created discontent by raising expectations to a level it was unable to fulfill.[1]

Mismanaging Workers' Expectations

The cynical inclination is to calibrate effort and involvement on the basis of "What's in it for me?" Plainly, unrealistic expectations have been fueled by the media and politicians, by educators and parents, and by society at large. In the world of work we find three ways in which companies mismanage the expectations of their work forces and reinforce their cynicism. One is by further inflating employees' hopes, to the point where they simply cannot be realized. The result is disillusionment. A second is to ignore people's aspirations. As a result, they learn to shield their dignity through cynicism. A final means of mismanaging expectations involves playing on people's ambitions, to the point where unbridled self-interest and swordlike cynicism define the corporate psyche. We will discuss each of these scenarios and then consider the alternatives.

Lost Loyalty in R&D. Listen to one company head, running a small corporation of five hundred people in the high-tech optics industry, describe his problems with R&D personnel:

> Those guys give me a royal pain. They all have Ph.D.'s in physics and think that they have a stranglehold over technological development. They have no damned understanding of what it takes to run a firm today.
>
> They get pissed off when I have to cut funding or stop projects in order to make the bottom line. They don't seem to understand or care that we're in a competitive business, and that their precious work is just one part of how this firm makes money. When I cut back, they start bitching and then fudge their budgets. They tell anybody who will listen that we're gonna be overtaken by the competition if we don't keep up our R&D support. That causes a lot of trouble in the sales force and starts rumors in the plant.
>
> They're really a bunch of prima donnas . . . who want to be treated like ''scientists'' even though they're just spoiled ''techies.''

This executive is harvesting seeds he had sown months before. He personally ''signed up'' many of the physicists with bright promises of independence and cutting-edge development work. Competition in the industry was keen for talented people, and promises of producing a breakthrough in optics appealed to many who would otherwise have had to wait their turns in larger corporations. When it came to specific projects, staff felt that they had been assured of the time and resources needed to accomplish something creative and important. All of this was suddenly (to their eyes) terminated. It seemed little more than a corporate power play—hence their anger, sense of betrayal, and jeremiads to the effect that the firm would no longer be competitive.

What the manager did not appreciate is the degree of frustration involved in shelving or cutting back on a promised R&D activity. When the physicists were hired, they were not told about the business cycles of the firm and the implications for R&D. On the contrary, that was deemed management information, and they were urged to busy themselves in their projects and cautioned not to nose around the financial aspects of the business. Furthermore, they were never privy to marketing or sales information.

Under the circumstances, they could be expected to have suspicions about the "real story" behind their setbacks and to protect their interests and integrity by challenging management's preemptive actions. That they would only fudge on their budgets and spread worrisome rumors is a measure of how unseasoned they are in the cynical world of high-tech gamesmanship: The high-tech industry is rife with stories of scientists taking technical talent and ideas to a competitor.

Management's error here is twofold. The first mistake is the boss's failure to empathize with the physicists and recognize how their frustration might lead to backbiting. He has simply lost sight of what truly motivates high-powered technical professionals and has miscast them as prima donnas and irritants. The second error is mismanaging the staff's expectations. Cynical managers "hype up" people's hopes with promises of a fast track to success and oversell the amount of time, resources, and freedom available to them. In this case, the boss never gave the physicists a realistic preview of their work, nor did he give them a clear picture before they were hired of the contingencies involved in the job. Some no doubt felt they had been duped by the president and now were paying back the company in kind.

Moreover, in the case of cutbacks, the R&D people were not fully apprised, through two-way communications, of the firm's financial condition. Instead, they heard vague references to unforeseen exigencies and problems. In the downsizing climate of the 1980s, many of the physicists read more into this talk than was intended. They were not, in any event, reassured that their futures were secure. Furthermore, they were given no indication that they were not the only ones suffering. Visible signs that management was "taking a bath" along with everyone else might have lessened their suspicions.

High plus false expectations equal frustration. That the staff was given neither a full disclosure about the reasons behind management's actions nor any reassurances about the implications for them naturally fueled their suspicions. It is no wonder that these employees reacted to management in a cynical, turf-protecting fashion. They put their cynicism to work through the bush telegraph and ultimately raised suspicion and concern throughout the firm. If the physicists had been educated about the business and had been given the chance to participate in decisions about its future, as well as their own, perhaps they could have coped better with the situation; and perhaps the boss would have found more loyalty in his company.

Dead-End Retail Dreams. At the other extreme are companies that downplay employees' expectations, to the point where they embrace cynicism to preserve their dignity. Cynical companies ignore the bona fide aspirations of the new work force and institute automation, controls, or procedures to eliminate, encapsulate, or circumvent the lazy ne'er-do-wells they seem to breed. This strategy deadens the work ethic, arouses passive and sometimes aggressive behavior, engenders mutual distrust between labor and management, and produces a self-fulfilling and self-defeating cycle.

This variety of cynical company hires people casually and fires them cruelly, experiences high turnover and low commitment, often produces shoddy products, and delivers poor service. It seldom confronts the problems posed by the high expectations of its employees, nor does it capitalize on the talents of the most able. The myopia and self-serving righteousness of executives in such companies, all of whom made it the hard way, only add to people's estrangement.

An owner of a mid-size electronics retail operation, age forty, has this to say about his employees:

These young kids coming into retailing today are
so indifferent. They want to do everything the easy

way. They don't have the drive, the get up and go, the sort of fire in the belly, that got me where I am today. They don't understand what it means to worry about customers who come into the store; they are more interested in proving to the customers that they're smarter than they are.

Look, everybody uses customers. But they use customers to show off: to communicate the idea that they are only temporarily in this kind of work—until something better comes along. Or to show them how technically sophisticated they are. They don't care about anything but themselves. It makes me sick.

Some smart-ass consultant told me once that I ought to lay out a career path to keep salespeople motivated. Hell, it's not my problem these kids don't think of retailing as a career.

In the case of this retail executive, the self-serving mind-set of his staff is predictable. They don't care about customers because they do not see any advantage in doing so; there is simply "nothing in it" for them to work hard, in contrast to just putting in time. This is too often the case in service industries, where the base pay is low and standardized procedures make it difficult for people to distinguish themselves in performance of their duties. As a result, these jobs are self-selected by many who are just bumping along without any hope for promotion or personal distinction.

Squeezed Cynics so prominent in service industries today are resigned to virtual anonymity on the job, as well as to routinized, dead-end employment. Hence they look to recreation and "partying" to express their creativity and blow off steam. It doesn't help when their superiors drive fancy cars or take long lunches, as is too often the case in retail sales-and-service outlets. This invites invidious comparisons among employees and leads them to ask, "Where's mine?" and to show off in front of customers.

What this executive needs to understand is that, as one informant told us, "cynicism starts with the paycheck." Studies show that the majority of working people do not believe that their hard work is rewarded, nor do they feel they are gaining a fair share of the company's profits.[2] Cynics believe, furthermore, that the reward system in their companies is rigged and that management simply doesn't value what they do on their jobs. Certainly the retail manager mentioned above hasn't done anything to alter that perception among his people, save for complaining about their laziness and indifference.

The best-managed organizations find innovative ways to reward merit and acknowledge accomplishment. They compensate people for acquiring skills or for proposing cost-saving ideas; they celebrate individual performance and initiative; and they respect young people's aspirations for more control over their time and space by instituting flextime programs, involving them in scheduling decisions, and providing time off in lieu of a bonus.

If such rewards are not available, then the job will not attract or sustain people who want a chance to become winners. On the contrary, the service work force will be peopled with losers who just go through the motions. Surely money matters to today's worker, but it is also important for managers to understand that people are equally interested in trying to distinguish themselves and gaining some measure of personal worth on the job. Our retail executive has failed to understand new cultural imperatives in American society. In the absence of an opportunity to distinguish themselves, people will buy time and seek their satisfactions elsewhere.

Unbridled Ambition. A third way that companies mismanage expectations is by failing to regulate people's self-interest. What characterizes a corporate culture based on unregulated ambition? It uses up many of its employees and spits them out, informants say. The cynics survive, having learned the rules of the game, and attrition takes care of the rest, leaving a cynical company with more cynical employees to match its cynical culture and management.

An important manifestation of unregulated ambition in corporate life is the promotion by managers and supervisors of a killer philosophy: Kill or be killed. This involves pushing the twin ideas that life is a jungle and winning is the only thing.

When winning at all costs is equated with profit at any cost, a company's ambition becomes exploitative.

When times are tough, ambitious and cynical managers will pressure employees or undertake layoffs without warning. They will also encourage backbiting and politics to create attrition. Even when times are good, exploitative and cynical managers will give several people the same assignment, in order to pick winners and losers. And they seldom, if ever, work with or on behalf of their employees. These are Command Cynics and unfettered Articulate Players.

All employees feel these killer imperatives, and the price of staying with such a firm is to assimilate the single-minded cynical life view, if only for psychological and economic survival. It means putting a face on things, getting by, and certainly not trying to change the system, the product, or personal relationships.

Consider the words of an executive vice-president, age fifty-five, who runs a division of a large packaged-goods company, complaining about the myopia, lack of sophistication, and what he calls the "pseudoidealism" of his direct reports:

> These people, vice-presidents all of them, are naive. They don't seem to realize that most of what we do is a game made up of fads and fashions. Don't they know that the executive suite in a marketing operation is a revolving door? Long-term brand building in the 1980s is out of style. Today it's all promotion. Nobody cares about what the brand is going to be like in a few years. By that time, most of us will be on another job and it won't make any difference to us.
>
> People have to learn that to get ahead in this business you've got to give the customers what they think they want, not what they should have. And that, sometimes, means sacrificing quality in order to cut the price and get sales. I don't want to hear any more of their complaints that we're milking brands. It makes us money—at least in the short run. And there isn't anything I can do if top management doesn't care about anything else.

This marketing executive is socializing his staff into the mind-set that customer loyalty doesn't really matter and thereby reinforcing their cynical proclivities. Certainly he was playing the jaded old pro for his vice-presidents, saying that the discipline of marketing involves holding one's finger to the wind and following the currents. He was disparaging their expertise and idealism—and therefore their dignity and professional standards.

The mistake of this manager is largely one of disrespect for his customers and his calling.[3] If executives have no respect for customers, it is very difficult to expect employees to have any either. This, of course, leads to the following perception: "If he says this about customers, what's he saying about us?"

Cynicism from senior management begets cynicism throughout an organization. The old pro was amorally signaling to his people that their decisions should be expeditious, since the only thing that matters is making a financial showing. With such an orientation, this manager has created a climate in which short-term opportunism has taken the place of long-term loyalty. For the vice-presidents, the price of staying is to assimilate this cynical mind-set for psychological and economic survival.

What a contrast this is to companies that are committed to long-term brand building and marketing excellence. In such firms, senior managers pride themselves on being positive role models and take pains to season hard-charging vice-presidents into high-minded corporate ideals. Such managers are sometimes seen as old-fashioned by young players. So be it. Better that than "dead meat," the way some were characterized by junior executives plotting to take their jobs.

Cynical Manifestations and Their Management

These executives, all in different industries, are looking for the same things from their people: loyalty and some appreciation of the "big picture," a measure of understanding, and a willingness to undertake change. Instead, they find themselves sabotaged by turfism, mistrust, scoffing, complacency, and alienation.

What these executives do not appreciate is that their employees have likely become disillusioned with company life and suspect the motives of their management. People are coping by acting as "their own best friends" and protecting their turf, identities, and dignity. And while all three executives feel victimized by these attitudes, they themselves are part and parcel of the problems they encounter. Stated simply, these executives are purveyors, as well as recipients, of cynicism at work.

This final account, of a vice-president in charge of manufacturing for a mid-size firm, illustrates the point:

> There are two kinds of people on the line. There are the old-timers, who pretty much stick to themselves. They don't say a hell of a lot and work at their own pace and in their own way, no matter what the hell we try to do to improve efficiency in the plant. No matter what equipment we bring in, or what kind of experts we use to tell them how to operate better, they seem to resist any change of any kind at all.
>
> The other group are the young fellows and gals. They just wanna put in time. They couldn't care less about what we do or what we say. They ignore directives and are far more interested in getting a long weekend than in joining any kind of a group effort to improve plant productivity.
>
> I've read the books about Japanese manufacturing and many of the things American companies are doing to be more competitive. None of that stuff seems to work in this plant. I'll tell you, people better wake up, cause we're going to become more productive with or without them.

The resistance to change that this vice-president encountered is based, in the minds of his employees, in the belief that change will lead to layoffs and dislocations, with the brunt of the pain borne by seemingly expendable blue-collar workers. The boss, a voracious reader of modern management tracts, has failed to understand the historical experiences of his work force. For years his predecessors had treated employees as "hands" and never solicited their suggestions or stimulated their initiative. On the contrary, blue-collar operatives had been told when to work, how to work, and how much to produce, with no questions asked. Management had scarcely invested in plant and equipment and had never considered any but the most basic investments in human capital. The older workers learned from experience that management doesn't give a damn about them. Many have become Obstinate Stoics who regard the new boss as something of a "kook." In their eyes, bosses come and go, and this one, too, will pass.

A more assertive attitude has been embraced by the younger workers. Some are, frankly, Hard-Bitten Cynics who see the boss as a self-aggrandizing promoter out to make himself look good. They, too, have seen bosses come and go and pride themselves on driving them out. No wonder the vice-president is frustrated.

Undaunted, the engineering vice-president initiated several new efforts at improving productivity. Stoical older workers looked upon them with suspicion, while younger workers dubbed them the "program of the month." Neither group was responsive to the slide shows delivered by so-called experts, nor were they given any reason to believe that the engineering vice-president would be any different from his predecessors.

Then the boss's rhetoric took on a tougher and more threatening tone. He vowed to make the organization "lean and mean," and the word went out to plant management that it was time to crack down on young malingerers and get rid of the older "deadwood." As a consequence, people began to lose confidence in the company and feared for their jobs.

The operative perception of employees at this and many other plants today is one of threat. Old-timers throughout heavy industry are under the microscope and have busied themselves with keeping their noses clean. They are worried that their skills are obsolete and have had their worries exacerbated by management's tough rhetoric and failure to communicate otherwise. The younger people who haven't yet developed a full range of manufacturing skills have even more reason to wonder whether they will be the last on and first off in the name of corporate efficiency.

It has not reached the point of layoffs or purges in the

manufacturing plant in question here, but neither have any of the productivity-raising initiatives yielded much success. The vice-president needs, through effective communication, to tell his employees what's in it for them to raise productivity. He cannot expect his workers to respond with enthusiasm when all he talks about is efficiency for the sake of the plant. He needs to talk about how productivity gains can be translated into more secure jobs and better incomes. Otherwise, he is saying that the company in the abstract is more important than the flesh-and-blood workers. He is also signaling that efficiency is more important than any long-term obligations the company may feel to its employees. This is always a danger when employers ask for loyalty and, at the same time, bring in experts to introduce change. It implies, too often, that the people in place cannot contribute to the change process and that their experience and skills are no longer relevant or important. Under these circumstances, it is small wonder that change is resisted by young and old alike.

The alternative, of course, is to involve blue-collar workers in the change process, to provide them with the training and support they need to upgrade current skills or develop new ones, and to guarantee them continuing employment. There are many instances of productivity-improvement programs under way in industry today that have succeeded in turning around floundering businesses and empowering lethargic work forces. The key to their success seems to be sensible investment in new technology coupled with extensive employee involvement in the change effort.

Cynicism at Work

Many managers today (and, to some extent, the four we have cited) operate in company cultures that create, reinforce, and sustain cynicism. The flavor of these cynical companies is well expressed in the following letter that reveals not only deleterious company practices but also their disillusioning impact on incipient cynics in the work force. The letter is entitled "How Working Stiffs Get the Short End."

Dear Ann Landers:

In response to the letter in your column about stealing, office style, perhaps the following might give you some added insight.

You speak of a fading morality, a lack of standards, acceptance of crooked practices such as inside trading on Wall Street and medical diplomas on sale for $500. May I suggest that you take a look at the executives running many of our large corporations? Then, take a look at our public officials. Several have been caught, convicted of crimes, and sent to jail. But they still keep collecting their pensions.

Executives cut their staffs by cutting employees after 20 and 30 years of service. They cheat them and their families out of their pensions and lifetime medical benefits. All the worker receives is a small vested benefit guaranteed by the Employee Retirement Income Security Act.

These same executives give themselves large salary increases, bonuses, trips, and other extras. I don't mind them getting a bigger share of the pie, but it shouldn't be at the expense of the little guy.

Double standards are at work everywhere. Workers may take small freebies, but it is nothing compared to what the corporate leaders are doing.

I do hope you will print this letter and start a groundswell to protect the workers and their families. You are one of the last honest people we can turn to. Please help us.

A Discouraged Worker in Flushing, N.Y.[4]

Culture of the Cynical Company. There are innumerable ways to characterize the work culture of a company. There are, for example, weak and strong cultures, rigid rule-based cultures, and innovative ones that foster independence; there are achievement-oriented cultures and cultures oriented to power or support; there are flexible cultures and cultures that resist being changed. It seems that descriptions of corporate culture are as varied as the ways of conceptualizing human affairs. But even though these descriptions stem from distinct intellectual traditions, they tend in their language and formulation to have one thing in common: They assign human attributes to the organization.

It is in this spirit that we add another dimension to the many existing descriptions of corporate culture—the values of the cynical company. Such a rendering necessarily anthropomorphizes the structure and operations of corporations. In so doing, it also enables us to see how this view of human nature is expressed in the way companies operate.[5]

To begin, it may seem strange today to think that companies could be idealized in the eyes of employees. But there are signs that many Americans once held large corporations in awe. Columnist Robert Samuelson makes the point: "World War II had seemed to vindicate big organizations: the military, wartime industry, and government agencies. More than 16 million Americans had been in uniform. Everyone knew big organization exacted a price, but the price seemed worth it. The war had been won." Today it is a very different story. Samuelson writes: "To be cynical about corporate motives is now normal, even chic."[6]

Our opinion is that many contemporary developments in business and the economy feed the cynic's outlook. Robert Reich, for example, speculates that there is widespread disillusion with the rise of "paper entrepreneurialism" in American industry. How should one view the widespread "shuffling" of corporate assets, the millions lost and gained in paper transactions, and the massive hirings, firings, and layoffs in industry today? Reich sees it as an insidious contributor to a "selfish attitude among directors, managers, and employees, an egoistic mentality which is seriously undermining American enterprise."[7]

Many mergers, acquisitions, and downsizing efforts have added to the perception that everyone must fend for him- or herself. Widespread reductions in force have confirmed for many their ingrained suspicions about the "real motives" of people

in charge today. Certainly this makes both managers and workers question what's behind the changes they experience and who
will gain what. It also makes many feel like fools for staying
loyal to their firms.

Within companies, there are also everyday practices—
concerning the company's philosophy, products, services, and
image—that can contribute to the disillusion of working people.
As we turn to them, the reader should recognize that, on the
surface, these practices can be cast as tough and realistic strategies for surviving in a competitive environment. At the core
of the corporate culture, however, these practices should be
recognized as manifesting both a cynical view of the world and
values that depreciate human character and advance naked
self-interest.

Greed over Ideals. Far and away the most frequent characterization we heard of the cynical company concerned its obsession with the bottom line. Companies that will seemingly do
or say anything for the sake of profit were marked by our
respondents as breeding grounds for cynicism. Those we talked
with offered many illustrations of the greedy company. Its practices included everything from selling shoddy merchandise to
polluting the environment.

Overall, the philosophy of the cynical company is that
greed predominates over high-minded ideals. This greed is most
manifest throughout the cynical corporation in its financial decisions and systems. Greedy companies will pay top dollar for
talented personnel but prey on the relatively low market value
of lesser-skilled employees. The message is: "If you don't like
it here, get another job." Greedy companies erect massive corporate edifices but replace domestic manufacturing facilities with
offshore sources whenever it seems more profitable. Managers
in greedy companies learn to pad their budgets, to operate on
"rubber margins," to do whatever it takes to make quarterly
results turn out right. Employees, in turn, cheat on their expense accounts, time cards, and production reports.

This emphasis on greed over idealism has subtle implications. The greedy company has no lasting vision of itself. Its
management is populated by short-term "vision killers" who

will do anything for a quick profit, regardless of the implications for future growth or the good of the firm. These include cynical marketing executives who rely upon quick fixes, such as promotions, rather than on long-term, customer-oriented, brand-building strategies, such as quality enhancement. Furthermore, plant managers who mindlessly automate, engineering heads who sacrifice R&D investment, and personnel managers who squander training money are all in their own ways vision killers. They send the message that money and machines are more important than people and long-term productivity.

Another variant of the cynical short-term approach is asset stripping. Nearly every day, the press recounts stories of financial raiders who buy companies and finance their purchases by selling off newly acquired assets. In this era of golden parachutes and stock options, moreover, the money is also needed to pay off senior management, who sold the company in the first place. To many working people, this all looks like the big boys are taking care of their own at the expense of the little people.

In a very real sense, vision killers and asset strippers are indulging in the same activity: They are mortgaging the future for present gains. It is an approach Americans are criticized for and one that the Japanese, by and large, reject out of hand. If the automotive and home electronics industries are typical (and we believe they are), the short-term expedient approach will in the long run bring trouble to owners and employees alike. The greedy company's lack of a lasting vision of itself carries with it, in our view, intimations of its own demise.

Shoddy Goods and Services. The Dalkon shield is a symbol of how dangerous American products can be. Add unsafe automobiles, cancerous food additives, and subsidized tobacco, and the list grows. A perusal of *Consumer Reports* attests to the questionable quality of many domestic products. "Made in America" no longer means high quality to many people in today's marketplace. What does it mean to employees? The majority of American workers say that the quality of American-made products is not as good as the quality of competing imported products. One in four American workers says that he or she personally is ashamed of the quality of goods he or she produces.[8] The decline in American services is felt equally by many service employees.

Many managers point the finger at employees on this count. They contend that the work ethic is dead; that quality doesn't matter to people anymore; that pride, craftsmanship, and care are gone. In turn, many employees point to their management, who, they say, set a poor example and are unwilling to listen to the ideas of otherwise well-intentioned employees.[9] In either case, the finger pointing over who is responsible for shoddy goods and botched services is just another earmark of a company in which all are presumed to be acting out of their own self-interest and nobody can really be trusted.

Companies that sell inferior or unsafe products are perforce cynical; they reveal a contempt for their buyers and their personnel and follow a strategy of short-term gain.[10] Companies that encourage their customers to finance their purchases through easy credit terms, regardless of a buyer's entire debt load, extend the cynical orientation directly to the retail marketplace.

Treating Customers Like Jerks. The film *Tin Men,* about aluminum-siding salesmen who have contempt for their purchasers, is an example of the cynic in the sales force. We trace some of this attitude back to cynical sales and marketing organizations. For example, many companies emphasize training in selling technique, at the expense of teaching the sales force product knowledge or stressing postsales service. The prevailing philosophy seems to be that customers can be readily manipulated and fooled. This brand of selling is not limited to siding salesmen, real-estate hustlers, or used-car higglers. In many large and well-respected companies, the culture is infused with the belief that customers are jerks who can be manipulated by sales staff into a purchasing mode.

This lack of respect for customers is a key ingredient in the cynical company.[11] Inevitably, the attitude generalizes throughout the organization. Surveys show that today many fewer supervisors than fifteen years ago have respect and confidence in their managers.[12] In turn, hourly and clerical workers have lost even more respect and confidence in their supervisors.

The biggest loser? Confidence in one's company has declined over 50 percent.

Ads That Create a False Public Aura. Employees of several companies told us they were embarrassed by corporate ads that made their companies appear benevolent, when the bottom line was all that really counted in their firms. They saw their companies as two-faced and hypocritical. Among the campaigns cited were self-congratulatory ads of oil companies that claimed to be in business for patriotic reasons—providing energy for a strong America. Other informants were outraged by insurance and pharmaceutical ads that portrayed their companies as unselfish and caring.

The effect of companies' advertising on employees' cynicism is a question that invites further investigation. We believe that ad campaigns like Avis's "We try harder . . . " might be morale boosters for employees. In the same way, ads that genuinely celebrate employees' contributions or innovative work arrangements may perhaps reinforce an upbeat mood. But ads that put the company in a false light in the eyes of employees may also be a source of cynicism to them.

Exploitative Management. There are, of course, many other managerial manifestations of the cynical outlook in organizations, in smaller offices, shops, and outlets, and in family firms. Michael Lombardo and Morgan McCall recently conducted a study of the characteristics of the "intolerable boss."[13] Bosses were faulted for being egoists, incompetents, martinets, and detail drones, but the most faulted were "snakes in the grass." These were managers who lied, failed to honor commitments, used their authority to extort confidences, and generally could not be trusted. These are, of course, our Command Cynics and Administrative Sideliners—the role models to Articulate Players in line and staff posts, respectively.

Everybody has had an encounter with an intolerable boss. When this is not the exception but the norm in a company, the company is befouled with exploitative management. It is led by supervisors and managers who are viewed as short-term and expedient—willing to sacrifice their everyday people for the sake of the bottom line, without remorse. The message is internalized, and it's every man for himself. Untrustworthy management begets a cynical work force. Opinion Research Corporation data indicate that nearly four out of five hourly and clerical workers find that their companies "play favorites," and most managers are of the same opinion.[14]

There remain, moreover, insidious signs of discrimination against women, blacks, and other minorities in today's workplace. They earn less than their white male counterparts and have less access to technical, professional, and managerial jobs. A cynical company operates within the letter but not the spirit of the law. A conspicuous example of this approach is the hiring of minorities and women to fill quotas rather than jobs. Flagrant exploitation of fellow workers (minorities or not) makes all workers feel vulnerable: Who might be next to get the treatment?

Institutionalized tokenism is not only morally bankrupt. It also signals to all workers that the firm's character is cynical: Managers seem to sneer and turn a blind eye to problems of general human dignity, with corresponding disregard even of product or service quality. It is a poor example to employees when they see their management working to rules or slyly complying with the law. This attitude encourages shoddiness in all aspects of the firm's operations.

We have seen the culturally imprinted contempt managers have for employees in cynical companies. Cynicism is manifest wherever supervisors or managers are unavailable during stressful periods (communicating, for example, by memo, bulletin board, or electronic media) but make themselves conspicuous during easy periods; it is manifest, too, wherever supervisors or managers do not try to make work life more pleasant (with better facilities and rest areas) but do enforce meaningless regulations and rules.

This mind-set is carried down through the ranks by cynics at every level in a company. At some point, the cynical style becomes part of the lifeblood of a company, and cynicism becomes a characteristic of a company's culture and takes on a momentum of its own. It is in this sense, then, that people's cynical predispositions are confirmed by company culture, and thus cynicism is embraced by new recruits and managerial trainees and becomes the way of life in a company.

The emergence of this attitude was aptly recognized by *Esquire* magazine in an article on how to get a job. The article offered the following ''hard truths about work'' to job seekers:

1. Your objective in a job is not self-expression but to put bread on the table. Knowing this will save you painful disillusionment later.
2. Staying happy on the job is your own responsibility.
3. There is only one perfect definition of doing a good job: Making your boss look good.
4. Don't expect thanks for a job well done. That is taken care of by the person who brings around your paycheck.[15]

It should come as no surprise that these recommendations have a cynical and self-serving beat. They are guides to survival in the cynical company.

3

The
Cynical
Society

The cynical outlook has always been part of the American character. Ambrose Bierce attested to its prominence in an earlier time in his *Devil's Dictionary* (originally titled *The Cynic's Word Book*). Today another popular book, *The Cynic's Lexicon,* gleans the writings and speeches of politicians, industrialists, and critics to exemplify the cynical mind at work.[1] These writings bear ample witness to American tendencies to deprecate institutions and satirize human foibles and reach an audience appreciative of wit and spite.

Yet there are historical epochs when cynicism is especially pervasive—when events are almost too profound for glib treatment and too palpable for derisive laughter. The U.S. Depression of the 1930s is an example of such a time. There was massive unemployment in this era; savings were wiped out and mortgages were foreclosed; people were sick, hungry, cold, and left to their own devices. Big business was blamed; government had failed; the Promised Land for many immigrants was lost. In this unique set of social and economic circumstances, seeds of disillusionment, sown earlier, in a more hopeful decade, sprouted into widespread cynicism.

The Cynical Cycle in the Twenties and Thirties

The 1920s were a period of wild optimism. This was a time of national expansionism and military victory. World War I was over. The industrial revolution was in full bloom. There were jobs and heretofore unimagined opportunities for the many. On the domestic front, there was a promise of "a chicken in every pot"; on the international front, tranquillity would be ensured through the League of Nations. As the decade began, Babe Ruth went to the Yankees and Man O'War went to stud. Women got to vote and Prohibition became the law of the land. America was being readied for its century, and Americans had soaring hopes of achieving the good life.

Soon thereafter, however, came the first signs that self-serving operators would exploit these hopes and ultimately undermine them. In political life, a powerful clique of U.S. senators played upon xenophobia and spitefully rejected U.S. membership in the League of Nations, while an ambitious district attorney and judiciary pressed ahead with the show trial of Sacco and Vanzetti. Crooked cronies brought disgrace to Warren Harding's presidency. And Chicago police and "pols" went on the take in service of Al Capone's booze-and-broads empire spawned by cynical disregard for Prohibition.

In business, a wave of mergers created a new generation of industrial empires. Rates of self-employment dropped dramatically, and an urban working class was formed. Scientific management techniques were used to mold these workers to the will of their employers, while less advanced but no less effective methods, including the use of secret police, were used to thwart their unions. Meanwhile, con men and bunco artists preyed upon workers' dreams of making it rich.

Still, skirts were shortened, the music was freer, and the 1920s were a time to throw caution to the winds. Big business was romanticized, and investors, large and small, began to buy stocks and properties "on the margin." It did not seem to matter that some flouted the law and others were victimized by it. Opportunities were there for the taking.

In the 1930s, of course, the ground gave way. The collapse of the stock market in 1929 gave rise to a sour period called the Great Depression. The shining expectations of the 1920s faded into the gloom of a worldwide economic collapse. There were songs of lament, like "Brother, Can You Spare a Dime?" that represented the plight of many Americans during this era. There were also hard realistic movies like *They Gave Him a Gun* and *The Grapes of Wrath* that reflected people's sense of betrayal and desperation.

We can see from American life in the 1930s how the high hopes of many were raised and then dashed, leading to their disillusionment. Yet there remained a wellspring of confidence and commitment to be tapped by the vigorous leadership of Roosevelt, the outreach of charitable groups, and, most of all, by the call to arms against Germany and Japan.

Rising Expectations: The Forties and Fifties

Victory in World War II proved a balm for the American psyche. Sociologist Seymour Sarason notes that, during the war, "things were accomplished which confirmed in people's minds the limitless possibilities of our society when the appropriate commitment was made."[2] The country built airplanes, warships, and tankers beyond all expectations. We demonstrated our scientific and technological prowess in harnessing the atom. He adds: "War, like the Great Depression, was a disaster for millions of Americans, but in its perversely dialectical way, the war broadened for millions horizons for themselves and their perceived world."

The many lessons of the war concerning organization, public opinion, and mass mobilization were readily incorporated into American industry, politics, and education. At the same time, America, perhaps too quickly, put the horrors of war behind it. The monstrosities of the Holocaust, the nuclear bomb-ing of Japanese cities, the slaughter of the air war over Europe, and even our own casualties seemed too quickly forgotten. In-stead, the public's attention shifted to the bright and promis-ing future.

The demobilizing and rehabilitation of the armed forces opened the way to upward social mobility for millions. The future in 1946 looked full of promise for a victorious America. Japan was reconstructed along democratic lines, and Europe was put back together through the generous-minded Marshall Plan. The hopes for peace were high, and American support for the United Nations was unstinting.

Subsequent events, though, make it seem that World War II and the enthusiastic worldview it fostered were all, so to speak, a setup for what was to come. After the heady euphoria of military triumph, a measure of disappointment was almost in-evitable. But the depth of cynicism that arose during the after-math of our intense and propaganda-reinforced effort to win illustrates what we believe is a familiar cycle: People's hopes and expectations were raised en masse and then broadly frus-trated and spoiled. In the next forty years of the American ex-perience, this cycle of cynicism, like so many other cycles, has been sped up by an expanding electronic media, an ever more trend-conscious public, and an increasingly interdependent global economy.

Making Up for Lost Time. In the war, there was the buddy system. Soldiers had to rely upon one another to survive, let alone to get home in one piece. Loyalty to the group, trust in one another, and obedience to those in command were integral parts of becoming a soldier. It was virtually unthinkable for a G.I. to publicize his self-interest in a crunch. After the war, by contrast, there was extraordinary competition to make oneself employable and a mad rush to make up for lost time. Coopera-tion and trust gave way to competitiveness and self-interest.

The social revolution that followed World War II was fueled by two essential elements. First, there was the G.I. Bill, which provided housing and university education for millions who before the war could never have imagined getting any form of higher education or owning, not renting, their homes at age thirty. Second, there was easy installment credit. This meant that ex-G.I.s, for very little down, could buy all kinds of goods, including autos for themselves and laborsaving devices for their wives.

Other factors as well contributed to rising expectations in society. For many married veterans, the desire to make up for lost time took the form of having children early. They expected that university life was going to be useful and pleasant and would coexist easily with family life. Many anticipated with relish the provider's role. Women, in turn, were charged with typing their husbands' papers and keeping the children quiet, but they looked forward to the future, when their husbands would provide them with enough material security to buy that treasured tract house in the suburbs.

All these economic and social advances were premised on America's continued achievements in science, technology, and productivity. With the atomic bomb, Americans had high hopes of keeping the peace. There were also high hopes that we would soon cure all diseases and rid the world of famine and pestilence. The broad point is that the 1950s gave rise to a new era of high hopes for individuals and for American society.

The realities were, in comparison, rather disappointing. The tin huts that appeared on most university campuses were uncomfortable, and students were herded into crowded classes on crowded campuses. Non–college-educated craftsmen and tradesmen had to compete for scarce jobs. They could only afford to live at home or move into cobbled-together homes in crowded developments. For most, these were tough times, replete with shortages of all kinds, including lack of money. They were unromantically difficult for women, and few men truly experienced the promised lush life-style. Still, it was a time when people were buoyed by an optimistic perspective. University men anticipated that their degrees would lead them to big jobs at important companies; blue-collar men counted on expanding opportunities in industry to support their dreams of getting ahead without having to strike. Women felt that, after the trials and tribulations of life in a trailer or with in-laws, surely something better would open up for them. More than this, the men and women of the 1950s seemed willing to delay their gratification, confident that better times were just ahead.

The Letdown of the Fifties. The future, however, proved a mixed blessing for many young veterans and their spouses. The first house was flimsy and scarcely private—not quite what they had anticipated, especially after the man of the house had obtained a better education than his parents. The appliances and expectations that were cast onto the woman stamped her in a subservient role. Her job was still to keep the children quiet, to defer, and provide meals, all this with the advanced technology of washing machines, dryers, blenders, and other labor-saving devices that the ex-G.I.'s mother could not have imagined. The wife, it was tacitly assumed by both marital partners, had it easier than either of their mothers and was therefore expected to be both fulfilled and grateful.

This was a time, then, of letdowns. The great American male disease—self-pity—appeared in epidemic proportions: Veterans found themselves in debt, compounded by buying a house for a growing family, laborsaving devices, and a car. Many had struggled through college with the view that there would be a payoff. The fantasies, to which wartime distance lent enchantment, of having children, owning a home, and getting on in the world seemed in reality to be more trying and less fulfilling than many ex-G.I.s had expected. Their life-styles were certainly in sharp contrast to those promulgated by *Playboy* magazine and to other depictions of the good life.

The American male's sense of letdown was increased by growing consumerism in society. Unanticipated sacrifices had to be made in order to keep up with the Joneses. Even the ostensibly successful "Man in the Gray Flannel Suit" was feeling psychologically pinched.[3] Ambitious and upwardly mobile veterans soon discovered that companies had rules and mores that constrained individual freedoms and occasionally strained moral inclinations, as William Whyte documented in *The Organization Man.*[4] Well-respected companies in the 1950s, like Procter & Gamble, often "advised" employees about which section of town to live in, as well as about when it was smart to marry—and whom. The white-shirt rule at Allstate Insurance and other companies was an example of imposed conformity. Many veterans questioned whether they had exchanged one uniform for another.

By no means, however, was cynicism as pervasive and palpable in the 1950s as it had been during the Great Depression. There were, after all, plenty of jobs for men, and suburban satisfactions seemed enough for many women. While the cozy domestic tranquility found in ''The Donna Reed Show'' and the goody-goody manners of the Mouseketeers scarcely represented the realities of the times, neither were home and family life marked by the upheaval and sense of disillusionment experienced in the Depression years. On the political front, however, there would be a sea change in our outlooks and confidence about the future.

From Victory to Vigilance. Suspicion and cynicism marked McCarthyism and the postwar Red Scare. These attitudes were brought into American homes by broadcasts of Senate investigations of alleged communists. Americans were told by Senators Richard Nixon and Joseph McCarthy that there were traitors among us. Russia's assertiveness was no accident, we were informed; it was manipulated by Alger Hiss and other East Coast, Ivy League hangers-on of Roosevelt's New Deal, producing the Yalta sellout to the Soviets and the communist takeover of China. Even General George C. Marshall was accused of disloyalty.

Senator McCarthy was the embodiment to many Americans of a healthy mistrust of ''dupes'' who did not share his views of the communist infiltration of the United States. Richard Rovere, the political columnist of *The New Yorker* magazine in 1959, wrote about McCarthy in this way: ''Whatever he did he did for an effect that he seemed either to have calculated or intuitively appraised with soundness. My own view was that whatever the wellsprings of his behavior and whatever tributaries fed them, he could be described as a true cynic and a true hypocrite. This seemed to me to make his a rather special case. True cynics—'those canine philosophers,' as St. Augustine called them—are very rare and true hypocrites are even rarer. Cynicism requires a disbelief in the possibility of sincerity. But to McCarthy everything was profane.''[5]

It would be grossly inaccurate, however, to conclude that the search for "Reds under the bed," including the case of the Hollywood 10 and blacklisting of entertainers, was the only source of disillusionment in our polity. Moderates and liberals of both parties also set themselves up for a fall when their trustful assumptions about people and beliefs in a just world were dashed. There was, for example, the shocking Suez invasion—a last cynical gasp of Britain's empire abetted by an opportunistic Israeli government. The Russians in Czechoslovakia and Hungary brought home the ruthless nature of the Soviet government to the heretofore trusting liberals. The continuing decline of the United Nations as an effective force was yet another blow to high-minded sensibilities, as was the realization that Sputnik would prove to be an orbiting symbol of an impending nuclear-arms race between the Soviets and the Western democracies.

These events, along with revelations about the Holocaust and South African apartheid, helped forge a jaundiced mindset in the American public. People began to question the motives of political leaders and what lay behind their maneuverings. More broadly, people began to question both the comprehensibility and the justice of a seemingly imperfectible world.

Yet there were many positive developments during this postwar era of domestic letdown and military vigilance. The women's movement grew partly from the sense of disillusion experienced by women who were treated as second-class citizens after their selfless participation in the war effort and their unrewarded efforts to help their husbands get ahead. In the same way, the civil rights movement gained ground through the leadership of black veterans who were treated hypocritically both during and after the war. Both of these movements drew strength from the need to have watershed postwar dreams and promises come true. All social change takes time; in the case of women and blacks, it took the children of the put-upon wives and put-down blacks to put these movements into motion.

These children had been raised on the rising tide of material and social expectations and with the knowledge that America could be a great country. As part of the "Now Generation," they would be impatient for social change, would find it harder to delay their gratifications, and would develop a new set of high expectations for themselves and their country. These children would, in their time, seek to change America's foreign and domestic policy and would gravitate to new life-styles, music, and modes of expression. They would also experience personal dismay and confusion, organized resistance to their organized protests, and deeper frustration and disillusionment than they or their parents could have imagined.

Hopes Renewed: The Sixties

There were attitudes and events in the early sixties that seemed to point to a different, more adventuresome, and less constricted way of life than, say, the fifties with their emphasis on short hair, narrow ties, and conformity. There were new ways of doing things that seemed far more promising and generous than those available in the competitive and materialistic postwar years. The idea that "father knows best" was doomed. Change was in the air, and the fifties values of home, hearth, and heaven seemed not only stiflingly dated but hypocritical, especially to those whose parents had "made it" financially but not emotionally. Never having known Depression-era hardship, many assumed that prosperity was easy to attain and that they should go for happiness and self-fulfillment.[6]

Symbolically and experientially, the sexual revolution was a breaking away from traditional authority. Moreover, the pill marked women's entry into sexual equality, with changed expectations. That both young men and women could participate in early sexual activities was in defiance of received wisdom and conventional morality. Young Americans began to experiment with new sexual practices and life-styles—including cohabitation and open homosexuality—all taboo to their elders. The anti-authoritarian qualities of the sexual revolution soon were translated into other areas of American life by the mid 1960s. It opened new vistas of thought, dress, and demeanor for young people.[7] The possibilities seemed endless. In essence, the revolution of rising emotional expectations was under way and seemingly genderless.

Then there were drugs. Mind-altering illegal substances of all kinds proliferated in the 1960s. Many young people at least tried the softer drugs, and many (alas) used serious mind-altering substances, such as LSD. In this they were urged on by ostensible gurus, who extolled the virtues of leaving the materialistic earth and its quotidian demands and tripping out to more celestial regions. What many had once considered outrageous behavior, illegal and unacceptable, became the thing to do for apostles and disciples of the new freedom.

The 1960s would also offer another means of reaching into oneself and connecting with other people and the surrounding world. This was the dawn of the human potential movement, with its myriad encounter groups and consciousness-raising experiences that were aimed at freeing people from their emotional barriers to self-expression and reaching out to others. To a large extent, the baby boomers thought of themselves as a new generation of Americans, bound to avoid the emotional bankruptcy and stultifying conformity of their parents, but also committed to establishing new frontiers of emotional and creative expression. In a sense, the transformation of the Beatles from the ''Fab Four'' into archetypes of the new consciousness mirrored and perhaps mapped that of the boomer generation.

Of course, there were other voices in the pop-music pantheon.[8] The tell-it-like-it-is lyrics of Bob Dylan delineated the cool and detached attitude that the baby boomers could apply to society, much as the tell-it-like-it-ought-to-be sound of Peter, Paul, and Mary evinced the warmer and more communal outlook of young idealists. Janis Joplin, the Jefferson Airplane, and Jimi Hendrix all put their oars in seas of rebellion, freedom, and sensitivity as they sang of racial injustice, excess materialism, hypocrisy, and other defects of that earlier generation.

Baby boomers found meaning in the slogan ''Don't trust anyone over thirty.'' Probably the Woodstock gathering was the bonding rite of the decade. Even for those who did not drop out in the sixties, who did not groove to pop music, and who did not regard their values as totally antithetical to those of their parents, the freer and more generous outlook was the mind-set of youth in the sixties.

Social Changes and Movements. There were many social changes in the 1960s that reached deeper into the polity and heightened the hopes of many far removed from young people's music and yearnings. One of the most salutary developments to come out of the communal burst was the civil rights movement. Blacks and whites marched together to break institutionalized segregation and, by 1963, the marchers had a new leader and he "had a dream."

This dream of a united America was noble, overdue, and unifying. The felicitous interracial attitudes that Martin Luther King, Jr., and others engendered were in the spirit of the new sensitivity. The Civil Rights Bill surely heightened blacks' aspirations and probably brought more enlightenment into white homes than any single legislative act. The sixties also brought the women's movement, the concept of sisterhood, and another set of national challenges and priorities. Public attention turned to the needs of the poor, the elderly, the handicapped. All this was part of the new sensitivity, and it inevitably fueled aspirations in these population groups. On the political front, the election of John F. Kennedy signaled that a new generation of twentieth-century Americans was taking power and embracing a broad social agenda, including a Peace Corps and a war on poverty.

The Sixties Begin to Unravel. Perhaps the unraveling of high hopes in the 1960s started when Kennedy was assassinated in 1963 and, on the following day, his assassin was murdered. The conspiracy theory concerning Kennedy's death lingers today. Many people worldwide believe that the government deliberately and cynically covered up the facts concerning the Kennedy assassination. The seeming subterfuge, whether true or not, sowed profound suspicion and doubt about legally constituted authority.[9] The death of JFK brought Lyndon Johnson to the White House and, early on, a spate of liberal legislation demarked the Great Society. But the Vietnam War soon preoccupied the Johnson presidency, and what seemed hopeful at the time turned dark as the war escalated and domestic progress was put on the back burner.

Toward the end of the sixties, many so-called alternative life-styles were beginning to play themselves out. Desperate searches for the good life were in part responsible for their own destruction. It was not just revelations that easy sex and drugs produced sordid lives and ruined middle-class children, nor was it that pop-music priests could overdose and pop-psychology nostrums about self-actualization would prove unattainable; it was also the realization that efforts to keep the world safe for democracy would have us propping us corrupt dictators, bombing heretofore peaceful villages, and napalming women and children. The Vietnam War was beginning to take its toll. It was also laying a foundation for the coming ideological split in the United States concerning the war and its conduct. Soil hospitable to deep and dark disillusionment was being tilled for the decade ahead.

The killing of Martin Luther King, Jr., in 1968 was as shrouded in mystery as President Kennedy's death. Senator Robert Kennedy's assassination, at the hands of a deranged Palestinian, was just as heartbreaking, if less mysterious. The loss of RFK, the most intense and idealistic of the Kennedys, was particularly disillusioning because he embodied the dreams of many of his generation. There was wonder also at the inability of the police forces to protect major public figures. This wonder, of course, would generalize to cynical suspicions about the power of monied special interests, foreign infiltration, and the competence of police and the criminal justice system itself.

Meanwhile, President Johnson was consumed by the country's inability to win the Vietnam War. The war was raging on TV sets in everyone's living room; on the battlefield, a disproportionate number of minorities and less privileged youth were leading the fight. University students were deferred, but working-class students went into service. To many, this added further injustice to what was being seen as an unjust war. Gradually, this rising wave of injustice led to massive draft dodging and then to organized protest. Mass protest of this sort in the United States was unprecedented in wartime. By 1967, it was so strong that Johnson withdrew from the upcoming race for the presidency.

To many, this was a politicians' war, a holdover from the days of the Red Scare, the legacy of the military-industrial complex and its influence on public officials and foreign policy.[10]

America was acting like a country whose foreign policy cynically suggested that the ends justified the means. Support for continued American involvement in Vietnam seemed confined to a minority of older nonfighting conservatives, who were nevertheless inflicting their will on increasingly reluctant youth. The system once again seemed both incomprehensible and unjust, all of which was leaving its residue of cynicism.

The nature of the Vietnam War left a legacy of mistrust, just as the assassinations had done. The confusion of our entry into the conflict under Presidents Kennedy and Johnson, the exploitation of the less privileged in society, the un-American way in which the war was conducted—all left their marks on the American people, and particularly on the baby boomers. For the first time, the majority of people began to question whether America was "wrong" and whether we had in some way lost our moral bearings. For the students, the ineptitude and hypocrisy of the American government in trying to justify the war and its methods left scars. This ineptitude led many to question the motivations and credibility of public officials. In important respects, this mistrust of government has hardly dissipated. It is another strand in the emerging skein of cynicism.

At the Democratic convention of 1968, the brutality of the Chicago police force and supporters of Mayor Richard Daley was a singular message for the youth of the country: It meant that protests could be crushed and that the utopian dreams of the new community could be shattered by force, if necessary. If the overreaction of the law-and-order forces was disheartening, the subsequent election of Richard Nixon, who had a "secret plan" to end the war, would lead to utter dismay.

Watergate and After: The Seventies. A majority put their faith in Nixon's pledge to lead us to peace with honor. But before the Vietnam War was over, there were episodes that still haunt the American conscience. The Cambodian incursion, with its merciless bombing of civilian targets, followed by double-talk and duplicity, was the salient feature of the determined Nixon and Kissinger effort to end the conflict with honor. The Kent State massacre, during which four student war protesters were shot by the Ohio National Guard, confirmed for many that the establishment would ruthlessly fight back. Vice-President Spiro Agnew attacked the press and students, purportedly representing the views of the "silent majority." It all seemed a sham—a sign that the establishment would do almost anything to advance its own agenda.

The presidential election of 1972 pitted an idealistic and hopelessly disorganized George McGovern against Richard Nixon. But by the time another two years had passed, Nixon would become the first American president to resign in disgrace, and his media-baiting vice-president would be chased from office by the threat of a felony conviction for political corruption.

Too much has been written about the cynical aftermath of Watergate to discuss it here.[11] It is enough to say that the spectacle—of a president protesting to the end, in the face of damning evidence bipartisanly derived, that he was "not a crook"—provoked more feelings of confusion and disillusionment on the part of the electorate. The revelation of the president's "enemy list" and the elaborate cover-up schemes he devised were viewed as confirming evidence by increasing numbers of cynics that the whole system was rotten and that everyone was a fake. The pardon of Nixon by President Gerald Ford added fuel to the fire. A disappointed and exhausted American public saw the machinations of the Nixon years as confirming a deeper, unwholesome, opportunistic pattern in American life.

When the OPEC oil embargo began in 1973 and helped to create the recession of 1974, it was more than a startled electorate that beheld the event. It was an American people who felt the center crumbling: Perhaps there was no basis for traditional American optimism, for faith in the government, belief in free competition, and regard for law. After Vietnam and Watergate, it was not hard for many to believe that America was now itself a victim, this time manipulated by Middle Eastern potentates. The rise in unemployment and in inflation that the oil embargo caused, along with long lines at the fuel pumps, certainly diminished confidence in America's economic invincibility.

The steady decline of Jimmy Carter's presidency, damaged as it was in the end by the Iranian hostage situation, was another step in the growing cynical disenchantment of the seventies. His presidency exacerbated feelings that America was unable to establish its control in a global economy. It was as if even an outsider, while trying to restore credibility to government, ironically failed because of his very lack of cynicism about the way things really work.

After Carter, people felt a tough pro was needed, even if it meant oversimplification. Big-time football became the winning metaphor: hard, simple, ruthless, and straight ahead. Ronald Reagan, the celluloid Gipper, fit that image.

The Cynical Decade: The Eighties

Americans in 1980 chose a new political package that promised to restore the country's might and leave them better off. Ronald Reagan's election and presidency signaled that a time for moral and economic pragmatism had arrived. The message was plain: You have to be tough and self-reliant in order to move up. Getting on in 1980s terms has meant, for most people, striving for material success. Tax cuts put more in some pocketbooks. But the broader economic policy gave rise to unprecedented business megamergers, myriad investment schemes and speculative ventures, and countless shakeups and restructurings.

Into the new economic order stepped the corporate raiders, making fortunes within the limits of the law, and the others, making millions outside of it. Young people particularly gravitated to the economic program and its values. This was a new generation with a new set of acquisitive aspirations. In the mid 1960s, for instance, campus polls showed that 80 percent believed that "developing a meaningful philosophy of life" and "doing something good for society" were the most important objectives. On the campus of the 1980s, by contrast, nearly 80 percent said that "making money" and "being successful" are what count.[12] The rise in business school applications, as well as the decline in the scholastic performance of those planning to go into teaching, social work, and government service, are signs that many of today's youth prefer dollars to ideals.

There is yet another aspect of the new economic order that appeals to a selfish public. The message is that people can have more things and better lives now, without worrying about future debt. The whole ethic of sacrificing for the sake of the next generation has been abandoned. Instead, people have been inclined to follow their self-interest and have been urged to get on with things without complicating them.

Robert Bellah and colleagues, in their study *Habits of the Heart,* make a compelling case that individualism, much more than collectivism, has marked the American psyche since the early days of this country. But since the days of Charles Horton Cooley, another scholar of American life, it has been postulated that our countrymen also gravitate to community feeling and collective life.[13] This thesis, while noble, was antithetical to the mood of America in the 1980s. Selfishness was in; public spirit, save for occasional displays of nationalism and Olympic glory, was plainly out.

Former Speaker of the House Thomas P. O'Neill put it this way: "Today, there are those who argue that the way to achieve the American Dream is to go it alone. This new morality claims that the young should forget about the old, that the healthy should ignore the sick, and that the wealthy should abandon the poor."[14]

We have seen how self-interest to the exclusion of public interest helped lead Americans into an emotional as well as an economic Depression in the 1930s and into a moral abyss and chilling generation gap in the late 1960s and early 1970s. The Reagan agenda in the 1980s again split private and public interest. However well intentioned in formulation, when embraced by a cynical public it introduced a larger wedge into American society: between, on the one hand, the well-to-do, savvy, and able who know how to get ahead and, on the other, the poor, guileless, and less able who depend on the commonweal and a generous spirit of common decency.

It is clear that Reagan's economic policies and social philosophies served some very well indeed. Command Cynics in many corporations embraced economic determinism and social Darwinism to legitimize massive restructuring in their industries for short-term gain. Sadly, even genuine efforts to make industry more competitive, lean, and mean were largely at the expense of middle-class and working people and their communities. In like fashion, the most ambitious and able honestly profited. But cynical Articulate Players profited at the expense of civility and sometimes, as we have seen, outside the rule of the law.

For many others, however, the Reagan recipe wrought pain and disappointment. The cynicism of the Squeezed, the Hard-Bittens, and even the Stoics comes from defeat and downward mobility. Steel and rubber towns of the upper Midwest literally rusted away in unemployment, and even the Sunbelt, fueled by oil demand, experienced a decline. Agriculture and the inner cities suffered. Among the young themselves, there is the widespread perception that they will not live as well as their parents and, according to polls, the widespread conclusion that their children will simply have to fend for themselves.[15] In this connection, it is interesting to note that pop music has largely abandoned the sensitivities of the 1970s and embraced 1980s-style punk nihilism.

On to Disillusionment. Several developments came to tarnish the flawless mirror President Reagan was holding up to the American people. Nineteen eighty-six witnessed the publication of *The Triumph of Politics,* by David Stockman, Reagan's former budget director, which recounted in detail the cynical machinations behind the first Reagan tax cut.[16] Stockman cited, among other elements in the manipulative ménage, the simplistic theories and self-serving counsel offered the president by supply-side advocates, the ideological hubris and PR mentality of presidential advisers who ''sold'' the cut to Congress and the public, and, of course, the political self-interest of members of his own party who willingly ran up almost unimaginable fiscal deficits. Stockman's book virtually recapitulated the views of many Americans about the endemic cynicism of Washington politicians and insiders. Stockman, a transparent Articulate Player, nevertheless portrayed himself as a dupe, prey to the urbane sophisticates and selfish schemers in the White House and Congress, who ripped off the righteous right and then foiled the program by failing to make deeper budget cuts.

Then the hypocritical story of trading arms for hostages with Iran emerged. Even as America was upbraiding Europeans for supporting terrorism, it turned out that a secret White House group had bypassed Congress and the American people to deal with known supporters of terrorism. That, however, was not the end of the scandal: It was revealed that some of the money from the Iranian arms deal was secretly diverted to the Nicaraguan contras, despite a Congressional prohibition.

This was all grist for the cynics' mill. Allegations of drug deals with Central American dictators and the publication of "kiss and tell" books by administration favorites Deaver, Speakes, and Regan have subsequently ground up the president's credibility, if not his personal popularity. In any event, we believe that the 1980s can be characterized as the cynical decade, and that the Reagan presidency, while contributing to a fast-paced cycle of high hopes and disillusionment, has been only one of many ingredients in the public's increasingly jaded outlook. Cynical operators on Wall Street and Main Street have led a free-market feeding frenzy in which asset shuffling and easy credit define American productivity and thrift. Holier-than-thou electronic preachers have been shown to be swindlers and fakes, and the public gloats at the spectacle. People have come to expect the setup. And cynicism, whether wielded like a sword or worn like a shield, helps them to cope with it. The election of 1988 is a case in point.

A Kinder, Gentler Nation. The campaign of George Bush demonstrated that fear and fantasy can beat complacency and generalities among that portion of the electorate that bothered to vote in the most recent presidential election. After leading Democratic contenders dropped out of the race because of hanky-panky and plagiarism, and after old Nixon advisers introduced negative campaigning into the Republican primaries, the public was left with Dukakis and Bush and what many saw as a "lesser of two evils" decision. Some 62 percent of voting-age Americans were displeased with the choice of candidates, while only half the eligible voters cast ballots. Pundits like David Broder and Flora Lewis saw the campaign as rife with cynicism, and Dukakis himself declared that Bush's cynical media campaign had largely done him in.

Again, initial appeals to idealism and community were forsaken for the expediency of negative campaigning, in the one case, and divisiveness, in the other. It was almost a repeat of the previous election, when a cynical electorate told Walter Mondale that looking out for oneself was more important than reaching out to the less privileged. Bush promised, however, to foster a "kinder, gentler America." But, in the aftermath of the election, the government sent out foreclosure warnings to 80,000 farmers.

No one can foretell how Americans will cope with the pain of reducing deficits or what new complications this will bring to the body politic. It is also uncertain whether George Bush can play his predecessor's role as a stand-tall optimist in the face of daunting domestic and international problems. We can only hope that Bush's "kinder and gentler" aspirations will mark his administration and its accomplishments. Otherwise, the age of cynicism will grind on, and discontent and disillusion will sink deeper into the American spirit.

Seeds of Cynicism

Cynicism in America today has its roots in the high hopes of the counterculture of the sixties, which gave way to disillusion in the seventies. The Reagan ethic in the eighties may have brightened the outlook of a new generation of Americans and made many other Americans feel good about themselves and their country again. But feeling good came to be equated with advancing one's own interest.

This pattern of emotional boom and bust, stemming from the end of World War II and carrying into the 1980s, has become an enduring fact of life in America and has helped to produce a cynical society.[17] A central question in America today is "Whom do you trust?" Which institutions, politicians, schoolmasters, employees, and managers are worthy of trust is an ongoing American issue. Trust is part of the bond that holds society together. As it deteriorates, respect for legitimate authority and confidence in enterprise, public and private, are undermined.

The emotional cycle was set up because of unreal expectations reinforced by politicians, the media, schoolteachers, and success-oriented lecturers and clergy. In America, one is expected to be happy and to win. When the inevitable happens and many people do not win, cynics have their built-in explanations, which scarcely take into account their own excessive expectations, personal shortcomings, or even rotten luck.

Cynicism is adaptive in the 1980s—it ices real and potential frustrations over. We have seen this in the emotional detachment of Command Cynics and Articulate Players, who are ever fearful of losing it and thus command and play to advance their power. We have also seen this in the wounded calculation of Squeezed Cynics and the Hard-Bittens, who have lowered their expectations of having it all and thus scoff and backbite to preserve their dignity and hold on to what they have acquired.

Some commentators project that this cynical wave will wash quickly over the public and that many Americans will be at least partly concerned again with compassion, commitment, and conscience. In our view, these Americans will be the most courageous members of the citizenry, those willing to sacrifice some of their personal interest in the service of public interest and the commonweal. Whether they will be helped in their private quests by a generous public ethos and leadership remains to be seen. From where we sit, *Newsweek* projections aside, greed is still fashionable, much as we might wish otherwise.[18]

In any event, the cynical society is not a serene one. Nor does it, in the face of economic ambiguity and polarization, provide much surcease to its members. In writing about cynicism and the jaundiced view of life, we realize that many people do not see the world as a grim, dog-eat-dog place. Still, a permeating lack of trust in society and in the future does mark many Americans.

Seymour Sarason makes the point that today's generation is "growing up old."[19] Just as young children are being pushed to read, write, and add faster than the norm for their peers, so also are teenagers being groomed for professional careers as early as junior high school, at least in the professional classes. Smart, hurried-up kids are expected not only to do well in school but also to gain the edge over classmates and position themselves to get into the right universities. It is not surprising, then, to find that cheating is rampant in schools at all levels, and that teenage suicides come in clusters. Young strivers embrace a "realistic" picture of what it takes to get ahead in today's competitive environment. It enables them to do whatever it takes to get the grade, the admission to college, even the degree.

This gritty picture of the world transforms self-reliance into self-service and work performance into self-promotion. Perspectives are shortened, and people strive to "get it now." This mind-set is being embraced by many in high schools and colleges today, who plan to climb and hope to command in their futures. Moreover, those who are in a position neither to command nor to climb have assumed a less ambitious orientation to the world around them. For them, self-reliance is at best equated with self-protection; hard work and accomplishment simply don't make it.

It is plain enough that working adults are struggling with analogous problems of self-definition and making fresh attempts to cope with urban overpopulation and anonymity, exaggerated business upturns and downturns, the decline of our manufacturing and farming base, and remote technology and institutions. People are seeking different means of achieving emotional equilibrium in a continuously clamorous world; this in turn brings about different ways of evaluating goods and services, choosing life options, and relating to other people. We see a pattern of consequences in response to a fast-changing total environment; we call it the "Europeanizing of America." It involves a loss of confidence in the environment and in the future and leads to a rise in immediate self-interest, with consequent manifestations in cynicism.[20]

The Europeanizing of America

Many Americans no longer believe we can control world events, nor do they want to. Bullishness and complacency have been replaced by European-style apprehension and doubt. European countries lost their colonies long ago and have felt the immediate destruction and dehumanization of two world wars. It is only relatively recently, however, that Americans have felt diminished control over world affairs, with all the concomitant threats to security and potency, collective and individual, that this implies. Terrorism and foreign cocaine cartels have become part of the collective consciousness, adding to feelings of general slippage and incapacity.

To this decline of perceived omnipotence one must add the realization that we have finite resources and competitive weaknesses in a world economy. Assumptions of unrestrained growth, unlimited affluence, boundless fuel, high productivity, a healthy trade balance, and a vision of the American consumer as insatiable no longer seem accurate. The promise of a rising standard of living for each generation may not be fulfilled.

Americans are less certain they can change things in the directions they wish. The French, for instance, have felt this for a long time, as one of their favorite aphorisms reveals: "The more things change, they more they are the same." Americans had never had military and diplomatic defeats approaching the magnitude of Vietnam. They had not, until quite recently, been privy to mass exposés like Watergate and the Iran/Contra Affair, been subject to an international oil cartel, lost so much in a volatile stock market, known such widespread street crime, drug abuse, and violence, faced hostile missiles and terrorists to such an unprecedented and newsworthy extent.

In turn, certain mainstream cultural assumptions have lost their validity: The life of everyday quiet desperation and smug security is not so easily managed in today's climate of job insecurity and marital unrest. What was formerly taken as an article of faith is now not widely accepted: Most people feel that they cannot manipulate their destinies as much. Without two incomes, for example, young marrieds often cannot afford to own a house, let alone a dream house. There seems to be less optimism about the possibilities of boundless material success. To Americans raised on the premise that everyone can be a winner with hard work and persistence, this feeling contributes to anxiety, anomie, and envy.[21]

The Rise of Fatalism. Psychologists would say that the American locus of control is shifting, by degrees, from self-certitude to the belief that life is controlled by external forces. Fatalism is pronounced among Europeans—a by-product of history and cultural assumptions. Today, however, we see it developing among the middle class in this country, where many high school graduates are less certain that they can reach their goals in life. Certainly, anecdotal evidence shows how a sense of fatalism and fear of the future mark the psyches of the upwardly mobile as well. In top universities, business school admissions are rising, but so are the tensions associated with the possibilities of real-world failure. Young MBAs and aspiring Articulate Players in corporations are wearing power ties and suits and yearning to make the right impression. Underneath it all, many say they are petrified of becoming losers.

Loserhood is the *bête noire* of Americans; it is the condition that MBAs and college students throughout the United States fear most. Even dropouts like to believe they have somehow beaten the system and emerged as some kind of winners. In America, trust and respect are only grudgingly given, if at all, to anyone who is not an obvious winner.

We hear this theme daily in our work, just as people no doubt hear it in offices and factories, markets, and service outlets. America's adult generation was raised to believe that you can be virtually anything you want to be, but today many people don't make it and many blame The System—parents, schools, government, industry—for their failures and disappointment. As a consequence, more Americans are moving toward fatalistic attitudes resembling those found in Europe *("que será, será")*. There are lowered expectations about the ability to manipulate one's destiny. A new attitude is emerging. Onward and upward to wealth and happiness through deferred pleasures has given way to a new viewpoint: "I want it now, because who can tell about tomorrow?"

An Orientation to Present Time. It has been said that Europeans live in the past and for the present. They savor everyday pleasures, always mindful of their origins, class, status, and stations in life. The traditional American orientation to time has been to live in the present but for the future. Today, the calculus has shifted. Many Americans live in and for today. No doubt some of this shift to present time has to do with the vulnerabilities people feel in a nuclear age, with our loss of innocence, and with the rise of fatalism in the American psyche. Living for today is a way of postponing the future and psychologically fending off grim possibilities.

Americans' priorities have changed. Not ten years ago, Americans had high hopes for their children. Surprisingly, surveys today show that their concern for their children has dropped significantly. Of primary importance to people today are their standard of living and personal health.[22] These preoccupations mark more than a new outlook on time. They fit together with a growing preoccupation with The Self in the American psyche and with one's self-interest.

The Rise in Self-Interest. The central aspect of the Europeanization of America is the rise of self-interest. People question other people's motives more than before. The role model of the blunt, reasonably skeptical, naively optimistic American is giving way to a worldly, mistrustful, hustling indifference in the 1980s. The attitude of "I'm from Missouri—show me!" has given way to "I've seen it all before—who cares?" Among other things, this means not revealing oneself at first, if ever; instead, one maintains an amiable facade, feigns ignorance, and doesn't trust anybody. This is historically the European peasant's protection. This kind of adaptation implies seeing through people and their real motives and putting emphasis on surfaces, style, and appearances.

One consequence is that traditional authority figures, and so-called experts and role models, are suspect. A study conducted by one of the authors to examine reactions to public service ads about illegal drugs is illustrative. In a group of TV commercials in the late 1970s, football stars (ostensibly role models) in effect said: "I can't do my thing if I'm high on drugs." These ads elicited disbelief in 88 percent of the grade-school children tested. When questioned further, the students felt that the revered athletes were lying.[23] One wonders whether today's antidrug appeals, however well intentioned, are not falling upon the same mistrusting ears. The point is this: Since fewer people in America know whom to trust, they suspect everyone. Seemingly everyone is for sale.

Street smarts are being celebrated in our society and defined by TV and films about mindless but instinctive self-centered heroes who know the score. Today's winner is often the realistic person who looks out for number one and takes advantage of gullibility, whether for money or for power. The new realism is fiscally oriented, without much moral questioning. Many Americans seem ready to adopt an untroubled, cynical shrewdness in their dealings with others. As a result, the immediate response, verbal or behavioral, is no longer a virtue. Wariness, caution, the fear of being suckered or caught off guard are in; spontaneity is out. From the customary American readiness for rapid closure, 1980s people tend to feel that it is unsafe to enter into new situations or to behave enthusiastically without waiting for events to clarify (if indeed they ever do).

Europeans have long lived with limited resources, fewer feelings of personal control, and more worries over their future security than most Americans. As Americans come to face limits on their futures, job opportunities, possessions, and power, their quest for viable modes to actualize themselves may be more or less Europeanized. This transformation hinges not only on objective environmental conditions but also on people's outlook on the society around them and on their views of their fellowman.

4

The Growth
of Cynicism
in American Industry

The seeds of cynicism in the American workplace have borne
their fruit in the sun and shadow of distinct historical epochs.
In this and the next two chapters, we will examine the cycle by
which working people's hopes are raised, then dashed, leading
to disappointment and disillusion. The cynical cycle does not
follow a neat progression across decades of American life. Instead,
its rhythm is in sync with patterns of industrial and technological
development, immigration and demographic changes, and shifts
in the character and outlook of the American work force. Here
we will see social, political, and economic conditions in society
breeding higher aspirations, and then personal and impersonal
forces in industry arising to frustrate them in the transformation
of America from an agrarian to an industrial society.

Work in Preindustrial America

The American vitality that Alexis de Tocqueville celebrated in
the 1830s was to be found on farms and in the crafts and was

95

proving to be a key ingredient in the country's budding commercial strength.[1] In his studies of the shipping industry, for example, which was more competitive than England's despite higher labor costs, he believed the key ingredients enabling Americans to sail their vessels at cheaper rates were inventiveness, risk taking, and our sailor's spirit. To appreciate that American drive and spirit, we must place them in a historical context. Immigrants coming to the land were fleeing religious persecution, rigid class structures, and economic hardship. Sea transport was hazardous, and few had relatives in the United States. It was the bold and hale who chanced the journey. Theirs was an escape to freedom and to economic opportunity in a new land. One immigrant of the period aptly summed up others' vision of America as "a golden land—so long as there is work."

Immigrants of that day found work, but work in a preindustrial America. The great majority were self-employed in the 1830s in farming, fishing, and forestry, where they toiled at their own pace, with much of their destiny in their own hands. Economic independence freed most from the tethers of employers. Thus dispirit centered on the weather, the soil, and the seed, rather than on exploitation by the still unformed "manufacturing aristocracy" Tocqueville anticipated.

There was a segment of the population employed in organizations during this era who encountered the same hard work and long hours as their agrarian counterparts. Many were craftsmen who were identified with their work and kept the fruit of their labors. Those employed in the mills, in ironworks, in shipbuilding, and in service to an owner were paid low wages and lived in relative poverty. Still, these laborers maintained close ties with their fellowmen and lived together in ethnic communities. And while their work life was monotonous, it was punctuated by days (often several days) off for religious holy days, for weddings and funerals, and for celebrating American holidays. These communal ties and gatherings relieved some of the burden of industrial life.

There were also many gestures of benevolence by employers in the era. The diary of one manufacturer illustrates: "I would prefer giving constant employment at some sacrifice to having a man of the village seen in the streets on a rainy day at leisure." Employers also encouraged churchgoing among their employees and sought to stamp out "vicious amusements" and "debaucheries." All this was part of what historians call the Moral Reform movement of this era.[2]

Nowhere were everyday working people's aspirations raised higher than in the mill town of Lowell, Massachusetts. The mill girls, employed by owners looking out for their betterment, were provided housing, religious instruction, and classroom education. This company town was visited from far and wide by leading industrialists and politicians and hailed as a model of what industry might be in the future.

Behind the pious-sounding motivations of the mill owners, however, other stratagems were in mind. "The wool business requires more man labour," one wrote, "and this we study to avoid. Women are much more ready to follow good regulations, are not captious, and do not clan as the men do against their overseers." Moreover, life in the mills and throughout industrial America would change in the next seventy years. The mill girls would be replaced by Irish immigrants, who were cheaper to employ, who paid for their housing, and who operated automatic machinery. Tocqueville presaged the consequences when he observed that the coming industrialization would make workers "more adroit" at specialized tasks but "less industrious" and would break theretofore communal bonds of obligation and duty. Moreover, he predicted that the object of the new "class of masters" would no longer be to govern the population; instead, it would be "to use it." The industrial revolution was coming to America, and as much as it would provide bright opportunities for the working populace, it would also leave shadows that would darken and disillusion the human spirit.

The Industrial Revolution

The late 1880s through the early 1900s were the age of invention and entrepreneurism. The number of patents and the rate of incorporation in this country skyrocketed. So did our gross national product and the opportunity for people to prosper, even gain great wealth. Visions of prosperity, of American streets paved with gold, along with the growing economy, proved a spur to immigration. By 1900, over 80 percent of New Yorkers were immigrants or the offspring of immigrants; nearly as high a proportion were to be found in St. Louis and San Francisco; and even larger proportions lived in Milwaukee, Cleveland, and Detroit. These immigrants had come to America fleeing poverty and persecution, like those who preceded them, but they also were to be enticed with a whole new way of looking at things.

Americans at the turn of the century were stimulated by what was called the New Thought movement, which held out the promise that success was within the reach of everyone.[3] One proponent wrote: "Anything is yours if you only want it hard enough. Just think of that. Anything! Try it. Try it in earnest and you will succeed. It is the operation of a mighty law." Hundreds of tracts promulgated this message of hope and paean to individual enterprise. The economic expansion and movement westward only reinforced the possibilities.

Industrial Realities. As American immigrants settled in, however, they discovered that Jeffersonian ideals of an agrarian democracy had been supplanted by industrial competition and urbanization. In turn, employers' sentimental commitments to benevolence and moral reform were being cast brusquely aside by a new intellectual movement: Social Darwinism.[4] Industry came to embrace this Spencerian notion, which dictated that only the most fit would survive in the economic struggle. This ethic stressed that success and riches were signs of progress, as well as evidence of elevation, and so admiration was the due of those who prospered in industry.[5] Scions of finance and industry, such as Jay Gould, J. P. Morgan, and, later, Henry Ford, epitomized this new ethos. Darwinian conceptions not only freed the captains of industry from the communitarian and moral responsibilities assumed by their predecessors but also justified them in adopting the law of the jungle. The challenge of industry called for men with cunning and strength—the Machiavellian traits of the fox and the lion. Gould used guile to build his empire; Morgan and Ford used ruthess power.

The Natural Order of Industry. The harsh doctrine of competitive survival served the interests of industrialists. At once they became role models for the ambitious in the society, who were eager to move to positions of greater status and social approval. Even their avaricious tastes and life-styles were celebrated and copied by many, leading to Thorstein Veblen's observations on the pathos of aping the "leisure class."[6] At the same time, their stature legitimized their absolute authority in the enterprise. Later, Henry Ford carried absolutism to its extreme by claiming the right to make every decision in the Ford Motor Company and by sending spies to monitor managers and thus ensure that none acted on their own authority.

The New Thought movement in turn also perversely served such purposes. It legitimized the harsh treatment of those unready or unable to subordinate themselves to the enterprise. Social Darwinism gave employers the right to weed out the unworthy. Elbert Hubbard, author of a popular book celebrating the loyalty of a soldier delivering a message to General García in the Cuban jungles during the Spanish-American War, stated the message thus: "Self-interest prompts every employer to keep the best—those who can carry a message to García."[7]

Of course, more than ideology defined the industrial revolution and dashed the dreams of working people. Automatic machinery and, later, the assembly line created vast numbers of low-paying and low-skill jobs. Hence craftsmen came to be identified with their products—steelworker, ironworker, autoworker. They flocked to the industrial cities and created urban ghettos. Strong local and communitarian ties fostered in village and rural life gave way to the dislocation of industrial urban living. Overall, these early-twentieth-century workers were seen as "a disorganized rabble" of individuals competing for scarce goods.[8] Americans were being divided, as Tocqueville predicted, into new classes of industrial masters and servants.

Evolution of Cynicism. Early industry was marked by immigrant workers, and by those leaving the farm to enter industry, with high hopes for material progress and the promise that a positive attitude would yield them rich rewards. Instead, most simply took their places on the industrial ladder, worked alongside their machines, lived in their urban ghettos, and suffered a working existence more palpable and inescapable than any imagined by the mill girls. The seeds of cynicism—high hopes dashed by grim realities—were thus firmly planted in the American work force by the industrial revolution.

Most Americans would not achieve prosperity or make their way up the economic ladder. For America's increasingly urbanized working classes in this era, depressions in 1890 and 1910 only deepened the lie and further dampened aspirations of ever escaping poverty and exploitation. What would happen to the power of positive thinking? It would give way to disillusion. Some immigrants would leave the country. Studies of the southern European settlements at the turn of the century show that for every hundred immigrants to the United States, forty-seven returned to their homelands.[9] Others would forbear, taking their places in what once promised to be a classless society, in hopes that their offspring might someday make something of themselves. Many, in our estimation, would become cynical.

Muckraking books reviled the naked self-interest of industrialists and fueled the cynic's belief that everyone was out for himself. Upton Sinclair's book *The Jungle* documented the brutal working conditions facing immigrants in the Chicago meat-packing industry and showed how greed and selfishness marked managers' motives.[10] The working public came to believe that owners and their managers should be regarded with suspicion and mistrust.

Goldbricking, petty thievery, and absenteeism were the active ways to fight back at exploitative management. More than this, there was a way for workers to respond collectively to mistreatment: They joined unions.

The Rise of Unions

American workers joined unions in massive numbers during the early 1900s. By 1920, over one-third of the work force would be unionized. Working people were fighting fire with fire. Unionism was marked by violence, coercion, and intimidation during its early days—on the part of both unions and management. Nevertheless, as much as unions gave vent to working people's frustration and disillusion, they also rekindled hopes and dreams that were shattered when industrialists abandoned notions of moral reform and adopted the law of the jungle.

Appeal of Unions. By contrast, union leaders summoned up Christian ideals in recruiting members; after all, it was Cain and not Abel who first promulgated "every man for himself." With unions, injury to one was the concern of all. Samuel Gompers promised his members "to bring about better conditions of life today."[11] Of course, he and other labor leaders also played to the growing cynicism of their members by castigating greedy capitalists. Along with the muckrakers, they succeeded in raising consciousness about the self-serving guile of America's once-revered industrial aristocrats.

Passage of legislation legalizing unions and strikes, spurred by a shift in public attitudes about capitalists and the rights of working people, signaled an end to industry's leonine response to the union movement. There would be no more use of the Pinkertons and other private police forces to break strikes. Management would need new tactics; it would emulate the fox.

Management Strikes Back. The industrialists' response to the changing political and social climate between 1910 and 1920 was threefold.[12] First, there was the open-shop campaign, wherein employers banded together to meet the challenge of the unions. This was a marked departure from their earlier individualistic and reactive posture. The National Association of Manufacturers devised a set of principles for undermining trade unionism and enlisted the offices of politicians and academics to speak against this growing movement. The president of Harvard College, among others, declared that unions degraded human character because they restricted output. Pamphlets detailed the costs of strikes and informed employees that unions prevented people from working for whom they pleased—hence, the open-shop campaign.

Behind these high-minded and informative appeals, the foxes of industry practiced more devious stratagems. Blacklists were used to identify labor "agitators" and forewarn other employers lest they hire them. Labor spies were hired to monitor union meetings and strike plans. Money and moral support were extended to employers suffering from labor unrest, and measures were taken to ostracize and defame those who cooperated with the unions.

The second step industrialists took was to embrace the principles of "scientific management" being advanced by Frederick Taylor. Taylor's principles were based on what social scientists call "rational economic" conceptions of human nature.[13] Victorian economists of the late nineteenth century advanced the notion of man as a calculating machine who would weigh incentives and compute how hard he would work for them. Taylor extended this machinelike imagery to cover all the basic human functions and thus proposed the scientific management of the "human machine." The principles, on the shop floor, were to divide the work of mass production into its simplest components, to specify a series of rules for the operation of the factory, and to provide financial incentives for productive results.

While there was much to recommend the theory of scientific management in its time, the mechanistic conception of human nature degraded human character. No longer were workers using tools or machines; instead, they themselves were treated as tools, and their machines were using them. Efficiency experts observed them with stopwatches, and psychologists perused their hourly performance records. They became surreptitious overseers in the princes' domain.

Finally, industrialists increased working people's wages while gaining even more control over their jobs. The wage increases of this era were related to the prosperity gained from the development of mass-production technology and the application of scientific management. As Taylor predicted, industrial profits did increase, and so did the workers' recompense. Yet the wage increases were also a cover for more deviousness during this era.

This deception is best exemplified in Henry Ford's announcement of the five-dollar-a-day wage for his workers. Ford undertook this payment as a sign of the continuance of his business and the desire to put more money in circulation. Newspapers heralded his humanitarianism. Yet behind this largess, Ford cut wages dramatically for all but the assemblers and undertook massive layoffs. To gain that 17 percent increase in pay, workers stepped up their production quotas by 47 percent. Furthermore, men needing work flooded into sweatshops offering less money, and Ford in turn began to subcontract work to these job shops.

To be sure, many industrialists in this era had good intentions and saw themselves as genuinely contributing to the common man's lot. But many others fit our profile of the Command Cynic. They disguised their naked self-interest in Darwinian ideology and scientific management and sought to smooth over exploitation through payoffs and public relations. Meanwhile, Taylor's well-intentioned recommendations that management show better care for workers were largely ignored. Perhaps Henry Ford had Taylor in mind when he said, "An idealist is one who helps the other fellow to make a profit."

Workers were just as cynical in their response. There was widespread resistance to applications of scientific management in the work force. Workers denounced the arbitrary layoffs and quota increases at Ford. "Soldiering"—the tactic of limiting output—spread among many workers. In a sense, the Hard-Bitten Cynic was coming to the fore. Some workers joined the Communist Party, and riots in Philadelphia and San Francisco closed those cities for several days. A tide of bolshevism swept through the work force after the Russian Revolution, leaving even union leaders in its wake.

There was, of course, no revolution in America and no workers' state. The resistance of most labor leaders to communism, the political and economic climate in the United States, the heterogeneity of the work force, the rising standard of living—all proved an uncongenial milieu for revolution. But the conditions were set for rising frustration and cynicism in the work force.

The Depression and its aftermath, and the world war and its victory over the Axis powers, set America on a new course. Conditions changed in society and in the way that management dealt with labor and with growth in its own ranks. Equally notable is how the elements and expression of cynicism were changed.

Human Relations Movement

The stock market crash and the Depression that followed it chastened industrialists in their quest for accumulation and sharply reduced organized labor's rolls.[14] It also scarred our population and, as we pointed out in our treatment of cynicism in society, led to despair for many of working age. At the same time, the federal government's response to unemployment and to mass suffering meant that people had a friend to turn to in FDR. More important, the soup and bread lines meant that people could turn to one another. A new set of expectations was forming that, together with management, working people could again prosper.

Visions of Community. America's recovery from the Depression and the victory in World War II proved to be a bonding experience, joining Americans together in common cause. Whereas the industrial revolution had pitted workers against management, ethnic group against ethnic group, and class against class, these two historic struggles bound our people together. The divisions between these groups did not disappear, of course, but the heat and hostility between them was tempered.

The image of America as a melting pot helped to reduce ethnic conflict, and economic recovery provided more opportunities for people's assimilation into industry. (Blacks continued to be denied the fruits of the economy, however, and still suffered from discrimination and prejudice.) The expansion of the working class and the creation of a middle class also provided many with the prospects of upward mobility, including home ownership and weekend leisure. While conflicts between management and unions remained sharp, with major strikes in the auto industry, the railroads, and coal, they were eased by the common destinies both assumed in recovering from the Depression and in defeating the Axis powers. Moreover, a new compact between them was devised, wherein both interests could be served in sharing the wealth of postwar booms.

More than economic and political factors, however, changed the face of management and labor relations in this country. This was the era of the human relations movement in industry. Studies by Elton Mayo and Fritz Roethlisberger at the Hawthorne Electric Works in New Jersey defined the limits of scientific management.[15] Experiments in lighting showed productivity to increase among a group of workers when the lights were turned up but also when they were dimmed. Thus it seemed that the special attention and care shown the workers, rather than the lighting, had promoted more production.

These studies introduced a new conception of what motivated people at work and how they should be managed. "We must remember that we are living in a democratic community. Managerial achievement in human organization is not dependent on mechanical devices nor routine methods. . . . We are leading men, not handling robots," wrote one new thinker. Mayo challenged the machinelike imagery and conceptions of people advanced by so-called scientific management. In addition, he called into question the rational-economic presuppositions of motivation and the "spurious principles of management" that followed from them.[16]

Thus social conceptions of man in the workplace entered the managerial vocabulary. Managers were urged to get to know their employees and their emotional makeup. Tracts such as Dale Carnegie's *How to Win Friends and Influence People* became essential guidebooks to the handling of human relations.[17] By the 1950s, companies were sponsoring bowling teams, picnics, and fairs as signs of their good association with people.

Make no mistake: The human relations movement was embraced in the spirit of self-interest. In a tract on "human engineering" that advanced its principles, one author commented: "Old mother nature has loaded us down with a bunch of feelings that we lug around with us through life, and it is the tramping on these feelings that causes most of the misunderstanding of the shop, and drives men into unions and Bolshevik gatherings, where they are received with 'false sympathy' and allowed to cuss the foreman and damn capital or do any other act of self-expression from heaving a brick at the loyal employees entering the plant to killing a cop or two." Thus the self-interested manager of this era was advised to personalize relations in the factory and, as Carnegie put it, "win people to your way of thinking."[18]

Inhuman Relations. Problems arose, however, when managers tried to put human relations precepts into action—their application, all too often, proved to be cynical and self-serving.

As an example, Carnegie's principles of "personality salesman-ship" led many managers to put on a face when dealing with their people and, indeed, with one another. Carnegie instructed his students to influence people by the arts of "tact, praise, modesty, and a little hypocrisy." The message was to play on the emotions of people and manipulate them "without giving offense or arousing resentment."

William H. Whyte, editor at *Fortune,* called attention to this duplicity in articles that ridiculed the fallacy of two-way com-munication in industry and the double-dealing of "social engi-neers."[19] Erich Fromm went even farther in his critique when he wrote that "the so-called 'human relations' are the most in-human ones, because they are 'reified and alienated' relations."[20]

Criticism of the human relations school reached its height in Whyte's *The Organization Man.* He reported that corporate man-agers were being stripped of their individual personalities and socialized to conform to an organizational role. His book criticized "scientism" for cultivating people's needs for "belongingness" and then sewing them in suffocating corporate straitjackets.[21]

Eugene Jennings, in an exposition on corporate leader-ship in this period, wrote that managers had become team men but were no less power seekers than before the fad of human relations started: "It is ironical but true that the human rela-tions movement enabled them to begin shifting from the more ruthless (lion-like) Machiavellian techniques to a more subtle (fox-like) set of techniques. . . . The crude princes of the past [gave] way to gentlemen of artful sophistication."[22] Here we see, then, a new source of cynicism arising in the workplace. Working people, searching for belonging, would be both "suc-cored" and "suckered" by the human relations ethic. Organiza-tion men, searching for a place, would lose their identities and subordinate themselves to the corporation. To be sure, the human relations movement would have its benefits. Workers would gain a measure of fraternity with management and the pleasure of sanctioned association with their mates. The orga-nization men, in turn, would enjoy great prosperity and life in suburbia. The stage was being set, however, for ever more cyn-icism in the workplace as the human relations movement would be overwhelmed by a far stronger and more pervasive development in industry.

Dawn of the Big Bureaucracy. The period from 1930 to 1960 saw the emergence of bureaucracy in American industry. This system rationalized the office in much the same way that scientific management had done in the factory. Bureaucratic principles, as articulated by Max Weber, were embraced in hopes of enhancing efficiency and promoting cooperation in the growing ranks of middle management and staff.[23] The aim was also to protect jobholders from capricious treatment and reduce nepotism and cronyism in organizations. Its precepts—dividing organizations by hierarchy and function, instituting rules and procedures, depersonalizing the operations of industry—were all designed to ensure the fair treatment of blue-collar workers and to promote expertise and meritocracy in the white-collar ranks. Like scientific management precepts, however, these principles were twisted in application and had, of themselves, cold and estranging consequences.

Anyone familiar with the red-tape rule-by-the-rule manifestations of bureaucracy knows those side effects and the cynicism they engender. While they are, of course, sources of despair both to the employees of bureaucratic life and to the consumers of its wares, our concern here is with the impact of bureaucracy on the rhythms of organization and character of the white-collar worker.

C. Wright Mills, in his penetrating study *White Collar,* points to three fundamental changes wrought by bureaucracy.[24] First, the rationalization of corporate structure passed authority from the hands of the owner or top manager to countless department and staff heads. These functionaries were not, however, the source of authority in organizations; they were "cog and beltline of the bureaucratic machinery." Mills writes of the bureaucrat's role: "Such power as you wield is a borrowed thing. Yours is the subordinate's mark; yours the canned talk. The money you handle is somebody else's money; the papers you sort and shuffle already bear somebody else's mark. You are the servant of the decision, the assistant of authority, the minion of management. You are closer to management than the wage workers are, but yours is seldom the last decision."[25]

Thus a first consequence of bureaucracy was the creation of a new class of petty bureaucrats. Their ranks grew between 1930 and 1960 as more and more people came to be employed in the white-collar ranks. The rationalization of the corporate structure gave them a shallow but legitimate power base from which to dispense orders and hear grievances. In a sense, then, the development of the modern organization brought to the fore a new cynical type: the Administrative Sideliner. Melville Dalton, in his studies of these operatives, describes their work as strengthening their positions ''upstairs'' by plugging leaks and ensuring that only good news passes upward. In turn, it involved discrediting rivals and building alliances with peers while monitoring staff attitudes and managing them with ''gossip, rumors, and confidences.''[26] At the same time, these cynical Sideliners, as we refer to them, sought to strengthen themselves ''downstairs'' by aiding the advancement of ''clamoring subordinates'' and singling out malcontents for ''special assignments.''

A second change wrought by bureaucracy involved the development of corporate functions. Deprived of any broad power base, department and staff heads built their own empires and fiefdoms within the corporate hierarchy. Functions became fetishes, and turfism came to dominate the enterprise. The consequences were nightmarish. The bureaucracy became, as Edmund Wilson observed, ''a vast system for passing the buck.'' We see in this, then, the institutionalization of the Sideliners' cynical style in the myriad rules and procedures of the modern organization.

Perhaps no writer has better captured the consequences than Franz Kafka in his depiction of *The Castle,* where decisions came from ''unforeseen places'' that could never be ''found . . . later on.''[27] The arbitrariness and impersonality of bureaucracy, along with the manipulativeness and turfism of petty bureaucrats, were seen as a fundamental source of alienation. They also became a focal point of cynicism for many middle managers and workers as well.

Mills's third point is that bureaucracy masked the source of authority and power in organizations and thus took on a life of its own. He writes: ''Under the system of explicit authority, in the round, solid nineteenth century, the victim knew he was being victimized, the misery and discontent of the powerless were explicit. In the amorphous twentieth-century world, where manipulation replaces authority, the victim does not recognize his status. The formal aim, implemented with the latest psychological equipment, is to have men internalize what the managerial cadres would have them do, without their knowing their own motives.''[28]

In this we can see, then, the creation of an environment conducive to the Obstinate Stoic. The regularities and rules of bureaucratic management provided everyday workers with the security and order needed to pursue their work ethic within the limits of their ambition. Bowling teams, social clubs, and the like proliferated—all of them company-sponsored, and all of them organized to allow workers to socialize with their kind. No doubt the cynically minded Obstinate Stoics were suspicious of all management's human relations and goodwill. It did not really matter, of course, because the bureaucratic order set them gyroscopically on course. In this sense, the power to manipulate had left the hands of owners, and even of managers, and had become simply part of bureaucratic life. So had the manifestation of cynical resistance. Goldbricking and working to rules on the shop floor were matched by long lunches and nine-to-five regularity in the offices. Industrial Relations was supplanted by Personnel Management, but the conflict between management and unions was now played out between various corporate offices and functions.

This juxtaposition of human relations and bureaucracy had perverse implications for organizations in this era. Take the case of General Electric. On the one hand, GE undertook a massive effort at human relations training for its managers in the 1950s. The communication handbook distributed to trainees stated that its purpose was to ''endow this mythical personality which employees call 'The Company' with the qualities of friendship, consideration, fairness, and competence.''[29] On the other hand, GE's efforts to institute measures of performance and to reward achievement had the contrary result of breeding a generation of organization men committed to playing it safe.

These men built their staff empires, reworked their corporate personae, and strove to fit into the GE mold. Functional autonomy marked GE's corporate life, and woe to the executive who sought to bring these functions together. GE, of course, enjoyed many of the benefits gained by human relations management and the rationalization of the corporate structure. In other firms, human relations were more disingenuous and bureaucracy served primarily to legitimize powermongering.

Organized Hypocrisy. We have seen, then, a new source of cynicism in the work force: organized hypocrisy. Early-twentieth-century industrialists may have been manipulative and guileful, but they never clothed themselves in camaraderie or wielded power so impersonally. On the contrary, institutionalized social distinctions were as important to them as the grand gesture and public killing. By contrast, Command Cynics in big bureaucracies would disguise their motives and wield their power behind a smokescreen of policies and procedures. Their followers and bidders, human relations managers and hatchet men alike, would in turn just be doing their jobs.

In the big offices, middle-level line managers had neither the power to command absolutely nor the prerogatives to manipulate so openly and with so much impunity. Thus many would perfect the practice of putting on a face when dealing with employees, pretending to listen while all the time persuading, seeming to care about people's emotions while instead playing on them. Another cadre of staff managers would learn to use the rules to their own advantage and, as Administrative Sideliners, protect their turfs and pensions. Hypocrisy was becoming institutionalized.

Our point is that middle managers and bureaucrats were as much manipulated as they were manipulators. The industrial system, in its bureaucratic form, established a set of rules in which people did not matter. Everyone was affected. Plainly, there would be payoffs for organization men who could fit into the mold. But there would also be payoffs for those who could mind their own business and keep to their own kind. Hard-Bitten Cynics in the workplace, outraged at the double-dealings of bosses decades before, were to some degree supplanted by Obstinate Stoics who would more or less go along.

By 1950, less than 20 percent of the American work force was self-employed. People depended on organizations for their material progress and had no recourse in returning to Europe or going back to agrarian life. Even private emotions were subject to analysis by managers practicing human relations. People retreated, accordingly, by adopting an equally false face. Organization men donned the mask of conformity. Administrative Sideliners hid behind their rule books. Obstinate Stoics worked to the letter of their job descriptions. The Hard-Bittens wore their company-provided uniforms. People became, as Roethlisberger observed, "the masters and victims of double-talk."

This hypocrisy was not lost on the offspring of the organization men and the sons and daughters of the cynical types born of bureaucracy. They would turn away from the false consciousness of the corporate world and seek to bring about the "greening of America" in the next decades. Nor was the hypocrisy lost on the new generation of future executives and climbers we will recognize as Articulate Players.

5

The Failed Promise
of Modern
Organization

The world of work in this country took a turn for the worse in the two decades between 1960 and 1980. Signs of economic trouble were apparent by 1970, when the rate of productivity increase in private industry began to decline and the investment in new plants, equipment, and R&D began to drop as well. On the employment front, there was a record rise in labor turnover, absenteeism, and grievances. For the first time, national surveys showed a decline in people's satisfaction with their jobs.[1]

A 1972 congressional inquiry into these matters focused broadly on the "problem of worker discontent and alienation" and squarely on a well-publicized indicator that something was amiss in the American workplace: a UAW wildcat strike of the General Motors plant at Lordstown, Ohio, in 1970.[2] The Lordstown plant had been GM's effort to build the most highly automated and efficient plant in existence. It proved to be a planner's dream but a worker's nightmare. Jobs were reduced in scope to simple and single operations, many with a cycle time of less than thirty seconds. Detailed records were kept of every operator's performance, and each step in the process was carefully monitored and controlled.

The result? Production of the Chevrolet Vega, once *Motor Trend*'s "Car of the Year," went to ruin. Downtime in the plant and defects in the product skyrocketed. Worse, there were many signs of careless workmanship and wanton sabotage by the work force.

The local union's complaint was not wages but working conditions. The plant had been designed for machines, not for people. Television's "60 Minutes" arrived to investigate the dispute. The show documented product sabotage and widespread absenteeism among workers. When Mike Wallace asked one worker why he came to the plant only four days a week, the free spirit replied, "Mr. Wallace, because I don't make enough money to work only three days." This disaffection was hardly limited to production workers at Lordstown. *Fortune* ran a cover story on the "blue-collar blues" rampant throughout American industry.[3] The conclusion of the article was simple: American companies and managers were out of step with the changing aspirations and outlooks of blue-collar workers.

At the same time, articles began to appear about the "white-collar woes." The University of Michigan's Survey Research Center showed job satisfaction to be lowest among blue-collar workers but declining most dramatically for those in the clerical, technical, and professional ranks.[4] The reason? The researchers attributed the decline to rising levels of education among people in these jobs that were not being matched by increases in their income, job opportunities, or challenges.

Rising Work-Force Expectations

In the introduction to their 1977 report on "Changing Worker Values," researchers from the Opinion Research Corporation wrote:

Employee attitudes in some important areas have
been worsening over the past 10, 15, even 25
years—in areas such as the evaluation of the
employee's company as a place to work, general
satisfaction with the work the employee does, the
fairness with which the employee is treated, the
believability of information given out by the company, and the company's willingness to listen to
the employee.

Undeniably, in some companies conditions
are such as to be the direct cause of increasingly
unfavorable employee attitudes. It seems unlikely,
however, that across scores of companies in many
industries the same unsatisfactory conditions would
prevail. Therefore, we have to look elsewhere to
understand what is fully happening. The fruit may
fall in the plant or office, but the roots of the problem often are external to the work situation.

A hallmark of our times is an increasingly
critical attitude toward much of what was previously
accepted or taken for granted. Communications
today are more plentiful, varied, and faster than
ever before and have sensitized people to flaws—
real or imagined—in the world about them—including the world of work. Also, a decade and a half
or so ago the economy was going well, all signs were
pointing up, and people were feeling optimistic
about the future. The public gave much of the
credit—perhaps more than was in fact deserved—to
business management for the rosy conditions. Today, with things going less well, it is not surprising to see business in on the receiving end of the
blame—again perhaps more than is deserved.[5]

What was behind this increasingly critical attitude toward
business and management practices? Surely high rates of inflation and unemployment and increased communications about
the flaws of business were contributing to a more critical and

more cynical perception of organizations in this period. Surely, too, media and corporate hype, along with permissive parents and various self-improvement gurus, were all heightening people's expectations to the point where they might never be satisfied.

But we must remember that there were fundamental changes in the composition and character of the work force during this era.[6] One change was the dramatic increase in the education level of the work force. From the postwar period to 1975, the average worker's education level increased 50 percent (from 8.7 to 12.7 years); the number of college graduates in the work force doubled; and by the mid 1970s over 60 percent of the entrants to the work force had some schooling beyond high school. All this education served to heighten people's aspirations for more interesting and challenging work.[7]

Moreover, many more women came into the workplace in this era as well. In 1960, some 33 percent of the work force was female. By 1976, that figure would increase to 41 percent, and over two-thirds of eligible young women would enter the work force to make a career. They, like many minorities, were aspiring to higher pay, higher status, and more meaningful jobs.[8]

Finally, the baby boomers entered the work force during this era. Born and bred during a time of affluence and having come of age in an era of social experimentation and protest, they brought new generational experiences and social outlooks into the workplace. They also embraced a new way of looking at work and its rewards. Up to the point of their arrival, the traditional work ethic was predominant: Work was seen as a necessity, to some degree a necessary evil. It was also seen as a means to achieve material security and comfort and a way to gain social standing and self-respect. To the boomers, however, work had to offer ''something more.'' Many defined it as an outlet of self-expression and a source of self-fulfillment. In important respects, this definition of work, along with new attitudes about management and authority, set up the new generation for disappointment.

New-Breed Workers. Charles Reich, author of *The Greening of America,* was the first observer to capture the changing values of younger and better-educated working people.[9] He found that the values and outlooks of many of the college-educated youth and free-thinking adults constituted "Consciousness III." These students-cum-workers were turning their backs on the life-styles and material orientations of their middle-class mothers and fathers. They despised the rat race, the regimented world of corporate life, and the status-conscious life-style of the corporate type. Instead, they wanted freedom, the opportunity to express themselves in their work, and the chance to do good for their fellow man.

Later, Daniel Yankelovich found a more encompassing change in the outlooks and aspirations of younger and better-educated workers in this period. He called it the "new breed" work ethic.[10] New-breed workers rejected the traditional work ethic. They wanted only psychologically meaningful work and would gain their dignity through independence and self-assertion. Such perspectives were actively cultivated in the life-styles of the 1960s. That the new breed's expectations may have been unfounded and unrealistic misses the point. These aspirations were so strong and so prevalent that they set up many in the work force for a precipitous fall into disappointment.

The quest for something more from a job was not limited to the younger, better-educated workers. Concurrent with the congressional hearings on alienation at work was the publication of the Department of Health, Education, and Welfare's study entitled *Work in America*. The summary of the report began: "Our nation is being challenged by a set of new issues having to do, in one way or another, with the quality of life. This theme emerges from the alienation and disenchantment of blue-collar workers, from the demands of minorities for equitable participation in 'the system,' from the search by women for a new identity and . . . the quest for the aged for a respected and useful social role, from the youth who seek a voice in their society, and from almost everyone who suffers from the frustrations of life in a mass society."[11]

Attitude Toward Management. Working people during this era were developing a more demanding set of expectations of their companies and standards for judging them. The civil rights and women's movements, supported by equal employment legislation, had surely heightened the expectations of minorities and women for fair treatment and a larger share of the pie. More broadly, this era witnessed an increase in employee rights concerning, among other practices, the right to privacy and due process, freedom from harassment and capricious treatment, and more say in the conditions of employment.[12]

Employees of all kinds, younger ones in particular, were less willing to accept traditional management prerogatives and authority. This new attitude was expressed through resentment over executive perks, such as assigned parking spots and private dining rooms. It was evident as well in challenges to autocratic management.

Thus a pattern emerges, in which working people expected and even demanded more from their employers. At the same time, they were not as loyal to their companies or as subservient to management as their fathers had been. Business, government, and labor leaders were slow to respond to these changes in the outlook and aspirations of the new work force and, to some degree, they were indifferent to them. They trivialized or dismissed many of the demographic and value changes as earmarks of "mau-mauing," "bra burning," or a "generation gap" that would subside once blacks and women settled down and baby boomers grew up.

The press for employee rights, constitutionalism at work, and quality of work life were given some attention but mostly lip service. Laments that the "work ethic is dead" were accompanied by calls for the use of more laborsaving technologies and methods to toughen up supervision.

Declining Satisfaction with Work

In the workplace, the *Work in America* report showed clearly, people's aspirations for quality in their work lives were not being met. The report's summary concluded: "Many workers at all occupational levels feel locked in, their mobility blocked, the opportunity to grow lacking in their jobs, challenge missing from their tasks. Young workers appear to be as committed to the institution of work as their elders have been, but many are rebelling against the anachronistic authoritarianism of the workplace. Minority workers similarly see authoritarian worksettings as evidence that society is falling short of its democratic ideals. Women, who are looking to work as an additional source of identity, are being frustrated by an opportunity structure that confines them to jobs damaging to their self-esteem. Older Americans suffer the ultimate in job dissatisfaction: they are denied meaningful jobs even when they have demonstrable skills and are physically capable of being productive.''[13]

Many observers analyzed this discontent and traced it to the value and demographic changes we have illustrated. We join the chorus, but with a new refrain: We believe that cynicism was at work in America between 1960 and 1980 and regard it as a key cause of the economic and human problems encountered in the workplace during that era and today.

Pollsters marked a broad shift in the American public's confidence in American business in this era. During this time, the great majority came to believe that power was concentrated in the hands of too few companies, that business leaders ranked low in terms of morals and ethics, and that companies were becoming cold and impersonal in their dealings with people. Indeed, Lipset and Schneider found that people were losing confidence in nearly all large and impersonal institutions.[14] We see in all of this signs of increasing cynicism about the motivations and performance of business and political leaders as well as of private and public organizations.

Surely this was also manifest in the workplace. In our view, many more young workers, blue collar and white collar, became estranged during this era. Not only did they resist being treated like numbers, they also railed against the system. Frayed Collars, now beginning to come on the scene, heeded Lily Tomlin's advice (''The trouble with the rat race is that even if you win, you're still a rat'') and essentially stopped running. The stage was also being readied for self-seekers to put themselves more visibly into action—many as self-interested Articulate Players.

Reich captured the widespread sense of disillusion that arose among America's Consciousness III generation thus: ''And when he stops believing in this mythic world, the breach

in his credulity is irreparable. The child of an earlier generation could get some unsettling shocks without coming to disbelieve everything . . . [now] he sees right through the form of
posture and pretense; he believes nothing he is told; he experiences . . . betrayal.''[15] The irony is that the material and
social progress wrought by industrialism sowed the seeds of this
disillusion. The education boom, integral to industrial progress,
heightened new-breed workers' expectations. Material comfort
freed people from the hard life and infused them with dreams
of self-fulfillment. Yet the organization man, who paid for their
college educations, in turn became an object of rebellion for
young people. And it was the opening of the American economic
dream to women and minorities that led them to aspire higher
and farther and thence to experience their frustration as betrayal.

There is irony, too, in the way corporations responded
to new-breed aspirations and to the economic dilemmas encountered in the 1970s. To be sure, many executives resented
the changes in working people's values and outlooks or failed
to understand the implications for their organizations. But others
launched new programs, seemingly responsive to the new mood,
and instituted changes in company policies and practices that
were aimed at meeting the new work force's needs. These were,
in our view, genuine attempts to respond to rising expectations.

Humanistic Management Theory

This period between 1960 and 1980 witnessed the dawn of a
new era of management theory. Douglas McGregor believed
the roots of morale and productivity problems could be traced
to the underlying assumptions managers held about people and
human nature.[16] The prevailing ideology of managers, which
he called Theory X, assumed that people had an inherent dislike
for work and thus had to be coerced and controlled on the job.
This he contrasted with a different set of Theory Y values, which
assumed that work was as natural as play or rest and that people would exercise self-direction and control toward ends that
they valued. Theory X saw working people as preferring direction, avoiding responsibility, and being driven by security and

material needs. In contrast, Theory Y assumed that needs for self-esteem and self-actualization were the prime motivators and that, under the right conditions, the highest potential of the worker could be called forth.

What was wrong with organizations? Chris Argyris addressed this issue in his study *Personality and Organization,* where he found that "healthy individuals will have their self-actualization blocked or inhibited because of the demands of the formal organization."[17] He argued that bureaucratic principles of task specialization and the chain of command, all based on Theory X logic, treated working people as children. Thus companies had bred childlike behavior—ranging from dependence and passivity to counterdependence and aggressiveness—throughout their ranks.

Between 1960 and 1980, McGregor and Argyris, among others, specified a humanistic model for managing people. They recognized that human relations training, à la Dale Carnegie, had not truly reached into the hearts of many executives. Thus the hope was that "sensitivity training" would awaken them to their own assumptions about people and cause them to respond more genuinely to the mature needs of their people.

T-groups and encounter sessions were popular in the 1960s.[18] In these "labs," managers could discard their "masks" and open up their "true selves" to scrutiny and counsel from fellow executives. These exercises were, of course, part of the larger human potential movement that was aimed at freeing people from emotional barriers to self-expression and true cooperation with their fellowman. In the 1970s, such encounters were brought in-house and took the form of corporate team development.

There were also broad efforts at organization-wide change. Organizational development programs were undertaken to free companies from their bureaucratic fetters and to involve people in diagnosing and addressing problems on the job. Efforts at job enlargement and enrichment were undertaken to counteract the tedium of assembly line and office work. Rensis Likert's proposals for team organization were implemented to build cooperation among workers and managers and to reduce bureaucratic turf.[19] Such an organization, moreover, was to be led by managers trained in "participative management" techniques.

There is no denying that managers took many steps to meet the needs of the new-breed worker and the rising expectations of so many already in their employ. That these initiatives were also launched in hopes of raising productivity, ensuring quality, and reducing the costs of absenteeism, grievances, and apathy only heightens their import. Indeed, studies showed that in many instances these programs did increase both production and morale, both quality and esprit de corps, in organizations.[20] Why, then, did they not meet the high expectations of the 1960s and 1970s workers or salve their cynicism?

The Theory–Practice Gap

One reason why the new management model failed to humanize work for so many is that so few companies embraced it. The New York Stock Exchange's Office of Economic Research estimates that only 15 percent of the companies employing a hundred or more persons had undertaken human resource programs as of 1980.[21] A second reason is that many companies undertook programs in hopes of gaining a quick fix for productivity and morale problems. Such innovations were marked by faddishness and easily recognized as a sham. Cynics aptly called this the "program of the month" approach to change. Third, in our view, even the better programs simply didn't go far enough. Only by the late 1970s had they reached the ranks of clerical and blue-collar workers and attracted the involvement of organized labor, and only by the 1980s had they come to focus on a major breeding ground of cynicism—the gap between what companies practice and what they preach.

Finally, the change programs of the 1960s and 1970s met with resistance. Many of the personal-growth programs, for example, never led to significant change in organizations. Studies showed that executives, feeling more open and authentic after an encounter session, would revert to their closed, self-protecting, turf-defending manner once back on the job. Similarly, more than a few organizational development programs were hindered by resistance to change by bureaucrats and bureaucratic organizations at large.[22]

What were envisioned as ways to humanize executives and corporations were often reduced to making life a little more livable for enlightened managers and a little better in their organizational areas. The point is that these programs, however well intentioned and implemented, were bucking a larger trend. Forces were at work in organizations and in the makeup of organization men that would limit the impact of the work-reform movement.

Technocracy on the Rise. Whereas the 1960s and 1970s saw small steps being taken to introduce humanistic management into organizations, there was a great leap forward in the technical aspects of management. Systems analysis, and the PERT and GANT charts it generated, helped to define the science of organizational planning and control and ultimately the science of management itself. Managers put it to work to understand their markets, forecast demand, and devise production functions to ensure the rational and efficient allocation of resources; hence, bureaucracy and technology were joined to create the modern "technocracy." On paper, it looked impressive. In practice, it was something else.

The cynical madness of technocratic management during this period was ably documented by two books. First there was *The Peter Principle,* by Laurence Peter and Raymond Hull, which explained "why things always go wrong."[23] It showed, for example, how executives had become consumed by "hierarchiology" at the expense of knowing what was going on in their firms. Executive work now involved "perpetual preparation, side-issue specialization, and ephemeral administrology" that amounted to, in the authors' words, "utter irrelevance." Accordingly, Peter and Hull recommended that people cultivate the "power of negative thinking" and practice "creative incompetence" in order to cope with the technocratic order. Their work became a cynic's handbook.

Then came John Gall's book on *Systemantics,* which showed how systems work but "especially how they fail."[24] This volume extended the "laws" of Murphy and Parkinson to encompass the full range of systemic failures in modern life. Their favorite arena was the modern corporation. Gall's basic message was that systems have a palpable lure for the rationally minded and quickly create their own reality in organizations. It was this reality in organizations of this era that led to a new division in society unimagined by Tocqueville—that between technocratic masters and victims.

Hard Drives Out Soft. The story of Robert McNamara's leadership of Ford Motor Company—and, later, his management of the Vietnam War—via statistical monitoring and modeling is testimony enough to the cold, detached, amoral quality of the technocrat in modern society. Systems analysis reduces all elements of a project—even of an organization—to variables that are in turn put into logic-driven models for analysis and implementation. American managers began to manage "by the numbers" in the 1960s.[25]

Accordingly, staff posts began to proliferate. It has been estimated that between 1965 and 1975 the ratio of staff personnel to production workers in American manufacturing companies increased from 35 per 100 to 41 per 100—all there to impose more paper requirements on line managers, who would then churn out ever more reports.[26] It is small wonder that corporate executives lost touch with their customers, their products, and their operations during this period. They also lost touch with their employees.

It was perhaps inevitable that advances in systems analysis and the new management sciences would prove ever more potent than efforts to promote personal and organizational development in enterprise during the 1960s and 1970s. "Hard drives out soft" became a business-school dictum. What was not so inevitable, however, was that the management of people, that one seeming "intangible," would be reduced to quantification and entered into the profit-maximization calculus.

Human Resource Management

Rensis Likert made the case that people were "assets" to an organization and should be managed accordingly. His expectation was that such an approach would justify increased investments in human capital. E. F. Schumacher's popular book, *Small Is Beautiful,* made human capital a centerpiece in a broad vision of economics "as if people mattered." The stage was being set, then, for human resource management.[27]

Along the way, however, the cold logic of technocracy took over. As an example, personnel departments, aided by advances in technology, began to amass huge data banks on the management of the human resource. Records were kept of employees' test scores, training, compensation rates, performance levels, attendance, and the like. Countless reports were prepared and issued, tracking individuals and functions. As people were seeking independence, meaningful work, and self-control, behind the scenes countless technocrats were studying them, reporting on them, cost-justifying them, and then evaluating their worth in the impersonal framework of economic rationality.

Personnel representatives, rather than listening to people, began to study the results of corporate attitude surveys. Moreover, their function, once the human center of the firm, was reclassified as a profit center. It is understandable, then, why people began to see themselves solely as numbers in the corporate world. This numeric logic was inevitably applied to the many workplace experiments that were undertaken in this era. On this point, sociologist Robert Cole notes that managers in Japan and Europe embraced changes in their industrial systems on the basis of their belief in people's inherent worth and the inherent soundness of the new management model. By contrast, he finds American managers to be skeptical of the management principles and embracing work humanization solely for its economic payoff.[28]

Critics go so far as to say that human resource management techniques, such as periodic attitude surveys, have replaced the stopwatch as tools of manipulation in our information age. We do not go so far. But it is clear that the technocrats seized on the human resource movement to expand their influence and that many managers viewed it solely for getting more out of their people. It reached the point where the human factor became just another variable in the managerial equation. In this impersonal world, investments in people were not distinguished from investments in plant. And, in time, the depreciation of plant was matched by the disillusionment of people.

Technocracy, even more than its bureaucratic forebear, frustrated the initiative and broke the spirit of many in industry. The tough-minded learned to work this ever more complex system; the tender-minded were worked over by it. For both, however, cynicism became part of the fabric of organizational life.

"People" Strike Back. It should not be surprising, then, to see the victims of this technocratic order striking back by advancing their own self-interest. Popular books, such as *Up the Down Staircase* and *Up the Organization,* rued the trials of institutional life and celebrated the qualities of the maverick schoolteacher and executive.[29] Self-help books urged people "to look out for number one" and to "pull their own strings." The management exemplar became the "gamesman."

The Gamesman was the new corporate persona of the 1970s. Michael Maccoby's study of the executive personality yielded four types. These were the Craftsmen, chiefly concerned with the technical functions of their jobs; the Jungle Fighters, throwbacks to the ruthless industrialists of an earlier era; Company Men, akin to those diagnosed by Whyte in the mid 1950s; and Gamesmen, who divide business into a set of games—the money game, the marketing game, the R&D game, and so forth. Accordingly, Gamesmen see people management as just another game.

Maccoby found that corporate Gamesmen in the 1970s worked through their management teams. They brought to their teams, however, a calculating edge and a cold orientation to human resources. Maccoby wrote: "Since he is so concerned about winning, the gamesman tends to evaluate his co-workers almost exclusively in terms of what they can do for the team. Unlike softer or more loyal company men, he is ready to replace a player as soon as he feels that person weakens the team. . . . 'The word "loyalty" is too emotional,' said one gamesman, 'and empathy and generosity get in the way of work.' "[30]

Gamesmen, at least those cynics we call Articulate Players, are consumed by the competitiveness of corporate life. They tend to see people only as winners and losers. These are not the cold corporate planners and bloodless staff types (Administrative Sideliners) who characterized the conglomerate technocracies of the sixties and seventies. Maccoby finds the Gamesmen prominent in high-tech companies, in industries undergoing massive changes—wherever there are action and high stakes. They manage with their heads, like their technocrat compatriots, but eschew the order and regularity of management by the numbers. Gamesmen are more hyped-up and independent. They play by the rules, so long as they can create their own.

Epochal Crosscurrents. We propose that there were strong crosscurrents between the warm humanistic management theories promulgated and the cold technocratic management practiced in the 1960s and 1970s. Such crosscurrents have marked several epochs of American enterprise. As such they were found:

- Between the Moral Reform movement and the greedy excesses of industrial capitalists in the 1800s
- Between scientific management principles and their exploitative application in the first quarter of the twentieth century
- Between human relations theories and bureaucratic organization principles in the second quarter of the twentieth century
- Between the work-reform movement and the technocratic management practices in the third quarter of the twentieth century.

Much as Henry Ford used Taylor's precepts to his own advantage, so also segments of corporate America came to use humanistic theories and coldly apply them through human resource management.

Tracy Kidder's book *The Soul of the New Machine* is a modern morality play about these crosscurrents in business in this high-tech/high-touch era. The protagonist, Tom West, a Data General project manager, assembled a team of young engineers to build the company's next generation of minicomputers. West designed the project so that each member had a piece of the action, the sense that each personally was building "the machine." His lieutenants hosted informal rap sessions and social events, built esprit de corps in their groups, and ensured that the team was getting up to eighty hours a week from each member. The high was exhilarating, and they did indeed get the machine out the door.

As a consummate Articulate Player, West knew what made the new workers tick and how to pull their strings. In a passage from the book, Kidder describes how one of West's lieutenants signed up recruits by testing their real interest in computers, their desire to build one, their inherent cockiness, and their taste for hard work and unrelenting hours. The interview winds down as follows:

> "It's gonna be tough [says the lieutenant]. If we hired you, you'd be working with a bunch of cynics and egotists and it'd be hard to keep up with them."
>
> "That doesn't scare me" [replies the recruit].
>
> "There's a lot of fast people in this group . . . it's gonna be a real hard job with lots of long hours. And I mean long hours."
>
> "No. . . . That's what I want to do, get in on the ground floor of a new architecture. I want to do a big machine. I want to be where the action is."
>
> "Well [says the lieutenant], we can only let in the best of this year's graduates. We've already let in some awfully fast people. We'll let you know."
>
> (We tell him that we only let in the best. Then we let him in.)
>
> "I don't know [says the lieutenant afterwards]. It was kind of like recruiting for a suicide mission. You're gonna die, but you're gonna die in glory."[31]

West and his charges got the machine out the door. In the end, however, there were few rewards for their effort; many left the company, burnt out, and the human toll in lost spouses and personal estrangement mounted. They had won, but many team members became cynical and promised ''never again.'' It is perhaps worth noting that, since then, Data General, West's employer, has made massive layoffs and lost its eminence in the computer industry.

In a sense, we have reached a transition point. Bureaucracy and technocracy are still the dominant structures in industry, but a new generation of pragmatic and cynical managers and workers is gaining a toehold on industrial life. The 1980s brought a new age, in which they had more say in setting the corporate agenda. Burr at People Express, Jobs at Apple Computer, Iacocca at Chrysler, and many other industrial leaders set a tone for the 1980s. So, too, did T. Boone Pickens, record numbers of MBAs, and Ronald Reagan. The times were a-changin', but not in the way that Dylan or other sixties dreamers had expected. Nor were the management theorists, once apostles of the people's self-actualization and now proponents of their empowerment, prepared for the chaos that would be wrought.

6

Managerial
Evangelism
and Exploitation

> We advocate a change from "tough-mindedness"
> to "tenderness," from concern with hard data and
> balance sheets to a concern for the "soft stuff"—
> values, vision, integrity. We have found that when
> it comes to achieving long-term success, soft is hard.

This is Tom Peters, coauthor of the best-selling business book
In Search of Excellence, speaking to executives about a new set of
American values and opportunities, with much the same fervor
that Russell Conwell mustered when promising "acres of diamonds" at the turn of the century.[1] Peters's audience is different:
It is well-heeled corporate managers, not immigrants or everyday people. The forum has changed: He speaks in the grandeur
of hotel ballrooms, whereas Conwell worked from a canvas tent.
Even the message has a different meaning: The opportunities
heralded are there for corporate "intrapreneurs," and the tools
of success involve closeness to customers, value-driven production, and "management by walking around."

Management by Faith

Management has entered an era of evangelism. In excellent companies, emphasis is on management by symbols: "Perception is all there is. There ain't no such thing as steak, sad to say, just the sizzle," or so says Peters. Executives are competing for the hearts and minds of knowledge workers; and the message is that only passionate leaders and excellent companies will survive in the new competitive environment.

The rhetoric fits our information age. Today physical labor has been supplanted by mental work, and mechanical imagery has given way to cognitive models of man as information processor. Executives are going to seminars on image management, dusting off Dale Carnegie's guide to personality salesmanship, and putting their oratorical skills to work—often in videotaped messages to their people. In turn, their companies are undertaking identity programs, formulating philosophy statements, and reaching out to people with bold visions and high-minded statements of purpose.

Is it all show? This new push to impassion executives and enliven company cultures, while smacking of revivalism, has been accompanied by action. Countless studies document widespread changes in the ways companies are run in the 1980s. The fledgling work-reform movement of the 1960s and 1970s has become a high priority on the corporate agenda in the 1980s. Many companies today are less bureaucratic and less dominated by turfism, and many are more participatively managed and more oriented toward people. Even unions have gotten into the act with joint labor–management programs.[2]

The new movement has even taken on technocracy—substituting friendly personal computers for impersonal mainframes and turning bloodless bureaucrats into corporate service representatives. It has tried to remove the paper-and-procedure barriers to people's achievement and fulfillment in the workplace. Certainly the press and the reading public have risen to the message. Whereas cynical depictions of managerial incompetence and organizational antics dominated bookshelves in the 1970s, today's values celebrate "change masters," "corporate pathfinders,'' ''transformational leaders,'' and the ''new competitors.''[3]

Two forces are behind the success of this new movement. For one, the rise of Japan, Inc., and the globalization of the economy have forced American executives to acknowledge the failings of technocracy and the adversarial model of labor-management relations. In turn, the new management model, when accompanied by prudent technological and marketing decisions, has shown it can yield a substantial payoff.

Second, there is evidence that the values and outlooks of top executives have changed in the past two decades.[4] More and more, they seem to espouse and practice a genuinely people-centered management philosophy. Some of this has to do with the arrival of the baby boomers into senior and middle-management levels. Apparently their earlier sensitivities have not been fully blunted by the climb up the corporate ladder. In addition, many high-tech executives have proved to be role models of this management outlook. Their high-tech/high-touch management style has been widely emulated.

While *Business Week* hails these developments as the ''new industrial relations'' and success stories abound in managerial periodicals and seminars, management by faith has its drawbacks.[5] Specifically, many of its followers have not been faithful to the precepts. Instead, they have emphasized the ''sizzle'' to the extent of burning up their credibility. Here we want to examine three ways that companies have sought to put the new evangelistic faith into practice and then to consider how some disingenuous practitioners have lost the hearts and minds of the laity.

Management by faith today has different followers and factions. Some companies have turned to Japanese-style management, drawing upon Japan's technical innovations and managerial concepts in hopes of keeping pace with their overseas competitors. Many more firms have embraced the principles of excellence, in anticipation of one-upping their competitors. Finally, there are plenty of examples of companies cultivating their own unique philosophies and practices and putting their own distinct brands of faith to work.

Japanese-Style Management

Much as Japan imported a whole set of American management principles during its reconstruction following World War II, some American managers are today bringing them back to reconstruct their own manufacturing base. The most modern American factories operate with just-in-time inventory arrangements—materials are ordered and delivered as needed, to reduce the costs of work in progress. Work flows are managed through "statistical process control," in order to monitor product quality on line, and scheduled through sophisticated computer programs—again, a common Japanese practice. All this, of course, relates to the "hard" side of business—the nuts and bolts. But American managers have also drawn from the "soft" side of Japanese management in the 1980s.

William Ouchi's *Theory Z,* a comparative study of Japanese and American management practices, illuminated the culture of Japanese management for an American audience.[6] With policies of lifetime employment, nonspecialized career paths, consensual decision making, and a broad-based concern for people's welfare, upper-tier Japanese companies are not only different but, in many respects, more effective than American companies in stimulating motivation and commitment in the work force. These practices are, of course, inextricably linked with Japanese history and national culture, and they depend as well on its technology base and economy. Nonetheless, Ouchi found Theory Z practices prominent in certain leading American companies, including IBM, Hewlett-Packard, and Eastman Kodak, and recommended them more broadly to American industry.

The main Japanese practice that American companies have adopted is quality circles. Q-circles are an effective way to involve workers in decisions in their areas of responsibility and to increase quality and productivity. In many U.S. plants, workers have formed circles, been taught the basics of group problem solving, and been put to work fixing problems and making improvements.

What about the other aspects of Japanese management? To be blunt, not many managers appear to have read *Theory Z.*

As publicity about the book picked up, however, the implication to many was that "the Japanese do it better." Then along came *In Search of Excellence* saying, figuratively, "We can do them one better!" and there were the makings of a phenomenal bestseller and a grass-roots management movement.

The homespun and sensibly simple advice proffered by Tom Peters and Bob Waterman in their eight lessons from excellent companies struck a responsive chord in the American manager's psyche. The message, in a phrase, fit the zeitgeist. President Reagan was promising a return to the good old days through self-reliance and the resurrection of traditional American values. The uplifting excellence message was that "we still had it," and countless numbers of companies, as varied as the U.S. Post Office and the Los Angeles Raiders, embraced the message and theme.

New-Age Entrepreneurs

In the 1980s—when soft is hard, yin is yang, and, as John Naisbitt observes, the "both/and" mind-set is operative—the excellence theme is an exemplar of what has come to be called "new age" management theory.[7] Companies, for instance, are supposed to be both loose and tight. Certainly there are tangible examples of this in the world of organizations.

In Digital Equipment's matrix structure, for example, people can work on a line project while still having a staff affiliation. At Hewlett-Packard, authority is decentralized by delegation and centralized by closely monitored objectives. The tensions created are regulated by a cohesive company culture. In many large manufacturing concerns, managers are charged with increasing productivity and promoting the quality of work life.

New-age management seeks to balance such competing pressures facing companies by aligning people with the firm's strategy and attuning them to one another.[8] The aim of alignment is to get people close to the customer, to establish hands-on, value-driven production, and to simplify structure and systems—all in service of meeting the needs of the firm. Nevertheless, aligned organizations may be properly directed but inhumanly oriented. Thus attunement allows people to make commitments to one another, collectively dedicate themselves to the company and customer, and thereby meet their own needs. This involves a corporate vision, lots of celebrating, a measure of communing, and compensation tied to getting the job done. All this, of course, sounds rosy in theory.

One company that fashioned its own new-age model was particularly celebrated in the press and business schools. The "Trailways of the Airways," People Express, perhaps best epitomized a home-grown solution to new economic problems. Donald Burr, founder of People Express, moved his company quickly into the deregulated air traffic market by providing low-cost service for the "smart traveler" and frequent flights to underserved markets. People Express made use of the hub concept, to ensure that flights were full, and charged for ancillary flight services, including food and baggage handling. It was no-frills flying but profitable beyond the imagination of the industry up to that point.

What fascinated observers most about People Express was its management philosophy and practices. The company was founded on six precepts that put profit and people on equal footing in the mission of the airline. The organizational structure was flat, and job responsibilities were broad. Compensation was relatively low, by industry standards, but all employees were stockholders, and the value of stock rose dramatically in the first years of operation. The company took the MBWA (management by walking around) principle to heart and transformed it into a central ideal: People Express was in the business of making a better world.

Donald Burr was featured on a cover of *Time*.[9] As much as any other CEO, he came to epitomize the new-age entrepreneur. Surely Burr had his detractors. Some called him a practitioner of "Kool-Aid Management," with reference to evangelist Jim Jones's totalitarian community. Others saw great promise in his example, and we do, too. But there are many other proponents and practitioners of new-age management and of excellence and Japanese-style management who have used the techniques to hype people up and then manipulate them in self-serving fashion. These are the faithless followers—cynical managers and manipulators who have given management by faith a bad name.

Fakery and Failings

As sensible as the Japanese management principles seem to be, it is important to note that American managers drew selectively from the roster of Theory Z practices. Japanese companies, for example, try to operate in an egalitarian fashion, minimizing distinctions between management and labor. Japanese managers may come to work in business suits, but they don the uniforms of members (employees) once in the plant. This practice is uncommon in American industry. Moreover, the gap between managers' and workers' salaries in Japan is much smaller than in the United States. We know of few attempts to lessen this gap in American firms. On the contrary, it seems to be widening in industry. Furthermore, Japan has many more supervisors per employee in the work force than in the United States, but many fewer upper managers. It has far fewer accountants and many more equivalents to human resource managers. Very few U.S. companies have guaranteed employees' job security or reorganized management and corporate structures in line with Japanese practices.

We are not suggesting that corporations should have made these changes in hopes of emulating the Japanese management system. There are far too many differences between our two cultures and work forces that make the forced fitting of Japanese management into American firms both impossible and imprudent. We do contend, however, that the practices American companies adopted, insofar as they concern human relations, represent to some degree another example of the big fast fix.

The case of quality circles makes this plain. Many companies embraced Q-circles because of their apparent payoff. Scant training was provided for circle leaders, however, and no structures were developed to ensure that ideas flowed up and authority came down. Thus many circles have been left to flounder with little management support and scant say-so about the important problems in organizations. It should not be surprising to see, then, that more circles are being phased out today than are being formed.

Up to this point, there has been a mix of successes and failures in companies undertaking the search for excellence. Committed and convincing managers, energetic and enthusiastic workers, well-orchestrated and participatively directed programs—all have contributed to the successes. In turn, doubtful and disingenuous managers, suspicious and disenchanted workers, and ill-conceived and poorly administered programs are at the root of the failures.

Beyond this, there are the majority of working people in the majority of companies who experience nothing akin to progressive management or people-oriented programs. That a few big, innovative companies have such management and programs only heightens frustration and feeds disillusion. Our point is simple: Rhetoric about excellence is well ahead of reality in industry and in most companies.

New-Age Realities. Surely many of the ideas that are advanced have strong theoretical foundations and promising potential for application. Of course, there is always some risk in how they will be applied. *Fortune,* for example, in an article on the management of corporate cultures, cited a case of a CEO's ordering his subordinates to get a strong, forward-looking culture in place—and quick.[10] It also referred to a growing industry of culture consultants, dubbed ''culture vultures.'' *Newsweek,* in turn, ran a story on new-age consultants practicing ''corporate mind control.''[11] Alignment and attunement may have some theoretical relevance, but they have mechanical connotations. Surely the emphasis of the 1960s and 1970s on human sensitivity and communal involvement seems rather quaint from the vantage of new-age management theory.

More than this, there are contending counterforces in the managerial world of the 1980s that threaten even the most genuine new-age management efforts. Big companies are merging, acquiring, reshaping, and resizing themselves to such an extent that efforts to align and attune people become hopeless and even disingenuous. Some see new-age management as an example of ''corpocrisy''—that is, hypocrisy in corporate life.

However laudable it may be in theory and even in practice, new-age management is being overwhelmed by new-age realities.

The sad saga of People Express Airlines illustrates. Cut-throat competition, unwise expansion, and egoistic leadership led to People's downfall. The company went broke and was purchased by Frank Lorenzo—a takeover artist and Burr's former boss. People employees, whose stock had been valued as high as $22 a share, received just $1.73 a share from their new owner.

Lorenzo also bought Eastern Airlines. Eastern had formed a joint labor-management committee to operate the company and had made impressive gains in productivity through negotiated wage reductions and a gain-sharing plan. It was not enough, and that company went bust, too. Famed union-buster Lorenzo took them over.

Business writer Bob Kuttner commented on the "human element" that is lost in all of this big-league finance:

> Most of us . . . don't play in that league. We want an honest day's pay for an honest day's work. We expect that tomorrow will be pretty much like to-day—indeed, we need that assurance in order to function. We expect that our home, our church, our kid's school, our bank, and the place where we work will stay put, unless we voluntarily opt for a change in order to improve our livelihood.
>
> America desperately needs an economy based upon notions of mutual obligation and reciprocity. Without that, well-intentioned bargains like those at Eastern and People Express are doomed to failure and decent people are played for suckers. Social contracts are impossible when every company is on the block. That is the hidden cost of the casino economy.[12]

New-age management is coincident with much broader developments that are wrenching established patterns in industry and provoking a return to Social Darwinism in management. Self-interest is back in the forefront, and it has a new playground.

The Second Industrial Revolution

Prognosticators have described America as moving into its second industrial revolution.[13] Our postindustrial society is dominated by the growth of the service sector and high-tech industries. Such transformations bring with them upheaval, losses, and gains. In the first industrial revolution, we lost our agrarian roots and identities, the social codes and mores of preindustrial life, and our close-knit communities. The gain was economic progress. In this second industrial revolution, many stand to prosper, but we are beginning to estimate our losses.

Loss of Heavy Industry. America is witnessing today what analysts call "de-industrialization," with the loss of over twenty million jobs in heavy industry in the past decade.[14] U.S. Steel is one cynical example of how business executives have coped with these changing conditions. Steel executives have offered regular paeans to free enterprise while seeking protectionist legislation and tax credits for capital investments in new facilities. But rather than invest in steel, the company has diversified with acquisitions in oil and chemicals, to the point where its steel business now accounts for less than 50 percent of its profits and the company has been renamed USX. How about steelworkers? Over 100,000 have been laid off or forced into early retirement. We suspect many have become, and rightly so, Hard-Bitten Cynics.

General Motors is another example. Ross Perrot unmasked the greed of GM's top executives, who took home massive bonuses while laying off nearly 30,000 workers. Ten years ago, GM workers were smashing Japanese cars to vent their frustration. They were promised progressive labor-management cooperation programs, and the UAW went along with wage reductions and concessions to build yet another factory of the future. Today, we suspect, many of the GM workers have become cynics—betrayed by swollen management bonuses and by significantly less innovation and investment, both in product and in the new-factory concept. This is in addition to the export of many autoworkers' jobs and the widespread importation of foreign parts for seemingly made-in-America automobiles.

The list could go on. The simple truth is that youth seeking blue-collar jobs will not find the opportunities or the recompense that were once available to their parents. That promise of a good job like the old man's has become a chimera. The world is, indeed, colder for them—and who can blame them for becoming cynical?

Rise of Service Industries. No doubt the blue-collar ranks will decline as we lose our heavy manufacturing base, but service, professional, and technical posts will increase as we gain world leadership in those industries. Will service jobs give people financial security, a sense of community at work, fulfillment of their dreams? At this point, the prospects are unsettling.[15]

As an example, service jobs pay less than industrial ones and offer much less in terms of fringe benefits and job security. Many of the service jobs, moreover, are found in small businesses that have a high failure rate. We risk becoming, according to one labor leader, a nation of "soda jerks" in a service-based economy. How about computers? High-tech industry, while appealing, employs less than 10 percent of the work force, and the coming shakeout in the industry makes its prospects less appealing. In turn, high-tech jobs, while engaging, are beyond the reach of the many who lack technical training or acumen.

The signs are that many going into the service sector face a future of downward mobility and will not achieve the occupational stature or security of their parents. Studies by Ralph Whitehead show that nearly half of them believe they are less able than their parents to find a job with long-term security.[16] We have labeled some of them as Squeezed Cynics and suspect that they are disillusioned about their prospects of owning a home, getting health care at a fair price, and sending their children to college.

There are, of course, many who will profit from work in the service sector. Jobs in finance, real estate, and specialized personal services pay handsomely, and there are many opportunities for the brightest, most energetic, and able to prosper in service jobs. Nevertheless, the postindustrial society has the potential of dividing working people into winners and losers, in even more dramatic fashion than we have witnessed heretofore, and it offers little in the way of enhancing people's outlooks on the future.

Corporate "Rationalization." One needn't look only at broad economic changes to see society being divided into winners and losers, for countless companies are dividing people along these lines in their moves to rationalize and restructure. "Rationalization" is a cynical euphemism for another cynical euphemism: "reductions in force." Companies are simply getting rid of people—notably, once secure white-collar clerical, professional, and technical personnel—in record numbers. Estimates are that the *Fortune* 500 companies have reduced their ranks by 2.2 million people in the 1980s alone. Why? The answers are many and varied, but for the "losers" they become a sound reason for cynicism.

There is reason to believe, however, that many of the putative winners are equally cynical. The rise in "asset shuffling" or "paper entrepreneurialism," as Robert Reich terms it, in companies today has added little to our productive capability while enriching a few. Reich looks at its human toll:

> Rearranging employees is analogous to rearranging paper assets. Some such shuffling is useful and often necessary. But when undertaken on a wide scale, when it becomes the automatic response to changes in the firm's environment, it is disastrous. . . . A high velocity of firings, hirings, layoffs, and rehirings at lower rates may enable the firm to adjust to short-term market fluctuations and appear to be more "dynamic," but it also serves as a deceptive palliative. It allows the firm to avoid undertaking more basic change. And it demoralizes everyone involved.
>
> Within a productive system that increasingly depends upon cooperation, good faith, and team spirit, the dominant ethic is coming to be cynical indifference and opportunism. The paper entrepreneurialism pursued by the firm as a whole inevitably finds reflection in personal manipulation

among people within the firm. "Beggar-thy-neigh-
bor" tactics which impose losses on people outside
the firm for the sake of short-term paper gains are
mirrored by similar tactics inside—a pattern of
behavior best described by the legal term "self-
dealing."[17]

In Reich's view, "We are witnessing an extraordinary
increase in self-dealing within the American enterprise." His
roster of such dealings includes the creation of complex golden
parachutes and cozy consulting relationships, as well as fraud,
embezzlement, and so on. Paul Hirsch provides sagacious
counsel for the self-interested in *Pack Your Own Parachute.*[18] We
see self-interest in less grandiose but no less malignant forms
in the self-dealings of Articulate Players when they put their
cynicism to work. They are winners, by American materialistic
standards, because they have learned how to cynically play the
new paper game.

Conditions Then and Now

There are, of course, deep parallels between the social and
political conditions of the first industrial revolution and this second one. Emphasis today, as at the turn of the century, is on
the unfettered accumulation of wealth. A French observer of
that earlier era was shocked to see a democratic country where
the rich had so little concern for the poor. Many observers express that same shock today over public attitudes toward the
uneducated, unemployed, and homeless. Business was marked
by a "let the public be damned" attitude during the first industrial revolution. With so many plant closures and consolida-
tions, that same attitude comes through today. Look at the case
of General Electric—once the hallmark of human relations
management. Its new president has been dubbed "Neutron
Jack"—after he visits a plant, the building is left standing, but
all the people are gone!
    As in that earlier time, there are intellectual and popular
movements in defense of Social Darwinism in industry. Workers
at the turn of the century were chided for their "laziness"; the

charge today is that many are "deadwood." And just as the accumulation of wealth was seen as ennobling then, today the argument is that wealth is essential to reducing poverty. Social Darwinism is surely at play in the marketplace, where manipulators like Ashur Edelman and Carl Icahn work the money game to buy and sell companies and, with them, working people's livelihoods. It is also at play within firms where intrapreneurs jealously advance their own projects and burn up their people in the service of their own advancement.

Now, it is fair to say that America needs more innovativeness, less deadwood in the corporate ranks, the motivating juice of a little competition, and fundamental changes in our industrial order and economy. In the scramble to move in these directions, however, we have created a scenario where it's every man for himself, and woe to those who don't get the message to García! As in the first industrial revolution, larger political and social developments are overwhelming the best intentions of reform-minded managers and serving to legitimize the actions of the most ruthless of industrial leaders and raiders.

It is small wonder to see the strength of cynicism in the work force. New-age management, gaining momentum in the 1980s, held out the promise of good, meaningful jobs for many in the work force. The Reagan revolution promised a return to the unencumbered land of milk and honey. But the former has been overmatched by larger political and economic forces, and the steak promised by the excellence evangelists seems to be only sizzle. The economic engine that Reagan fired, moreover, shows signs of being slowed by debt and doubt.

Psychological Shoals

To understand how the cycle of cynicism has started afresh, we need also to look at what the "experts" projected for the work force in the 1980s. Many, for example, predicted that baby boomers—facing increasing job competition, raising families, and striving for economic security—would lessen their "expressive" orientations in the 1980s and temper their expectations to the new economic realities. It was also expected that women and minorities would learn to fit into the traditional passive mold.

Furthermore, it was also projected that the young workers, seemingly more conservative than their baby boomer brothers and sisters, would see through the folly of aquarian ideals and participate in their own green revolution, wherein money would be the name of the game. The larger point is this: It was anticipated that the pursuit of self-fulfillment through work would wane and that workers—managers, clerical, and blue collar— would be forming aspirations wholly in keeping with the materialist thrust in the society.

But data from surveys, depth interviews, and case studies show that this return to traditional pursuits simply has not occurred. Studies of workers in the 1980s counter predictions that people have swung back to an era of discipline and self-sacrifice. The era of high aspirations, then, is hardly dead; on the contrary, it continues to extend throughout the work force. Workers today have not yielded to the lure of economic security and creature comfort at the expense of self-fulfillment. They still want it all.[19]

We believe that many, therefore, are further setting themselves up for disillusion. Our study finds high levels of cynicism among the young and the baby boomers, particularly the least educated and least advantaged of them, who want it all but can't find it in the economy and society of today. Clearly this disappointment has cast many on psychological shoals. Maslow's hierarchy is still at work, and many are focusing their energies on making a living and providing for their households.[20] At the same time, the loss of their dreams has left them cynical and embittered.

There is a second and profound disappointment afflicting working people today, particularly the young and the baby boomers who have higher levels of education and income. Many self-seekers have focused so sharply on their own needs that they have grown apart from others, lost the capacity for intimacy and community, and discovered that their "inner journey" has brought them loneliness and depression.

Another cost is increased cynicism. In our view, the search for self-fulfillment has raised people's expectations about what

the corporation workplace can offer. That some organizations
have developed more humane and inspiring work cultures has
further fired the imagination. What so many people have encountered, instead, is that the grim realities of economic life
in the 1980s limit their possibilities and make corporate promises of self-fulfillment illusory. The promise of the human potential movement was that everybody could be a winner—"I'm
OK, you're OK!" The realities in the social and economic
marketplace are that we also have many losers. We see this in
the mistrust and suspicion people have of their fellow man.

Unlike their forebears in the early part of this century,
today's self-oriented workers have no tight-knit community or
extended family to fall back on and few to turn to, save psycho-
therapists and fellow self-seekers, for emotional sustenance. The
"entitled" generation has limited capacity to delay its gratifications and no desire to sacrifice for the next generation. We can
see, then, that the seeds of bitterness have been nourished not
only by national policy and industry's response to competition
but also by individual ambition and self-seeking.

The saving grace is that many have prospered and others
have coped with the larger social changes by tempering their
aspirations and redirecting their inner journeys in more fruit-
ful ways in the 1980s. In that sense, then, we see both cynicism
and optimism in the American working population as a function of today's crosscurrents.

Today's Crosscurrents

By focusing on the downside of the economy of the 1980s and
the disappointments for America's psyche, we do not in any
way discount the more salutary developments of the decade. In
many quarters, an ethos of community is taking hold. There
are signs, for example, that yuppie-ism is no longer fashionable,
and more than a few T-shirts worn by youth proclaim, "Greed
Is Out." Private–public partnerships flourish, with the expressed
aim of meeting both economic and human needs. Community
is coming into currency in many companies, too, a topic we
will examine in the final section of this book. We believe that
its progress has been slowed, limited, and constrained by cyni-

cism in management and labor, and certainly by the cynical dog-eat-dog environment in the society and the economy, but this is not to gainsay what has been accomplished.

Some company downsizing efforts have been accomplished with compassion and are providing more secure jobs for heretofore anxious workers and managers. Some mergers are invigorating industry competition and signaling that American companies can compete in a global economy. Many organizational innovations have yielded workplace designs that emphasize teamwork and new work structures that break down bureaucratic barriers and connect people to people again.

The Gamesman mentality is being encouraged in companies, but not all Gamesmen are cynical Articulate Players. Some of the model managers are those who, according to Maccoby, manage with both their heads and their hearts. Many Command Cynics are in the lead of the asset shuffling and corporate restructuring that are under way, but there are also visionary leaders rebuilding flagging industries and restructuring them in more competitive and humane fashion.

These developments promise to provide jobs, opportunities, and a measure of community for most working people in this country. The absence of such developments throughout industry and particularly in the service sector, however, threatens to deepen the despair of those who have not and will not have the chance to participate in them.

Finally, let us be clear about our biases. We find an element of "smoke and mirrors" in today's corporate revivalism. Too many companies have used it as a smokescreen to manipulate people, and too many companies exploit the Darwinian environment. Work is undergoing a revolution-producing ambiguity. We simply do not know what to believe, whom to believe, whom to trust, and whom to turn to in the face of massive changes. The cynicism cycle of high hopes and disillusion has, as we have suggested, become a national biorhythm. One implication is clear: A nearly equal number of Americans are cynical as are upbeat. It would seem that some have coped with ambiguity with honor, while others have turned to cynicism. The new age is bringing out the best and the worst in us.

7

Profiles
of Today's
Cynics

As society and conditions of work have changed over the past decades, so too have people's experience of hope and handling of disappointment varied according to time, employment situation, and personal circumstances. To see the consequences of cynicism, we need to detect its prevalence in selected pockets of the work force and to consider why it has spread disproportionately through the American populace. Here we focus on the results of our national survey to profile cynics in the country today.

There are at least three reasons to expect levels of cynicism to differ among segments of our society. First, members of selected groups have had distinct life experiences: Their expectations have been born and their frustrations bred in particular historical and sociocultural contexts. We have noted how today's baby boomers came of age in an era of rapidly rising expectations and how many became disillusioned by the scar-

146

ring events of the 1960s and early 1970s. The historical experiences of older and younger workers have been different. Some flavor of the youthful mind-set, at least for college-educated youth, can be found in the T-shirt and billboard "art" of Jenny Holzer, one of whose aphorisms reads as follows:

> AFFLUENT COLLEGE-BOUND STUDENTS FACE THE REAL PROSPECT OF DOWNWARD MOBILITY. FEELINGS OF ENTITLEMENT CLASH WITH THE AWARENESS OF IMMINENT SCARCITY. THERE IS RESENTMENT AT GROWING UP AT THE END OF AN ERA OF PLENTY COUPLED WITH REASSESSMENT OF CONVENTIONAL MEASURES OF SUCCESS.

We will indeed find that cynicism varies across age groups in the work force.

Another force influencing the spread of cynicism in society concerns one's personality and frame of reference. There is a body of theory and research, for example, suggesting that women form attitudes and make moral judgments in a pattern somewhat different from men's. In our national survey data, we find that women are less likely than men to agree that people are by nature dishonest or to believe that people are basically out for themselves. They are far more likely, however, to think that it is getting harder to make true friends and, in general, they find the world to be colder than men do. We believe these different perceptions can, to some extent, be traced to differing male and female patterns of attribution and frames of reference.[1] We introduce this point at the risk of stereotyping people on the basis of their gender, race, or social class and can only plead for appreciation of our intent: The data imply only attitudinal tendencies in society's subpopulations and are in no way freighted with evaluation on our part—good or bad.

A final factor influencing the spread of cynicism in our society concerns the way the media, opinion leaders, and members of various population groups themselves reinforce a cynical versus an upbeat outlook. It is interesting to note, on this point, that a current debate rages as to whether baby boomers of the 1960s were truly caring idealists or rather self-centered pleasure seekers. In turn, there are more and less salutary appraisals of leaders of the women's and civil rights movements as they reach out to women filling traditional roles and form the ''Rainbow Coalition.'' Our point is that some people take cynicism as the appropriate outlook of their peer group. Others follow a different drummer or do the drumming themselves.

Cynicism and Age

Figure 4. Younger Workers More Cynical Than Older.

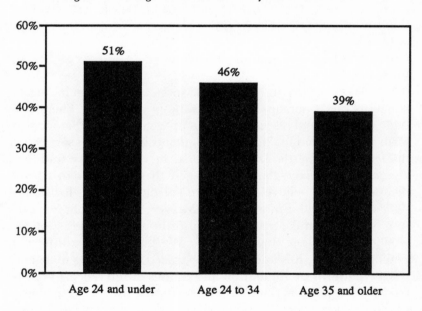

Figure 4 shows that there are significant differences in the cynicism of different age groups in our society. To summarize, 51 percent of workers aged eighteen to twenty-four fit the profile of the true cynic, 46 percent of those aged twenty-five to thirty-four are cynics, and 39 percent of those over age thirty-five fit that categorization. In turn, there are more upbeat workers in the older age cluster (46 percent) and proportionately fewer (31 percent) in the youngest age group. (A full report on all the statistics in this chapter can be found in Appendix E.)

Young Cynics. Youth is supposed to be a time of idealism. We expected our younger respondents to have a more upbeat outlook on people; instead, they are more cynical than other age groups. At first glance, this finding runs counter to popular depictions of young people showing up to employers as better dressed and better mannered than their baby-boomer brothers and sisters. Furthermore, pollsters find that the young respect and share many of their parents' values and, like their folks, resonate with conservative politics and traditional views of success.

A closer look at national polling data, however, shows that the expectations of today's young people, particularly with regard to money and financial success, far exceed those of their parents.[2] By contrast, the prospects of reaching them are, for many, rather grim. Heywood Broun wrote: "The most prolific period of pessimism comes at twenty-one, or thereabouts, when the first attempt is made to translate dreams into reality."[3] Surely he was speaking of a universal component of youthful cynicism. Today, however, there are very specific and particularly disillusioning ingredients.

Time-honored routes to material betterment and security, for example, are more precarious for the young in our increasingly service-based economy. Studies show that entry-level jobs now being created pay less, are less secure, and offer fewer chances for advancement than in previous decades.[4] Moreover, younger people, particularly those with high school or trade school degrees, cannot anticipate the opportunities to earn and advance that were available to their parents.

In turn, college graduates, beginning with their preprofessional curricula, seem to have adopted a more personally pragmatic, career-oriented set of priorities. The character of Alex in TV's "Family Ties" is one example. Hard-driving young materialists like him seem to prosper in today's political, economic, and cultural environment. They value success, and some want to attain it at any price. More than a few have become young lawyers and stockbrokers, consummate Articulate Players, who are thrilled with the money game and the big payoff. Youth who are less well off turn to the trappings of success—high-priced stereos and fashions—and say to hell with saving money or reaching out a helping hand. They are, of course, the Squeezed Cynics.

Pundits call this the Me Generation. We worry that its emphasis on me-ness, along with the incessant hype of materialism and careerism pitched to young people today, has bred a generation of self-oriented cynics. Politicians and educators, no more or less than beer commercials, are telling young people that they can "have it all." In turn, young people at every education and income level want more than their forebears and seem more dissatisfied with what they get. We suspect that many of the young conclude they have been cheated by the system.

Today's young also bear cynical scars that have desensitized them to signs of manipulation and deception by politicians, executives, and others in power. Many have lowered their expectations of honesty and integrity in public figures. Statistics confirm the manifestations: Young people are not as inclined to vote or volunteer for political campaigns as older Americans.

Young cynics have seemingly embraced disillusioned realism as the answer. They have a cool, self-absorbed outlook that is as contemptuous of the baby boomer's altruism as it is of older folks' naiveté. David Leavitt gives a poignant picture of today's young people in his essay "The New Lost Generation": "There are advantages to growing up, as we did, on the cusp of two violently dislocated ages; advantages to becoming conscious just as one decade is burning out, and another is rising, phoenixlike, from the ashes of its dissolution—or disillusion. If the Sixties was an age of naive hope, the Eighties is an age of ironic hopelessness."[5]

Indeed, the image of the lonely outsider has become an accepted icon among young people. Madonna embraced it in *Desperately Seeking Susan,* as did the heroine in *Liquid Sky*—two films pitched to young cynical viewers. This type is familiar in song, as in Billy Idol's "Dancing with Myself," and its depressive qualities are substantial in the Ramones' "I Wanna Be

Sedated." David Leavitt observes: "Mine is a generation perfectly willing to admit its contemptible qualities. But our self-contempt is self-congratulatory. The buzz in the background, every minute of our lives, is that detached, ironic voice telling us: At least you're not faking it, as they did, at least you're not pretending, as they did. It's okay to be selfish as long as you're up front about it. . . . Our parents imagined they could satisfy this urge by marrying and raising children; our older brothers and sisters through community and revolution. We have seen how far those alternatives go. We trust ourselves, and money. Period."[6]

Baby Boomers. The baby boomers, (that portion between twenty-five and thirty-four when surveyed), were raised in a time of "great expectations," and suffered great disillusionment from the world they encountered.[7] The Vietnam veterans' slogan, "We are the unwilling, led by the unqualified, doing the unnecessary, for the ungrateful," exemplifies the gritty cynicism that some embraced to cope with their experiences. Many others have lived out their peer group's anthem, "Tune in, turn on, drop out," and used cynicism to escape from the world around them.

Apart from the historical bases for their disillusionment, many boomers encounter contemporary sources of cynicism. Baby boomers grew up with the traditional birthright that their economic well-being would exceed that of their parents. Today they find it harder to buy homes and harder to find well-paying jobs than their parents did. Their numbers have swelled the job ranks and reduced their earning power. To many, the cancellation of this birthright is seen as an injustice. Their sense of being ripped off accounts partly for the relatively high level of cynicism reported by this age group.

Yet our data show that baby boomers are not as cynical as young people and have many more upbeat souls in their ranks. What has happened? One popular interpretation is that the boomers have simply grown up and become members of that "over thirty" age group that could not be trusted. William F. Buckley, Jr., has made the point thus: "Idealism is fine, but as it approaches reality the cost becomes prohibitive." We cannot agree that baby boomers have shed their ideals. There are signs, however, that the majority have shed their deepest suspicions of the system and have come to grips with working within it.

Ralph Whitehead's study comparing ''Bright Collar'' and ''New Collar'' baby boomers summarizes the distinct forces shaping their outlook today. The bad news, notes Whitehead, is that boomers are getting less in their lunch pails. This, we believe, has undermined their birthright and left many of them embittered. The good news is that Bright Collar baby boomers are getting more out of life, he adds.[8] Indeed, those with socially oriented values and life-styles have experienced the freedom to express them in their work and lives. We believe that this enables those boomers to cope more optimistically with the world around them and accounts for the relatively higher proportion in their ranks of those with an upbeat outlook.

Older Workers. Wage earners thirty-five and older have an even less cynical and more upbeat outlook on life. Nevertheless, the worldviews of this age group are not uniformly more

Figure 5. Cynicism Varies for Older Workers.

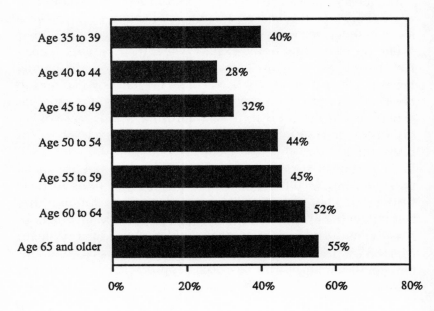

sunny. Indeed, when we look more closely at older workers, distinctive patterns of cynicism emerge. Figure 5 shows that the group aged thirty-five to thirty-nine, for example, has a relatively high number of cynics (40 percent)—not surprising, for its members are part of the postwar baby boom. By contrast, age segments forty to forty-four and forty-five to forty-nine have a lower proportion of cynics (30 percent). Some in this age group came of age in the 1950s and embraced the reigned-in expectations of that generation. Men and women in this age group are also comparatively more affluent than other age groups.

The most striking findings emerge for workers over age fifty. In the age groups fifty to fifty-four and fifty-five to fifty-nine, we find a large proportion of cynics (44 percent), and in the age groups over sixty years, that figure increases to over 50 percent. Even more striking is the low number of upbeat people in these upper-age cohorts. Several factors influence the higher levels of cynicism found in this over-fifty age group. First, its members have less education and, for those over sixty, lower incomes than those in other age groups. Second, a greater proportion of its members are blue-collar workers. Third, more of its members are widows or widowers. As we will see, all these variables are associated with higher levels of cynicism.

There are, moreover, generational reasons to expect higher levels of frustration among older people. As H. H. Munro notes, ''The young have aspirations that never come to pass, the old have reminiscences of what never happened.''[9] Beyond this, we believe that specific social and economic factors have affected these age groups. The oldest members of our sample had direct experience with the Depression and all the apprehension and disillusionment that it wrought. Moreover, there is evidence to suggest that older workers today are suffering disproportionately in the current economic restructuring. Plant shutdowns and corporate downsizing efforts have put the squeeze on workers over fifty, forcing some into early retirement but many more into belt-tightening life-styles. Frankly, there are signs that corporate America has forgotten the contributions of its senior workers. Many have been callously labeled as deadwood and passed over for promotion and raises in order to meet the demands of the record numbers of baby boomers in corporations today.

This is all part of the age discrimination that older workers experience beginning at age fifty, a prejudice that haunts them the rest of their lives. It is based, like sex and race discrimination, on stereotypical conceptions of older workers—that they are unproductive, health risks, too expensive, and less energetic. No matter that researchers have systematically discredited these myths;[10] what does matter is that older workers encounter them daily and find them disillusioning.

Men Versus Women

Figure 6. Men More Cynical Than Women.

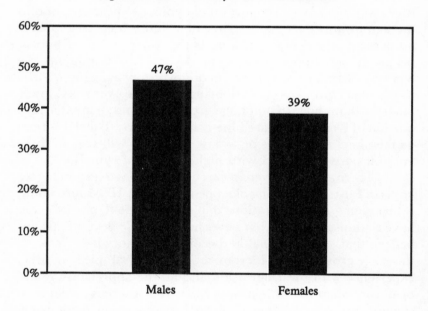

Figure 6 shows that 47 percent of the men in the sample profess attitudes about life and other people that classify them as cynics. A statistically significant smaller proportion of women (39 percent) fits that profile. What accounts for the somewhat higher proportion of cynics among men?

To begin, we find that our society's predominant image of the cynic is male. Cynical characters in the movies and television (as played by James Dean in *Giant* or Caroll O'Connor in "All in the Family"), in country and western ballads and pop-music videos (sung by Merle Haggard and Elvis Costello), and in comic books and newspaper cartoons (the oafish Duffy or savvy P. J. McFey) come in all shapes and sizes, but they are usually male. In this book, too, most of our exemplars of the Command Cynics, the Articulate Players, the Hard-Bittens, and even the Obstinate Stoics are men. We admit this bias in our selections, and we see it throughout the media and society. It is true, as these data show, that there are plenty of cynical women. Our point is that cynicism among men is a more visible and socially sanctioned orientation to life. Men are simply not discouraged from being cynics. This is particularly true when their cynicism can be equated with a macho type of realism and worldliness.

Significantly, these cynical males seldom triumph against the system. Either they end up beaten by it (Jack Nicholson in *Five Easy Pieces*) or else join in the duplicitous games (Robert Morse in *How to Succeed in Business Without Really Trying*). We are beginning to see portrayals of women disillusioned by their work who are tough rather than touching, vengeful rather than forgiving. Sally Fields in *Norma Rae,* Jane Fonda in *The China Syndrome,* and Fonda, Lily Tomlin, and Dolly Parton in *9 to 5* all play potentially cynical characters. What is notable, however, is that these women are depicted as initially naive and innocent, seemingly victimized by their environment. In the end, moreover, they triumph over their nemeses.

Of course, Hollywood has given us tough and cynical women. Joan Crawford and Bette Davis played classic schemers, and Faye Dunaway in *Network* showed us the Articulate Player at work. These are the exceptions. Few everyday female film characters, save Meryl Streep playing Karen Silkwood, start out as hard-bitten and end up beaten by the system. And we know of few films, save some of the countercultural or cinema vérité sort, in which everyday women gain the audience's respect for their cynical-cum-realistic outlook on life. More often, women in films save families, farms, and even their men's self-esteem. It is not just Hollywood's preference for a happy ending. Our culture, again in our opinion, simply insists that its women assume a sunnier outlook on life.

We are suggesting, then, that although the differences in the amount of cynicism reported by men versus women are modest, there are stronger differences in how each gender expresses its cynical inclinations. This cultural imperative—that men can be visible and vocal cynics, whereas women should appear to be sunnier and more generous-minded—has roots in the distinct psychosocial makeup of each gender. Carol Gilligan's studies, in which subjects are asked to make judgments about the motives of other people and describe their own moral reasoning in real-life crises, suggest that women are less judgmental and emotionally distant than men. Studies at Duke University, moreover, show that men who fit the cynical profile are more apt to be aggressive and hostile in their attitudes and behavior.[11]

These findings reinforce the stereotype that men's cynicism is more likely to be anchored in the belief that it's a tough world populated by self-serving people. In important respects, this outlook permits men to fight back and put their cynicism to work with more gusto and less apology. Women, we suspect, are more relativistic in their judgments about what motivates people and more circumspect in how they manifest their cynicism.

Such interpretations are speculative, we acknowledge, and by no means apply to all men or women. We needn't be so speculative when it comes to differences in cynicism for racial groups in our society.

Whites Versus Minorities

Figure 7 shows that 61 percent of the minorities in our sample fit the profile of the cynic, as compared with 40 percent of the whites. Whites are also much more likely to hold an upbeat outlook. These differences in cynicism by race are more significant than those found in comparisons of men versus women. No doubt, present-day aspects of culture and socialization influence how cynicism is expressed by whites and by minorities. Higher levels of cynicism among minorities can also be traced clearly to historical experiences of disillusionment.

We recognize that minorities are less well off than whites

Figure 7. Minorities More Cynical Than Whites.

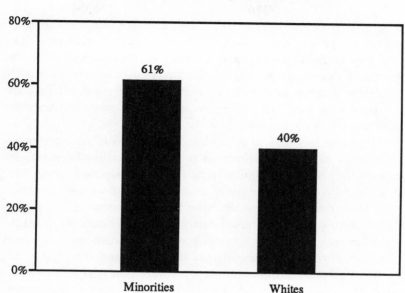

for nearly all indicators of economic well-being. They earn less, have lesser status and less secure jobs, and are more likely to be unemployed. In national studies, minorities report less satisfaction with their jobs than whites do, and they see themselves as having a bleaker future.[12] Such factors, coupled with the history of racism and discrimination that many minority groups have faced in this country, all contribute to the findings we report here.

There is ample evidence in modern times of the costs of frustration and disappointment among minority groups, where rates of criminal activity, drug abuse, school dropout, teen pregnancy, and such are disproportionately higher. Cynicism is partly cause and partly consequence of this grim roster. These are, of course, the most exaggerated and sociopathic manifestations of cynical estrangement. Most members of minority groups, however, cope with an objectively tougher, harder, white-dominated world by using cynicism to shield their psyches and preserve their self-respect.

Cynicism and Social Class

Maxims from the popular culture make it plain enough that people of means versus the less advantaged have different lives and therefore different outlooks on life. Manx poet Thomas Brown, for example, wrote, "A rich man's joke is always funny," while the French writer Anatole France observed, "It is only the poor who pay cash, and that not from virtue, but because they are refused credit."[13]

When it comes to everyday experiences, moreover, winners seem to be everywhere in the mass media—being interviewed, lionized, and shown in their materialistic splendor. The role model is not the person of moderation, who takes the bitter with the better, but the person who wins and savors all the recognition that winning brings. Losing, then, becomes intolerable. And because relatively few people can be winners, envy and bitterness are one legacy of this media hyping.

We are making the case, of course, that people's perceptions of winning are related to their socioeconomic status and prospects. It is clear today that those with less education and those who earn less income have a far less comfortable lot and face a much less promising future than the better educated and better off. Some have, of course, adapted to their stations in life and adjusted their expectations to current realities. Many others, however, have turned to cynicism in the 1980s.

Figure 8 shows clearly that higher levels of cynicism are reported by people with lesser levels of education and income. Some 58 percent of those lacking a high school diploma hold a cynical outlook on life, as do a majority of those who are high school graduates. By contrast, only 29 percent of those who have graduated from college or attained more schooling are cynical. As for income, less than 33 percent of those who earn over $30,000 a year are cynical, whereas about 50 percent of those who earn less are cynics.

In today's highly technical and more competitive economic environment, higher education more than ever is a prerequisite for success. The distinction between the haves and have-nots increasingly lies between those who have earned a college

Figure 8. Less Education and Income = More Cynicism.

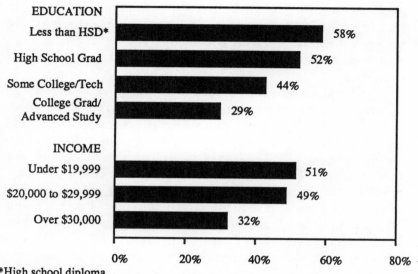

EDUCATION
Less than HSD*   58%
High School Grad   52%
Some College/Tech   44%
College Grad/
Advanced Study   29%
INCOME
Under $19,999   51%
$20,000 to $29,999   49%
Over $30,000   32%

0%   20%   40%   60%   80%

*High school diploma

degree and those who have not.[14] In the same fashion, more
money is now required to sustain a middle-class life-style.

The tragedy of polarized prosperity is that, in a phrase,
it kills the American Dream that so long sustained the worker's
optimism, work ethic, and ambition. To dampen the attitude
that hard work and temporary sacrifice will yield rewards is to
change the belief system that undergirds initiative and enterprise in this country. Yet there is evidence that this is precisely
what is happening. It is expressed vividly in the selfish "Where's
mine?" attitude of Squeezed Cynics in the work force and in
society, and in the cold calculations of tough-minded realists
who look out only for themselves. In a country that keeps score
and measures success by acquisition, the cynical consequences
are hard to overstate.

It is not merely our hunch that aspirations for the good
life mark all social classes in America today. When asked what
is "most important" to them on the job, people at all education levels place heavy emphasis on good pay, of course; but polls

also show that less educated men and women look for nearly as much stimulation and challenge from their jobs as college graduates do. But the gap between what is important to people on the job and "how satisfied" they are widens dramatically between the most and least educated.[15] We see in this gap between expectations and satisfaction the main ingredients of cynicism.

Our data also show that those who have some college education are far more cynical than college graduates. Many are, of course, Squeezed Cynics who are downwardly mobile and for whom a year or two of higher education has had no measurable payoff. The ranks of college attendees (but not graduates) also include people who have taken courses at community colleges, earned trade certificates, or, through other educational means, tried to better themselves. Like so many others hoping to advance themselves through education, they have encountered instead frustration and disillusion. A sampling of education-related trends reinforces the point that those with a high school diploma or some college education have very concrete reasons for being cynical.

First, it must be recognized that the American work force today is better educated than ever before, academic standards notwithstanding. Consequently, there are simply many more high school graduates who are employed in jobs once filled by less educated workers, and many who have attended college or trade schools have taken jobs once filled by high school graduates. Moreover, there are in the work force many more college graduates and people who have been to graduate school. Thus we are witnessing the phenomenon of overeducation in the work force. Estimates are that over one in three workers have more formal education than required by their jobs.[16]

Vocational overeducation tells only half the story. Higher-paying and higher-status jobs simply are not available to as many workers today as in the past. Not twenty years ago, over 75 percent of those seeking professional, technical, or managerial jobs could find them. Today that figure is less than 60 percent.[17] Roughly 40 percent of the new jobs created in the country in the past several years pay less than $7,500. One psychological consequence of having overeducated workers in underpaying and understimulating jobs is, in our view, cynicism.

We do not imply, of course, that higher education per se makes people less cynical. Indeed, in some respects, the current collegiate environment is a breeding ground for young, self-interested strivers, the Articulate Players in business. Our point is that those with college credentials have more opportunities to get ahead and put their education to work. Still, a substantial segment of the best educated have embraced the cynical outlook.

Our data also show that income figures significantly into levels of cynicism: Those earning over $30,000 per year are far more upbeat and certainly less estranged than those at lower income levels. There is considerable evidence that income is a primary cause of people's satisfaction, not only with their jobs but also with their lives.[18] Those who earn more can afford better transportation and child care, can avail themselves of more personal services, and can take better vacations. With omnipresent credit cards, they can "master the possibilities."

Money is the way our society keeps score. Lack of money in turn connotes loserhood, with all the concomitant threats to self-esteem. Cynicism is one way that people protect their self-esteem and preserve their self-picture. In many respects, too, those with less income are the "marks" for today's come-on artists and con men, not to mention electronic preachers and assorted "bill consolidators." They may suffer further at the hands of uncaring supervisors and uninterested union stewards and are treated with less respect by sales clerks and service representatives. In their less advantaged and more hassled life-styles, working-class and lower-middle-class people simply encounter more cynical treatment than those in higher socioeconomic strata do.

Life-Styles and Locales

To complete our profile of the cynic in America today, we turn to the indicators of how Americans live and where they reside: marital status, house ownership and locale, and region of the country.

Figure 9. Widowed and Divorced More Cynical.

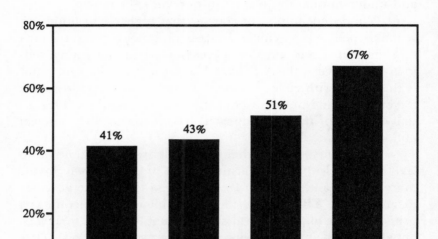

Marital Status. Divorced members of our sample are more cynical than those who are married or single, as Figure 9 shows. Perhaps this should not be surprising: Several years ago, an advertising agency in London conducted a study of the attitudes of divorced persons and labeled them ''divorcynics.''[19] Many analysts have identified the additional demands that people face after a divorce, including the need to find or expand child-care service and to adjust budgets and life-styles to new material circumstances. But the agency researchers also found changes in people's attitudes and behavior after a divorce.

Specifically, they found that divorced people went through a period of disillusionment that, for many, was prolonged by the travails of the singles scene. The consultants reported that divorced people were more contemptuous of advertisements that played exclusively to the married or fun-loving singles market, and they generally held a more depressed attitude toward life.

The investigators concluded, though, that many divorced people lose their jaded edge once remarried or established as single persons. We have no way of checking that conclusion in our data.

Figure 10. Homeowners and Suburbanites Less Cynical.

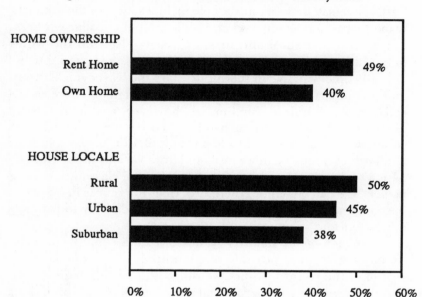

House Ownership and Locale. Socioeconomic factors help to explain the finding that those who own their own homes are less cynical than those who rent (Figure 10). Interestingly, Figure 10 also shows that people who live in rural areas are more cynical than those who live in other environs. This finding is, of course, contrary to received mythology about rural life and all that goes with happy times down on the farm. Many have chronicled the plight of the farmer today and noted the rising disillusion in small-town rural America. The sheer productivity of American farmers, coupled with a worldwide "green revolution," has kept the price of agricultural products low and limited their export. Today there are heretofore unimagined numbers of farm bankruptcies and bank foreclosures in America and few jobs for those who move from their farms to small rural towns. Salutary efforts like Farm Aid concerts do little to leaven the economic depression and moral disillusion experienced on the farm today.

Urban dwellers, too, are comparatively cynical. Certainly the trials of urban life in the 1980s bear no recounting here. Suffice it to say that this subsample includes most of the minority respondents and lesser-paid and -educated blue-collar workers. Let us add that rural and urban dwellers also find the world to be colder and less engaging than those living in the suburbs.

People who live in the suburbs are the least cynical group in this comparison. Our suburban sample has many more white-collar professionals and managers, however, and its members are more educated and earn more. To be sure, those in the suburbs may be exposed to less manipulation at the hands of landlords and may be more insulated from various urban hustles. Much of this, however, is a function of social class and earning power. We can conclude, therefore, that differences in cynicism based on house ownership and locale relate directly to people's education and income.

Region of the Country. Since our data come from a national sample, it is possible to examine levels of cynicism by region of the country. Since we did not draw this sample with specific reference to geographical sampling, any interpretations about levels of cynicism within a region are speculative. Nonetheless, the findings are interesting, and we present them mindful of that caution.

Demographers have been studying regions of the country for decades to examine social class, education, health, income, and other important signs of people's well-being. Recently, however, studies have been undertaken to explore the emotional life and political orientations of people in different regions.[20] Several studies have focused on people's level of stress and satisfaction with life.

A profile of cynicism in nine distinct regions in the country is shown in Figure 11. Three regional ratings—from people in the Mid-Atlantic, New England, and West North Central areas of the country—track the national trend. As the figure

Figure 11. Cynicism by Region of the Country.

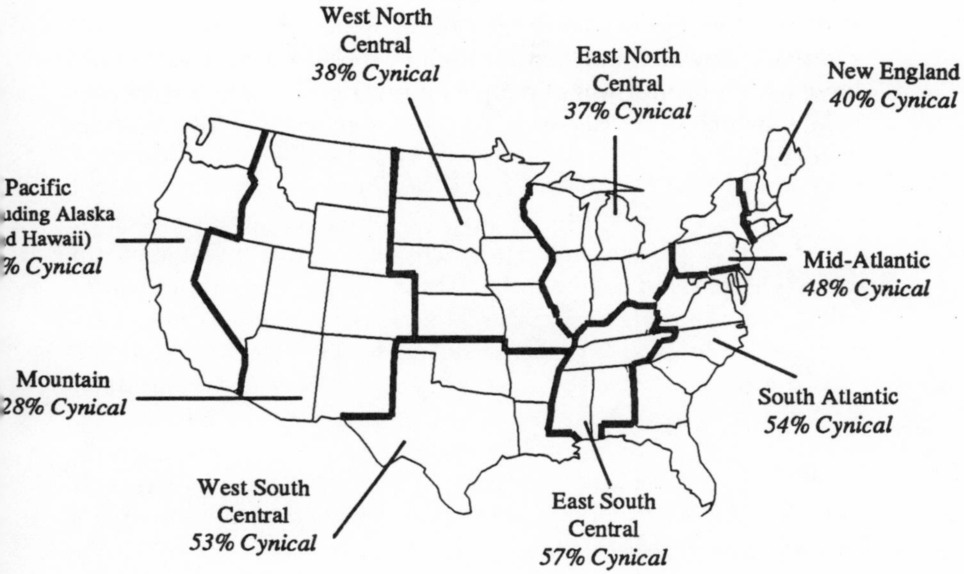

West North
Central
38% Cynical

East North
Central
37% Cynical

New England
40% Cynical

Pacific
luding Alaska
d Hawaii)
% Cynical

Mid-Atlantic
48% Cynical

Mountain
28% Cynical

South Atlantic
54% Cynical

West South
Central
53% Cynical

East South
Central
57% Cynical

shows, the most cynicism is to be found in the East South Central region, comprising Mississippi, Alabama, Tennessee, and Kentucky, and in the South Atlantic region. The levels of cynicism reported here correlate with regional data that show stress to be quite high and satisfaction relatively low for people in these areas. People in our sample from the southern tier, moreover, also have lower levels of education and income than those in other regions.

The Mountain states and the Pacific region report the least cynicism. These areas also score favorably on ratings of stress and satisfaction in other research. There are, however, two regions where cynicism ratings do not match other regional indicators of stress and satisfaction. We find, for example, that 37 percent of the people living in the East North Central region— Michigan, Wisconsin, Ohio, Indiana, and Illinois—can be classified as cynics. People in these states score high on stress and relatively low on satisfaction in regional studies. By contrast,

53 percent in the West South Central region—Texas, Louisiana, Arkansas, and Oklahoma—can be classified as cynics. This statistic does not equate with studies which show that stress is relatively low and satisfaction high in these states. These states have a high proportion of people at lower education and income levels, which may account for the higher level of cynicism reported.

8

Cynical Attitudes
About Work, Management,
and Organizations

Like other workers, cynics grouse about their pay, begrudge
their chances of advancement, often find management distant
and uncommunicative, and do not believe they are getting the
respect they deserve. In a manner unlike that of the upbeat
employee or even the wary one, however, cynics purport to see
through what's behind their frustrations on the job. And they
see things through a cynical lens: The company's compensation system is rigged; getting ahead depends on whom you know,
not on what you do; the bosses clan together and stick it to the
workers; and nobody cares about them, respects them, or even
gives a damn, so they'd better look out for themselves. In short,
to the cynics, company life is a jungle.

   This is the put-upon and put-down outlook of the tough-
cum-realistic cynic, perhaps the Hard-Bitten factory worker or
cop on the beat. Add the perception of conspiratorial calculation and the attitude of righteous indignation and we have a

Squeezed Cynic, the chronic complainer found in every office and retail outlet. Soften the tone, dull the edge, and this is the outlook of the Obstinate Stoic, ever phlegmatic and often forlorn. All these personality types use cynicism as a shield to protect their dignity and preserve their self-respect.

Other types of cynics, as we have seen, wield cynicism as a sword. They are the lions, not the lambs, the players, not those who are played on. We have characterized them as Command Cynics, Administrative Sideliners, or Articulate Players, and we find them wherever the choice seems to be "eat or be eaten." They know how to manipulate the reward system, whom to know and how to be known by the people who count, when to fawn over bosses and when to stab them, how to win respect and engender fear, and, above all, how to take care of themselves.

What kinds of jobs seem to attract cynics and reinforce the cynical outlook? In what occupations and industries are cynics most likely to work? Do cynics have different attitudes about work than, say, more upbeat employees? Drawing on our national survey, we first profile the cynical American at work. Note that in reporting levels of cynicism found in different jobs and organizations, we can only speculate to what extent people's self-selection versus socialization by certain work environments accounts for the levels of cynicism shown. Obviously, cynics bring their mind-set into the workplace. Yet the way people are treated and managed in organizations surely has a bearing on their cynical outlook.[1]

The Cynical Work Force

As Figure 12 shows, cynicism is more prevalent in blue- than in white-collar ranks in the American work force. (A full reporting of data can be found in Appendixes F and G.) On the basis of the survey questions, the majority of the blue-collar respondents (54 percent) believe that most people are manipulators, will lie and pretend to care if it is to their advantage, and are basically out for themselves. By contrast, a smaller proportion (40 percent) of the white-collar respondents regard such attributes as fundamental to human nature.

Figure 12. Blue Collar More Cynical.

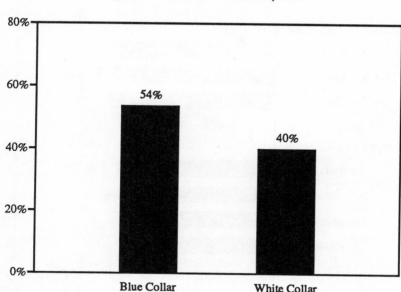

To a large extent, the differences in cynicism between white- and blue-collar workers represent differences in people's education and income. Blue-collar workers have less education and earn less money—key factors in the general profile of the cynic presented in the previous chapter.

A closer look at occupations within the blue-collar ranks shows cynicism to be most prominent among service, maintenance, and security personnel—cooks, gardeners, barbers, custodians, guards, and those in the fire and police service, among others (see Figure 13). It is just as pronounced among technicians and tradespeople—computer operators, repair people, mechanics, and plumbers. Factory workers, machine operators, and truck drivers are not quite so cynical as the other blue-collar workers.

It is notable that cynicism is highest among blue-collar service workers—those in the front line of commercial and public service. People who go into such jobs say that "working with people" is important to them. At the same time, they report that they are "underappreciated" by their employers and the

Figure 13. Cynicism by Occupation.

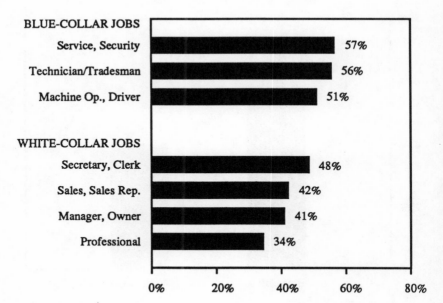

BLUE-COLLAR JOBS
- Service, Security — 57%
- Technician/Tradesman — 56%
- Machine Op., Driver — 51%

WHITE-COLLAR JOBS
- Secretary, Clerk — 48%
- Sales, Sales Rep. — 42%
- Manager, Owner — 41%
- Professional — 34%

0%   20%   40%   60%   80%

public and "overworked" on their jobs. It may be that their initial high hopes of serving have soured many of them.

It is worth noting, too, that these service people have the most contact with cynical consumers. The rude, pushy, and petty customers encountered by service personnel, the crooks that cops must deal with, the complainers that tradespeople put up with— all serve to feed their cynical mind-sets. Yet it's a vicious cycle. Survey after survey shows that Americans find themselves under-served by service personnel and mistrustful of repair people and those in the trades.[2] People have concluded that service personnel simply do not care about doing a good job. This cycle of cynicism may be contributing to an erosion of performance in the service sector and to the decline in the service ethic among workers.

As shown in Figure 13, more variability in the levels of cynicism is found in the white-collar work force. Cynicism is most pronounced among secretaries, office workers, and clerks. Income may be an important cause of cynicism here—these office workers earn substantially less than those in other white-collar jobs. Sales representatives, managers, and supervisors are less cynical than office workers. Their higher levels of education and income partially account for their relatively more upbeat outlook. Still, over 40 percent of the people in these jobs subscribe to the cynical view.

It is interesting to note, on the basis of the survey questions, that many people in these job groups seem to be "situational" cynics. For example, sales representatives believe that people are basically honest and will put themselves out for other people. Yet most of them also believe that people will lie when they can gain by it and will abandon their standards of morality if money is at stake. Thus salespersons may not be cynics at heart—but they are when it comes to making a sale. In turn, managers and supervisors have faith in people's honesty and integrity. Yet a majority of them also believe that lying and cheating are commonplace when people can gain by them. They, too, seem to differentiate between human nature in the abstract and what is expedient for people in an employment situation.[3]

Finally, Figure 13 shows cynicism to be lowest among professional people and engineers. These are the most educated members of our sample and the best paid. It is also worth noting that a larger proportion of these people are self-employed or enjoy more autonomy on their jobs, which, along with professional status, may be a mediating factor in their judgments about life.

Cynicism and Union Membership. Figure 14 shows that union members are more cynical than those who do not belong to a union. We have noted, for example, how union leaders historically rallied their members with charges that the bosses were taking advantage of working people and were only out for themselves. The rhetoric is less strident today, to be sure, but the message basically is the same: Management is still viewed as the enemy, and the union is seen as the worker's friend.

At the same time, unions are under attack from many quarters. Charges of union involvement with organized crime and convictions of labor leaders on charges of racketeering are not uncommon. Many business and political leaders are lashing

Figure 14. Union Members More Cynical.

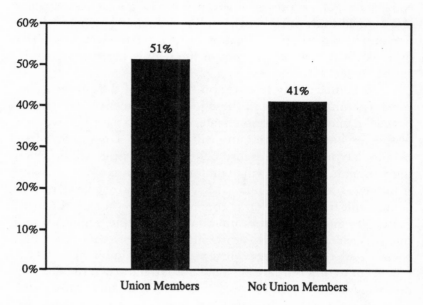

out at union wages and work regulations as the source of our lack of competitiveness in the global economy. However justified these claims (and we believe the evidence is mixed and surely not the whole story), they have put union members on the defensive.

Beyond this, there are signs of corrosion within the union movement. A large proportion of union members say their leaders are out of touch with the rank and file, and a substantial minority believe that union officials are most interested in feathering their own nests.[4] Furthermore, many union members have lost confidence in their unions and find them filled with politics and cronyism.

The failure of 1984 presidential candidate Walter Mondale, despite union endorsements, to obtain the support of the rank and file is one example of how unions hold less sway over their members than previously. Being an individual seems to be more important than being part of a collective to many union members today. Our data show that a large proportion of union members have also concluded that most look out for themselves.

Cynicism and Industry. Our analysis showed no significant differences among the levels of cynicism reported by people working in government, manufacturing, retail trades, or service industries.[5] There were, however, significant differences within industry sectors. Figure 15 provides a breakdown of cynicism in the service sector that reveals one interesting pattern.

Figure 15. Cynicism in Service Industries.

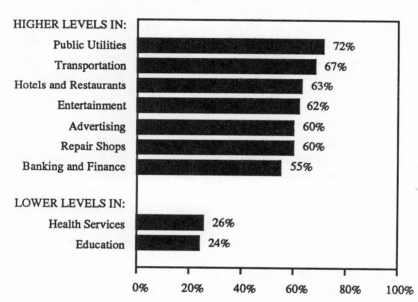

This figure shows very high levels of cynicism in certain service industries—well above the national average. Cynicism is quite pronounced, for example, in transportation services, hotels and restaurants, and repair shops. Here we see the blue-collar service cynics—our Squeezed types. Cynicism is high in entertainment and advertising concerns, where we see the Articulate Players and less facile hustlers at work. Finally, cynicism is very high in public utilities and, to some extent, in banking and financial concerns.

In the lower-end service jobs, paltry wages, poor benefits, and poor working conditions are often exacerbated by bosses who rule like petty tyrants and showboat their relative status and income. We wonder, at the higher end, to what extent deregulation and the many mergers in the financial sector have left people frustrated and jaded. Certainly, a customer-be-damned attitude has developed in segments of the financial sector, not to mention in the airlines.

Figure 15 also shows that cynicism is markedly lower in health services and education. The high number of professionals in these industries is one explanation. Furthermore, studies of these white-collar workers show that they have many of the same commitments to service as those going into government work. They are not as frustrated by their jobs, however, or as hampered by red tape and bureaucracy. They are also in the business of healing and teaching—causes bound to attract more idealists and, in our estimation, more upbeat types.

Finally, there were no consistent differences in the level of cynicism reported by people who work in companies of varying size. Cynicism, it would seem, is equally pronounced in big companies and small ones. There is some evidence, however, to suggest that bureaucracies, with tall hierarchies and a technocratic bent, are breeding grounds for cynics. Over 56 percent of the people who work in companies ranging from 5,000 to 15,000 employees fit our profile of the cynic. People in even larger companies, however, are not nearly so cynical. It may be that these megacorporations are more decentralized and simply offer more to working people or attract a more upbeat type of employee.

It should be noted, too, that people who work in smallish firms, including mom-and-pop shops, can be just as cynical as their corporate counterparts. Even tiny operations can have their own mind-numbing rules and scapegoating rituals, as well as their share of interpersonal and managerial gamesmanship. Company size, our data suggest, is not a key to cynicism in the workplace.

Consequences for Work Attitudes

In our national survey, we asked about people's attitudes toward their work, their companies, and their treatment on the job. Here we will examine how cynical versus upbeat working people view their companies, their management, and their working conditions. Measures of people's attitudes toward work covered these subjects:

1.   Trust in management
2.   Trust in co-workers
3.   Fairness of rewards
4.   Management style
5.   Views of the job and organization

Trust in Management. To measure people's trust in management, we asked respondents whether they often doubted the truth of management and whether they believed that management would take advantage of them if given a chance. "Does management in your company tell half-truths, put a face on things, dissemble and equivocate, trade in disinformation, or obfuscate communications to the point that they lack credibility? Do management's actions seem self-serving, aimed at one-upping people and taking advantage of them?"

Cynics have significantly less trust in their management than do upbeat respondents. As Figure 16 shows, fully 40 percent of the cynics doubt the truth of what management tells them and believe that management will take advantage of them if given a chance. This figure compares with 25 percent of the upbeat respondents.

These statistics illustrate the corrosive impact of cynicism on people's perceptions of management's credibility and intentions.[6] The entry-level assumption of cynics is that they will be lied to and ripped off; our data show that a sizable proportion of cynics finds these assumptions confirmed in dealings with management.

Authority creates problems (and opportunities) for the many varieties of cynics. The Command Cynics use it to manipulate their underlings. Administrative Sideliners become obsequious toadies in front of the boss and ruthless rule-enforcers in their own dominions. These cynics are, by position, the power brokers and rule administrators in companies. Articulate Players, by contrast, use authority to set their own rules of the game.

Figure 16. Trust in Management.

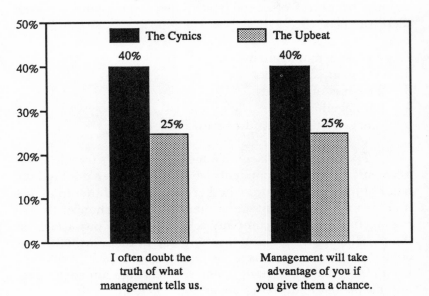

Other cynical types found in lower echelons embrace cynicism as a means of coping with management's power. Scoffing, backbiting, working to rules, incessantly asking, "What's in it for me?"—all extract revenge. "Paying them no mind," "keeping your nose clean," and lowering expectations, in turn, lessen disappointment and disillusion.

Furthermore, that one out of four upbeat members of the work force mistrusts management (and that fewer than a third of workers affirm that management is trustworthy) is a telling and troubling indictment of American management practices. In our view, this is a product of cynical forces at work in organizations throughout this century and certainly an earmark of the prominence of the cynical company in today's Darwinian environment.

Trust in Co-Workers. Many working people (68 percent) have more trust in members of their work groups than they do in management. To measure people's trust in members of their work groups, the survey asked whether members of the respondents' work groups had "trust and confidence" in one another and whether they cooperated to get the job done. Figure 17 shows that cynics have somewhat less trust and confidence in work-

Figure 17. Trust in Co-Workers.

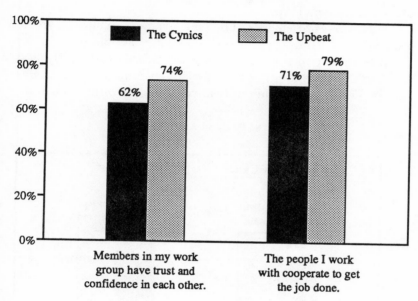

group members than do upbeat respondents and find them somewhat less cooperative. Cynicism is less corrosive in this regard, as the majority of cynics also take a favorable view of their workmates.

There are several reasons why cynicism is less potent in people's dealings with their co-workers. For one thing, it is simply harder to hold cynical stereotypes about people you work with every day.[7] Research on prejudice, for example, shows that people can hold stereotypes about general groups of others (say, management) but often modify or abandon them when dealing with individual members of the stereotyped group. Workers are more apt to have everyday dealings with their work groups than with management and hence may have an informed, less stereotyped view of their trustworthiness.

Furthermore, in many factories and offices, cynicism about the big shots is good currency. Indeed, it is sometimes essential to gaining true membership in a work group.[8] By contrast, people can only backbite or put down their co-workers so much. Malcontents are ostracized by work groups, and they often transfer or leave.

Fairness of Rewards. The measurement of fairness in organizations is composed of two questions. People were asked whether their concerns about pay were dealt with fairly and whether they had a fair chance for advancement in their companies. Fewer cynics than upbeat respondents think their indi-

Figure 18. Pay and Advancement.

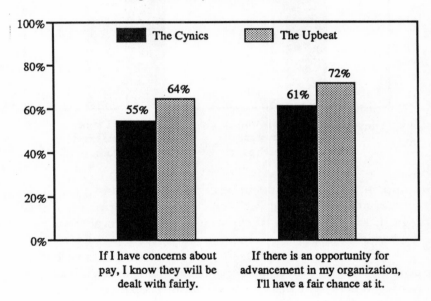

vidual concerns about pay and chances for advancement are handled fairly, as Figure 18 reveals. Although these differences are statistically significant, they are not as pronounced as might be expected given the cynic's sharply disparaging views of management's trustworthiness and evenhandedness. National surveys consistently show that most Americans, whether cynical or not, question the way compensation and rewards are handled in their companies.[9] We suspect that cynics have a substantially more suspicious view of how their companies operate in these regards, but we asked them only about their personal experiences.

In any case, people have diverse ways of coping with perceived injustice and inequities. One way of coping is through indifference and lowered expectations. This protective coloration is pronounced among Obstinate Stoics and Squeezed Cynics. Stoical types, for instance, are much more concerned about getting a fair day's pay for a fair day's work—a question not addressed in our study. Squeezed Cynics, in turn, fixate on whether the system is fair—a topic worthy of study but not investigated directly in our survey.

Quite another way of coping with unfairness is to even the score. This is the proactive strategy of Articulate Players, who might make a deal with the boss about their pay or get into the right power networks in order to get ahead. It is also the tactic of Hard-Bitten Cynics, who get even by goldbricking, goofing off, taking home tools and supplies, inventing overtime, or having a friend (or the supervisor) punch them out long after they've left the job. These active cynics know how to make things ''fair'' where they work.

Management Style. In our survey, we asked people how management relates with people. Specifically, people were asked if management listened to them, if people at the top were aware of problems at their levels of the organization, and if they received sufficient recognition for doing their jobs. As Figure 19 shows, significantly fewer cynics believe that sufficient effort is made to get the opinions and thinking of people who work in their organizations. This perception may be more pronounced among negative and vocal cynics—those always ready to dismiss ideas and scoff at management's efforts to solicit their own. Such cynics are predisposed to believe that nobody is listening to them—and often with good reason. Their explanations of why nothing will work or improve their lot become tiresome, and many managers and co-workers simply tune them out.

Cynics are also somewhat less inclined to believe that they have received sufficient recognition for their contributions. This

Figure 19. Management Practices.

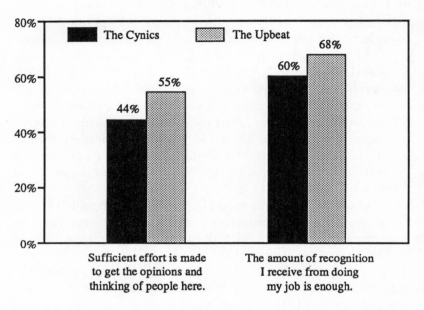

attitude is understandable when we remember that cynics believe
that people pretend to care more than they really do. Thus they
may discount whatever recognition they receive as insincere or
as an effort to ''butter them up.''

Cynics (51 percent) are no more or less inclined to believe
that the information they receive from management is satisfactory than upbeat workers are (55 percent), nor do they view
management as any more or less aware of problems at their levels
of the company (53 versus 55 percent). The absolute levels of
these ratings (low in our opinion) seem more important than differences between cynical and upeat workers' mind-sets. Still, it
may be that certain cynics are quite successful in making their
particular concerns and causes known to management. In many
organizations, for example, meetings are dominated by nay-
sayers and self-interested turf protectors. Yet, in many other
instances, both cynical and upbeat workers find themselves disenfranchised and neglected. We will see, however, that other factors, specifically the worker's age and ability to negotiate the envi-

ronment, are crucial predictors of attitudes toward management.
   Views of the Job and Organization. In the final measures
of this part of our survey, we asked people about the importance of their jobs and about their satisfaction with their organizations. Fewer cynics than upbeat workers think their jobs are

Figure 20. Jobs and Organizations.

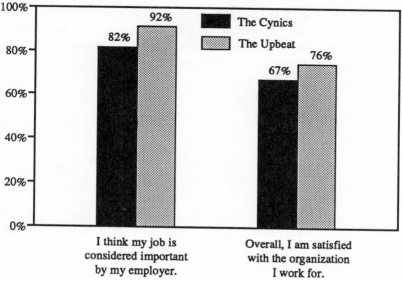

considered important by their employers. As Figure 20 indicates,
cynics are also less satisfied with their employers. Even though
a substantial percentage of cynics believe their jobs are valued
(82 percent) and express a measure of satisfaction with their companies (67 percent), their outlook should not be confused with
equanimity or commitment. Some people cope with devaluing
jobs and uncaring companies by lowering their expectations,
by becoming lethargic, and by blindly going about their business
and simply marking time.[10] Some cynics no doubt detach themselves emotionally from work and conclude that involvement
has no real payoff. In this way, they protect their dignity by
lowering their sights and coming to an uneasy peace with their

employers. As we will see, age and commitment to the work ethic, more than cynicism, figure into people's satisfaction with their jobs and organizations.

What is most important to note here is that nearly 30 percent of the U.S. work force (whether cynical, wary, or upbeat) have a middling or dissatisfied attitude about their places of work. Such a sizable proportion surely depresses levels of productivity and quality and proves a drain on morale and esprit de corps. In the next chapter, we conclude our analysis of the consequences of cynicism by examining to what extent cynicism, versus other views about life and work, contributes to people's work attitudes and discontent.

9

Cynicism Versus Traditional Values About Work

It is apparent that America's so-called traditional values have undergone substantial change throughout this century, but particularly since World War II, the baby boom, and all that followed. We have developed this point with reference to people's cynicism and their concomitant loss of trust and confidence in other people, institutions, and authority.

Many others have generalized the point and noted wholesale changes in American outlooks and values. More than a few have made the claim, for example, that Americans have become less friendly and outgoing, that our sense of self-esteem has been lowered, that our work ethic is dead, that people have increasingly lost control over their destinies.

To assess where the American work force stands today vis-à-vis traditional values, our national survey asked respondents to indicate how much they agreed or disagreed with questions grouped into the following areas:

1. Estrangement from the world: To what degree do people find a loss of trust and faith in the world and find it harder to make true friends?
2. Sense of self-esteem: To what degree do people believe that what they say or do counts for something in the world?
3. Belief in the work ethic: To what degree do people believe that work is necessary, is useful, and makes them feel good about themselves?
4. People's locus of control: To what degree do people believe that others think for themselves, can reach their goals, and are masters of their fate?
5. People's ambition versus complacency: To what degree do people think about their futures and want to be more than a face in the crowd?

Americans' Outlook on Life

The results of these measurements, as we will see, suggest that the more extreme conclusions of the hand-wringers are off target. Our data affirm that the great majority of Americans continue to find hard work valuable and useful, believe that people can reach their goals in life, and want to be more than just a face in the crowd. In short, most people in the work force today remain committed to the traditional values that encourage self-reliance, promote productivity and accomplishment, and sustain our economy and society.

At the same time, there is a loss of basic trust and faith in other people, which goes hand in hand with the high levels of cynicism registered by the American work force. This raises the question of the extent to which people's pursuits of personal gain and a better future are becoming enveloped in their perceptions of the world as unfriendly and unstable, a place where one does things and gets things for oneself and others must fend for themselves.

We think it crucial to give careful attention to these findings. At once they suggest to leaders and managers in the private and public sectors that there continues to be a strong base of commitment and motivation, as well as ambition, in the American work force that can and must be tapped to build our economic strength and strengthen our social fabric.

Here we see an opportunity for leaders to encourage more salutary qualities in the populace and the work force. The need is to build structures and develop environments that reinforce the work ethic and promote responsible independence. The challenge is to build realistic optimism, not inflated hopes, and to channel ambition to generally productive rather than simply self-serving ends. The goal is not only to restore America's economic might but also to rebuild bonds of trust between companies and workers and to resurrect, to the extent possible, people's faith in their fellow man.[1]

Estrangement Versus Connection. Our telephone interviews assessed people's beliefs that the world is getting colder and less hospitable. Respondents were asked to indicate how much they agreed that there is a growing loss of basic trust and faith in other people in today's world, that it's getting harder to make true friends, that most people feel alone, and so on. This is a measure of people's sense of estrangement, a form of alienation.[2] It applies to people who not only find their environment to be foreign but also dissociate themselves from it and hence are in varying degrees removed from the world around them.

The national survey found rather high levels of estrangement in the populace overall. Some 72 percent of the working population agrees (either strongly or slightly) that there is a growing loss of basic trust and faith in other people. The majority also find it's getting harder to make true friends. Over 40 percent believe that outside of their homes most people feel alone, and nearly 33 percent say it is hardly fair to bring a child into the world the way things look for the future.

We divided the sample into three categories, based on sense of coldness in the world. The categories roughly segment the population into thirds—with 32 percent fully estranged from the cold world they find and 33 percent connected to a world they find considerably warmer and more engaging. The remaining 35 percent see the world somewhere between these two extremes.

Figure 21 shows that the majority (55 percent) of those who are cynical are also estranged by the cold world around them.

Figure 21. Estrangement from Cold World.

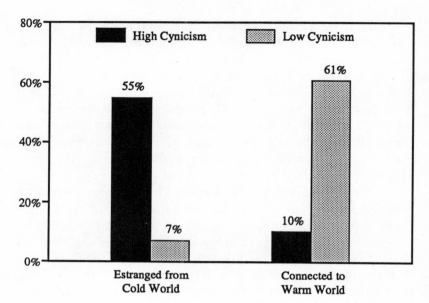

Interestingly, only 10 percent of the cynics find the world to be warm and engaging. Thus we find a large number of estranged cynics in our sample. In turn, the majority of those we call upbeat (61 percent) find themselves to be highly connected to their environment and other people; less than 7 percent of the upbeat find the world to be cold and lonely.

These analyses show, then, that within the species known as the cynic we can identify two distinct brands of cynicism. First, there are cynics who seem to be brokenhearted about life. These are estranged cynics who have been let down by other people and retreat into themselves to escape from the cold world. Many of these estranged cynics, we believe, find the world not so much hazardous as hopeless. They do not define others as their enemies. But they do find themselves isolated and powerless in the face of selfishness and sham. We have represented them most prominently as Squeezed Cynics, but their ranks include many of the Stoics and Hard-Bittens who are not peer leaders or strongly connected to social groups.

Estranged cynics cope by distancing themselves from other people. They include the truly lonely crowd, those who suffer in quiet desperation, and the many lonely hearts—all well chronicled in literature and the social sciences. Furthermore, in the affairs of commerce and politics they are the outsiders and the voiceless.

A second prominent version of the cynical types is neither estranged from the world nor connected to it. Instead, they seem to be tough-minded about life. These cynics are downbeat about their fellowman but hard-nosed about the cold world. We characterize them in the upper echelons as Command Cynics, Administrative Sideliners, or Articulate Players, and we find them among the most Hard-Bitten on the lower rungs of industry. These are the cynical realists. They bring to mind Sydney J. Harris's dictum: "You may be sure that when a man begins to call himself a realist he is prepared to do something he is secretly ashamed of doing." Roughly 40 percent of the cynics in our sample fall into this category. We speculate that many of them see the world as impersonal and gritty and cope with it through the realist's brand of cynicism. These tough-minded cynics hustle and will risk being hustled. They roll with the punches and handle life's ups and downs because they suffer no illusions about other people. These self-styled realists do not distance themselves. Instead, they see things as they are and look out for themselves and their own interests.

Sense of Self-Esteem. A second measure examined people's sense of self-esteem—their perceived potency versus depersonalization. Here the focus is on the psychological phenomena of becoming faceless and defining oneself simply as part of the masses.[3] The national survey data on depersonalization are not so desolate as those on estrangement. Some 31 percent of our sample see themselves to be just a face in the crowd, but fewer than 20 percent conclude that what they do or say doesn't count for much. Putting these measures together, we label only 14 percent of the sample as completely depersonalized or faceless, while the great majority (70 percent) are more or less self-respecting.

Among the species of cynics, then, there are those who have more and less self-esteem, as Figure 22 shows. The majority of people in our sample, whether cynical (55 percent) or

Figure 22. Depersonalization in the Work Force.

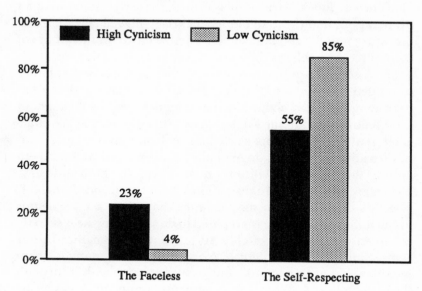

upbeat (85 percent), are self-respecting and believe that their ideas and actions count for something in this world. Yet 23 percent of the cynics in this sample are faceless. Their self-picture is depressed and dehumanized. Faceless cynics see themselves as helpless victims of their environment. Many have given up trying to operate in our complex world. Studies of the depersonalized and faceless show that they do not relate well with other people and chronically isolate themselves. Moreover, they cannot commit themselves to causes and ideas and ultimately lose their self-esteem.

These faceless cynics and their estranged brethren epitomize the jaundiced view of life in today's world. Remember, though, that there are many cynics who are not so estranged, and many more who respect themselves and their agency in life. All share, however, the common perception that the world around them is full of fakery and hucksters and that other people just cannot be trusted.

The Work Ethic. Respondents in our survey were asked four questions pertaining to the work ethic. Nearly three out of four (72 percent) strongly agreed that "being involved in work makes you feel good about yourself." Moreover, there was strong agreement with this statement by men and women, whites and minorities, in all age groups, and across socioeconomic strata. This finding clearly supports Yankelovich's contention that Americans of all types now value work as a form of self-expression.[4]

At the same time, there is somewhat less conviction that work should be regarded as a necessity of life. A smaller proportion (61 percent) of the sample strongly agreed that "work is something people have to do much of their adult lives whether they want to or not." Younger workers and baby boomers were least apt to agree with this facet of the work ethic. These new-breed workers simply reject the notion that people have to work and instead value work primarily as a means of affirming oneself.

The other two questions about work show as well that the traditional work ethic continues to be strong but holds less sway among different segments of the population. Roughly 50 percent of the sample strongly agreed that "no matter how hard or boring, work is good for people to do as long as they can." Some 46 percent strongly agreed that "others think better of me if I am working." Again, baby boomers, young workers, and the better educated were less inclined to agree strongly with these statements about the work ethic.

Putting these four questions together, we find that 30 percent of the American population strongly embraces all aspects of the work ethic, while another 44 percent believes in the value of work but is less committed to the necessity of working as an end in itself. Finally, 27 percent of the work force rejects the value of work out of hand.

Interestingly, there were no differences between cynical and upbeat workers in their commitment to the work ethic. Cynicism is, of course, only one view of life. It relates primarily to people's views on the motivations and makeup of other people. Values about the work ethic, by contrast, are formed in relation to the material, rather than personal, side of life. In this survey population (and, we suspect, more generally), questions about cynicism and the work ethic tap different aspects of the psyche.

Locus of Control. The next worldview under study concerns people's locus of control. People with an "internal" locus of control believe that the average person is master of his or her own fate and that with enough effort people can reach their goals in life. By contrast, those with an "external" locus of control believe that the environment to a large extent determines people's lot in life.[5]

Three questions in the survey addressed people's beliefs about personal control. "Do you believe that the average person is largely master of his or her own fate?" Some 32 percent of the respondents in our sample strongly agreed with this statement, and another 45 percent expressed some agreement. "Do you believe that most people think for themselves?" Some 60 percent either strongly or slightly agreed. "Do you find that if people try hard enough, they will usually reach their goals in life?" On this question, 88 percent strongly or slightly agreed.

There are some interesting trends in these data. On the one hand, self-reliance and the can-do spirit of many Americans are quite pronounced. On the other hand, there seems to be less blind faith that people are captains of their own ships and some doubt that people really think for themselves. It would appear that, broadly speaking, American attitudes about control have become more relativistic.

Again, we grouped respondents according to the strength of their convictions in these regards. One in four Americans (24 percent) is very firm in the belief that people control the world around them. This group consists of the "internals." The young embrace most firmly the notion that they are masters of their fate. This may be an earmark of youthful exuberance or, said another way, naiveté. Another 44 percent of our sample has a more relativistic view of the locus of control. This group contains the best-educated members of the sample. It may be that their worldliness gives them a more circumspect picture of a person's prospects of controlling the environment. Finally, one in three (32 percent) is a fatalist who thinks people are manipulated by the environment. This "external" group concludes that people cannot think for themselves, master their fate, or reach their goals. Research indicates that people of this mind have lower levels of motivation and self-esteem and find it harder to cope with the stresses of life.[6] Again, it is notable that cynics are no more or less inclined to be fatalistic than upbeat respondents.

Ambition Versus Complacency. Our survey asked respondents two questions concerning their ambition. The first asked whether it was important to them to be "more than just a face in the crowd." Some 62 percent of the national sample strongly agreed that it was important. The second asked whether they thought about their future a lot. Some 61 percent strongly agreed that they did. Putting these two questions together, we created an index of people's ambition. Nearly 50 percent of the respondents in this sample strongly agreed with both of the statements; we call them the ambitious. Another 15 percent only slightly agreed with the statements; we can classify them as moderately ambitious. Finally, 35 percent of the population expressed little ambition at all.

Cynicism in the Context of Other Attitudes

On the basis of the data we have seen concerning cynicism and people's estrangement, self-esteem, adherence to the work ethic, locus of control, and levels of ambition, we can draw the following conclusions:

- Americans have more faith in the value of work than they do in the generosity and goodheartedness of their fellowman. In the same fashion, they have more faith in their absolute or relative capacities to master the world around them.
- Said another way, a healthy majority has a firm belief in traditional American values, while a substantial minority is plainly cynical about the outlooks and motives of their fellowman.

Certainly there are many frames of reference people use in evaluating the world of work. To what extent does people's cynicism versus their commitment to traditional values influence their attitudes about work? To answer this question, we undertook a statistical analysis to determine how much each of the measured worldviews contributes to Americans' attitudes about their work. (A summary of the findings appears in Appendix H.)

Predictors of Work Attitudes

Through a statistical technique called regression analysis, we entered into an equation all the attitudes we measured (concerning cynicism, estrangement, self-esteem, work ethic, locus of control, and ambition) and many of the demographic factors (sex, race, age, income, and education). This technique enables us to see to what extent each of these factors contributes to the ratings people give to aspects of their jobs.

Trust in Management and Co-Workers. The survey contained two indexes measuring trust in management and co-workers. Based on regression analysis, the following life attitudes and demographic factors prove most predictive of people's trust at work:

Predictors of Having More Trust in Management

1. An upbeat versus cynical worldview
2. A connected versus estranged worldview
3. A higher versus lower education level
4. An internal versus fatalistic orientation to control

The most significant predictor of people's trust in management is their relative degree of cynicism about life and their fellowman. People's degree of connection versus estrangement to the world around them is the second-best predictor. It appears that trust in management hinges primarily on people's judgment of the motives and intentions of their fellowman. No doubt, selfish and self-serving management reinforces cynics' predispositions to mistrust the motives of others. Furthermore, trust in management relates to people's estimates of the friendliness and warmth they find in the world around them. Cold and impersonal companies can in turn make the world seem even colder to estranged souls.[7]

Educational level is the third most significant predictor of trust in management: Better-educated people find more trust in their bosses than do those with less education. This finding relates, of course, to the kinds of jobs those with higher education hold and to their income levels. As for the less educated, a significant segment of people in less skilled and lower-paying jobs feel ripped off by their companies. Some are the Hard-Bittens and the Squeezed downwardly mobile types, to be sure, but those who are not cynics at heart also feel downtrodden and exploited on their jobs. Many are the front-line blue-collar service personnel.

Finally, locus of control is a predictor of trust in management. It seems that those internals who can take charge of their lives also find management more evenhanded and trustworthy.[8] Such individualism and self-confidence can be very healthy. The risk is that individualists may go their own way to such an extent that they will lack any sense of company loyalty or community. We have suggested how some self-starters can become self-seeking Articulate Players.

The second index most predictive of people's trust in coworkers and finding cooperation is the following:

Predictors of Having More Trust in a Work Group

1. An upbeat versus cynical worldview
2. An internal versus fatalistic orientation to control
3. A strong versus weak work ethic

Again, people's upbeat versus cynical outlook is the prime predictor. Estrangement is no longer a significant predictor. We suspect that people feel connected to their workmates, however much the world seems cold. Surely cynicism can have a corrosive effect on group morale in organizations large and small. Many of today's management practices, ranging from participatory management to quality circles, require supervisors without proper training to handle negative employees. Surely they need to learn how to handle cynics who can become rotten apples and spoil the entire barrel.

Two traditional values, an internal locus of control and commitment to the work ethic, are the next strongest predictors of having trusting and cooperative group relations. People who believe in the value of work and who take responsibility for their lives simply make the best co-workers and likely earn the respect and support of their peers. By contrast, lazy and fatalistic people make the worst kind of colleagues and often are ostracized or ignored by their peers.[9]

It is notable here that no demographic factors predict work-group relationships. Certainly there are special difficulties in building groups with men and women, blacks and whites, and people from different socioeconomic strata. Our data show, however, that these demographic factors do not themselves predict how much people will trust and cooperate with their workmates.

Fairness at Work. In assessing people's perceptions of the fairness of their opportunities and rewards, the following life attitudes and demographic factors prove most predictive:

Predictors of Finding Rewards and Opportunities to Be Fair

1. An internal versus fatalistic orientation to control
2. Being self-respecting versus depersonalized

Locus of control is the most significant predictor of people's ratings of fairness in their companies. Those internals who believe they are masters of their fate find that supervisors are responsive to their concerns about pay and that they will be given a fair shake at getting ahead in their companies. Our survey found that those with less income were especially troubled by fairness in the handling of rewards in their companies. In this connection, though, remember that many on the lower economic rungs also have a strong belief that they are masters of their own fates. In good times, they will leave companies to gain better pay and a chance to get ahead. In bad times, however, they can become locked in to jobs. Such employees can then create their own standards of fairness—by goldbricking, maneuvering, and looking out for themselves.[10]

The second predictor of people's views of the fairness of their rewards concerns their sense of self-respect versus depersonalization. People who respect themselves and say that their opinions count find much more fairness in companies than those we call depersonalized. Statistics show that many Americans find that pay and promotion decisions in organizations hinge on politics rather than performance. It appears that depersonalized members of the work force, those who see themselves as powerless and faceless, simply feel victimized by the politics.

View of Management Style. The index of management style measured people's perceptions that management solicited their opinions and recognized their contributions. These factors proved predictive of ratings of management's style:

Predictors of Finding an Agreeable Management Style

1. Being an older versus a younger worker
2. An internal versus fatalistic orientation to control
3. A complacent versus ambitious attitude
4. An upbeat versus cynical worldview

Age emerges as the most significant predictor of general attitudes about management. Older workers simply have more confidence in their bosses than younger ones do and find communications from management more agreeable. Baby boomers' attitudes fall between these two extremes. We have commented on how attitudes toward authority and cynicism in general vary across these age groups. It is possible, for example, that older workers in this sample are more responsive to the predominant styles of management found in this country or, alternatively, have lower expectations of management's communicativeness and responsiveness to their concerns.

Certainly today's baby boomers and younger workers have more demanding expectations of their bosses and use different standards for evaluating them.[11] It is important for them to gain a voice in company matters and to hear the straight dope from company leaders. The young especially may be nurturing restless hopes about management's responsiveness, while young cynics may have lost all illusions about their companies' leadership.

An internal locus of control also contributes to a more positive image of management. We suspect that the internals are simply better equipped to maneuver and operate in organizations and to take charge of their work lives as a result of their inner direction. They may also obtain more recognition and gain greater voice in their companies. By contrast, fatalists find themselves outmaneuvered and underappreciated.

What we find particularly notable is that ambition is a negative predictor of attitudes toward management. Ambitious workers simply do not gain the input or obtain the recognition they seek from management. We have described how ambitious Articulate Players will use their cynicism to their own advantage. Granted that companies need and want ambitious people, the challenge is how to meet their expectations and channel their energy in desired directions.

Finally, cynicism is also a predictor of ratings of management. Since cynics have less trust in management, it seems that their negativism spills over into ratings of management style.

Job Satisfaction. Our survey contained two indexes measuring people's satisfaction with their job situations. The most significant predictors of how workers rate their jobs and importance to management are as follows:

Predictors of Having a Favorable
View of One's Job and Its Importance

1. Being an older versus a younger worker
2. A strong versus weak work ethic
3. An upbeat versus cynical worldview

Again we see that age is a prime predictor of people's ratings of the job and its importance. Just as the young are less willing to put up with insensitive, incompetent, and uncommunicative managers (in their estimation), so too are they put off by boring jobs that lack importance. Baby boomers and older workers in turn are more likely to have reached posts of greater challenge and recognition. There are signs within these data, however, that many baby boomers still lack satisfactory jobs. Older workers, by contrast, have fewer employment options, and many more have seemingly come to terms with their current jobs, however unchallenging they might be.

The work ethic also figures into people's ratings of their jobs. Those who value work in general also value what they do on the job. Those who have a commitment to the traditional work ethic clearly value their own jobs in whatever form. Those with the new-breed work ethic, however, are responsive to jobs that match their interests and talents. Finally, those who find no value in work per se are bored by their current jobs.

When cynics feel that their jobs are not considered important by management, they focus their negativism on the kind of work they do. We believe such views are most pronounced among the Hard-Bittens, including many public service workers, and the Squeezed Cynics. The strong work ethic of the Obstinate Stoics lessens the effects of cynicism on their jobs.[12]

The other index measuring job satisfaction is whether people like or don't like their organizations. Consider:

Predictors of Satisfaction with One's Organization

1. A higher versus lower income
2. An internal versus fatalistic orientation to control
3. Being white versus minority
4. Being self-respecting versus depersonalized

Here cynicism drops out as a significant predictor. After all, cynicism reflects a view of human nature and thus crops up more prominently in questions pertaining to how other humans behave. Cynicism is activated when the subject concerns trust, evenhandedness, communication, and regard—all aspects of human relations. By contrast, evaluations of one's organization concern many other material facets of company life.

Income is the most significant predictor of satisfaction with one's organization. Studies at the University of Michigan's Institute for Social Research affirm how important income is to people's lives and satisfaction.[13] It means comfort, leisure, a better life-style, and status, not to mention groceries. Moreover, higher earners generally have better jobs and better working conditions. It should be no surprise, then, that how much people earn is more important than their psychological makeup in predicting satisfaction with their organizations.

Locus of control emerges as another potent predictor. Earlier we saw that those with a high internal sense of control find rewards and opportunities to be fair in their companies. Apparently those who believe they can reach their goals in life simply navigate organizational waters more effectively. They have a great deal more satisfaction with their companies than do people who believe they are controlled by their environment.

Race is the third most significant predictor of satisfaction with one's organization. We have described how blacks and other minorities objectively find their work in organizations less satisfactory. Here we see that race influences satisfaction independently of people's income. Perhaps opportunity and sense of estrangement also enter into judgments of company life.[14]

Optimism and self-respect are also important ingredients in people's satisfaction with their companies. Do I count for much? This is a question people ask of themselves and calibrate in rating organizational life. Self-respecting people value their organizations. The depersonalized do not. The risk of the corporate restructuring efforts—as well as the risk in programs that bring high tech to the factory and office, develop "intrapreneurship" in companies, or just "jazz up" products and advertising—is that fundamentals such as respect for people are not entering the strategic calculus. We are not saying that people risk becoming depersonalized per se by the current shakeup and shakeout in the economy. But concern over money and machinery does loom large in corporations, and concern for people has a lower profile.[15]

Attitudes of Cynical Subgroups

What happens when people view their work through the lens of cynicism and interpose their other negative views of life and the future?[16] Do cynics who are estranged have an even more negative view of their organizations? How much do a weak work ethic and a sense of fatalism further depress cynics' attitudes about the job? To investigate these questions, we examined certain work attitudes of cynics who also feel estranged and depersonalized and do not hold traditional values about work, control, and the future.

Estranged and Faceless Cynics. In our sample, estranged respondents see a basic loss of trust and faith in other people in the world today; they feel alone and find it hard to make friends. In turn, estranged cynics trace this coldness to the selfish motivations of other people and come to see callousness as basic human nature.

These are not the cynical realists, who take a tough-minded attitude and jaundiced stance to their dealings with a troublesome world. Nor are they the idealistic and compassionate, who have become distant and turned inward in the face of a cold and inhospitable environment. Rather, they are the brooders and blameful, the depressed and embittered. We found that this estrangement, coupled with cynicism, produces in them an even bleaker picture of their work and employers.

Another group we have identified (small in number) are those lacking in self-esteem who believe they are just a face in the crowd and that their opinions don't count for much. Faceless cynics attribute this feeling to the naked self-interest of others—especially those in power. They, too, have an even more jaundiced view of the workplace.

Figure 23 shows that 52 percent of the upbeat respondents find management to be honest and evenhanded in dealings with people. By contrast, some 32 percent of the cynics find their management honest and evenhanded. More corrosively, only 24 percent of the estranged cynics and 17 percent of the faceless cynics find management trustworthy.

Estranged cynics find the world cold and manipulative. It should come as no surprise, then, that so few of them find management credible and equitable. Faceless cynics are outsiders who find their powerlessness exacerbated by management that deceives and exploits them. Estrangement and low self-esteem darken the cynics' views of many attitudes about work, especially management's style and the importance assigned to their jobs.

Lazy and Fatalistic Cynics. Our sample contains cynics with a strong work ethic and cynics with a weak one. Over 40 percent of those we classify as cynics also report high commit-

Figure 23. Estrangement and Depersonalization
Lessen Cynics' Trust in Management.

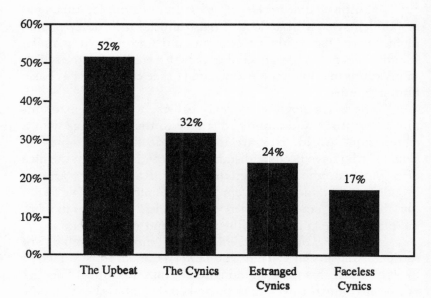

ment to the work ethic. We call them hardworking cynics. These types are deeply committed to work but see the world around them as full of self-interested and manipulative people. Their ranks no doubt include the Command Cynics, Administrative Sideliners, and Articulate Players who believe in work and wield their cynicism actively on the job. Some may be Obstinate Stoics who are careful to attend to their jobs and their kind but are ever suspicious of others.

Another 25 percent of the cynics have a weak work ethic. This group sees no value in work and thinks that manipulation and self-interest predominate in the world about them. We call them lazy cynics. In our estimation many of these are Hard-Bitten Cynics—vocal about the exploitation of management but not particularly concerned about their own work and accomplishments. Some young Squeezed Cynics are no doubt part of this group as well.

The analyses also show that there is a subgroup of cynics who have an internal locus of control and another subgroup who see the environment as controlling them. Specifically, one in three cynics subscribes to a belief in people's capacity to master their environment. They see manipulation around them but believe that people can determine their success nevertheless. We call them cynical strivers. We suspect that there are some Articulate Players in this subgroup—cynics who are out for themselves and know how to advance their own interests—as well as a few Command Cynics. We want to add, however, that Hard-Bitten Cynics also fit in this category.

In turn, another one in four cynics in this subgroup believes that people lack such personal agency. Such cynics see manipulation and self-interest all about but believe that people cannot control their destinies. We call them cynical fatalists. No doubt some of the Obstinate Stoics are fatalists, but we suspect that many downwardly mobile Squeezed types are also prominent in this subgroup.

The key question is: To what extent do laziness and fatalism interact with cynicism in shaping people's views of life in their organizations? Figure 24 presents a graph showing how

**Figure 24. Fatalism and a Low Work Ethic Lessen
Cynics' Satisfaction with Their Jobs and Their Importance.**

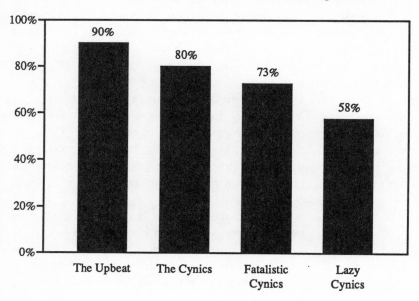

fatalism and a weak work ethic further depress cynics' ratings of their jobs and their importance. It shows that while most upbeat workers find their jobs satisfactory, ratings decline for cynics (80 percent satisfied) and even more for cynics who lack inner drive (73 percent) and a commitment to the work ethic (53 percent). These mistrustful and unmotivated employees are the bane of productivity and morale.

Fatalism and laziness depress cynics' ratings of fairness and management's style, too. Unfair treatment, whether real or imagined, is grist for the mill to the Hard-Bitten Cynics and another sign to the Squeezed Cynics that life isn't fair. To some extent, both find themselves powerless to master the environment around them. By contrast, Articulate Players, exemplars of the cynical strivers, find more fairness in their companies than cynics do in general. They may have figured out how to get pay increases and promotions in their own self-interested fashion.

Ambitious Versus Complacent Cynics. When we also divide the cynics into two subgroups based on their levels of ambition, 50 percent can be categorized as ambitious cynics. These are people who suspect the motives of others around them but think a lot about the future and are dedicated to getting ahead. Here again, we find many Articulate Players and Squeezed Cynics. Ambitious cynics tend to be young, and many have some college education but not a degree. They are ambitious, to be sure, but lack the opportunities and the credentials to put their ambition to work.

By contrast, 30 percent of the cynics may be called complacent cynics. This group is just as suspicious of others but has no strong drive toward accomplishment in the future. Here we find some Obstinate Stoics, Hard-Bittens, and Squeezed types that have given up on the future. These are by no means the Articulate Players: Cynicism is not a weapon in their arsenal for getting ahead.

Ambition and complacency have a distinct impact on cynics' attitudes toward management, as Figure 25 shows. Ambitious cynics (51 percent favorable) are a bit more critical of management's style, for example, than are cynics (59 percent) in general. Many no doubt believe that if they were in charge,

Figure 25. Ambitious Cynics Find Their Companies to Be
Less Well Managed Than Complacent Cynics.

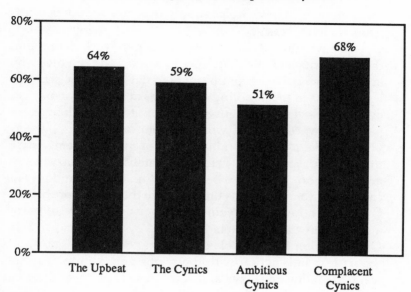

they could do it better. We suspect that these are Articulate Players and Squeezed Cynics chafing at the pace and inefficacy of management. Interestingly, complacent cynics (68 percent) have more favorable views of management's style than cynics do in general. They also trust management more, find their rewards a bit fairer, and are more satisfied with their organizations.

The trends on ambition and complacency bespeak the heating up of cynicism in the 1980s for the ambitious types and the cooling-down effects for the complacent. Whereas ambitious cynics are always looking for the edge, the complacent cynics may simply be making do with less, which dulls their disappointment.

To sum up these findings, consider:

• Cynics, compared with more upbeat respondents, have less trust in management. Cold and faceless cynics have even less trust. Perhaps they see management as to some extent an agent of their own estrangement and powerlessness. Complacent cynics, by contrast, are not so inclined to distrust management. These Stoics simply may not expect as much from their leaders.

- Cynics have somewhat less trust in their co-workers and find their rewards less fair than upbeat workers do. Cynics who lack an inner drive or commitment to the work ethic see even less fairness in the handling of rewards at work. By contrast, cynical strivers have figured out how to make their companies' reward systems work for them.
- Cynics have a less favorable rating of management's style than upbeat workers do. Estranged, fatalistic, and lazy cynics are even more inclined to believe that management does not care about their opinions or recognize their work problems. Cynics with low self-esteem have a very grim view of management on these counts.
- Cynics assign lower levels of importance to their jobs and report less satisfaction with their jobs and companies. Estranged, fatalistic, lazy, and faceless cynics have an even less sanguine view of their work. Complacent cynics have a more favorable view than cynics do in general. This means that cynics are more inclined to leave their jobs. But, if locked in to them or complacently griping about them, they are more apt to passively disparage their companies or actively look for ways to loaf and otherwise even the score.

Implications for Management

We see many implications for management in these data on the interactive effects of cynicism and other views on people's attitudes toward work. Plainly, management has an opportunity to build on the strength of the work ethic, channel people's sense of personal control, and give positive direction to their ambition. To respond to the cynic, however, poses special challenges. Cynics in general, for example, and estranged and depersonalized cynics in particular, seem to focus their dispirit on management. To earn trust and build morale among these types, management simply has to reach out to them. This approach has implications for managing the atmosphere in companies. (Cold and cynical companies breed cold and cynical workers.) It also has implications for the design of company compensation and reward packages (estranged cynics think they're being taken advantage of) and company communication practices (depersonalized cynics don't trust what management tells them and don't think their own opinions count for much).

Reward systems send messages to people. We propose that companies make reward systems clearer to people and give them more control over their compensation and career planning. This increased clarity and say-so addresses the importance of internal locus of control in people's ratings of fairness in their firms (while countering fatalistic cynics' claims that reward systems are rigged). As for stimulating the work ethic, our data show that such innovations as job enrichment and participatory management might well contribute to people's sense of control and motivation (while challenging lazy cynics who don't think their opinions count or that their jobs are considered important).

10

Creating
Work Cultures
That Counter Cynicism

What can companies do to manage an increasingly cynical work force? How can they temper people's expectations, counter their suspicions, and gain their confidence? We acknowledge that cynicism has always been part of the human condition and recognize that its causes lie largely in personality development and social situations experienced outside the workplace. Still, given its prevalence in the American work force and the consequences for working life, we want to address ourselves to coping with it and even to suggest a few remedies. Our review of historical and contemporary conditions in society and the workplace has highlighted how cynicism is bred and reinforced among working people. The primary challenge, then, is to reverse these conditions—literally, to manage our way back to credibility.

We have no illusions that more honest and evenhanded management per se will eliminate cynicism at work. But it may lessen people's sense of disillusionment, neutralize their negativism to a degree, convert a few cynics into skeptics, and perhaps influence some to the point where they will be more trustworthy colleagues, stronger contributors, and better company citizens.

It is always risky to prescribe remedies for what ails companies and people at work. Most prescriptions are commonsensical and, when reduced to text, often sound self-righteous, ivory towerish, trite, or all of these. Moreover, thousands of books, articles, and seminars have appeared in this decade, telling managers how to manage better and instructing companies in what to do to win over disaffected managers and workers. We see no need to join the bandwagon.

Instead, drawing from our research study and consulting experiences, we will present some modest counsel to those who lead, manage, and work in companies and must contend with cynicism at work. At once, the key message is to build on strengths. Our survey showed that people's belief in the value of work and sense of control over their lives have a great deal to do with positive attitudes about their companies and jobs. Clearly companies need to create and maintain cultures that promote the work ethic and give people more influence over their work and work-related decisions. Moreover, a company whose culture reinforces people's upbeat outlooks is also apt to retain the approbation of goodhearted employees and gain a measure of surcease from cynics in the fold. Our recommendation: Companies must create cultures that counter cynicism.

Cynical Realism Versus Realistic Idealism

Our research revealed a sharp distinction between the values of cynical versus upbeat companies. In the former, managers, professionals, clerical, and blue-collar employees, as well as sales personnel, all described their companies as dominated by a grim, narrow, and gritty view of things. Descriptions of company life revolved primarily around money and machinery, rather than around purpose and people. Accounts of how things ''really got done'' were rife with politics, positioning, self-promotion, and backstabbing. No one was to be trusted; everybody seemed to be out for him- or herself. What's more, this was accepted as the way things are—as though such conduct was par for the course—and no better or worse than what could be expected. Hence, we label the dominant value of these companies *cynical realism*.

By contrast, people in upbeat companies talked unabashedly about corporate ideals. High-minded purpose seemed to mark these companies' cultures, and people said they were proud of what they were trying to accomplish on the job. These were work-hard/play-hard companies, places where people contributed their best efforts on the job and socialized quite freely with peers, superiors, and subordinates, without regard to rank or social status. Management was described as open and honest; co-workers were seen as trustworthy and caring. People's accounts of life in the upbeat companies seemed to us to be neither Pollyannaish nor pious. Certainly these companies emphasize finance, technology, and bottom-line results, but in doing so they also push "people development." We label the dominant value in these upbeat companies *realistic idealism*.

Values About People in the Upbeat Company. Why do people work? Surely to put food on the table. We have seen that cynical companies often magnify this essential human need to the point where the quest for bread alone defines the outlook of top, middle, and first-line managers in dealing with one another and their employees. But common sense and reams of research show that people also work to maintain ties with colleagues and friends, to attain occupational identity, to develop their talents, and to obtain self-esteem.[1] Plainly, the so-called excellent companies embody these aspirations in the way they do business. Firms with a strong, innovative, achievement-oriented culture demonstrate a deep and abiding faith in the self-motivating qualities of the work ethic and the capabilities of their people.

This people-oriented idealism, while a central value of the upbeat company culture, does not itself embody the full range of aspirations people have for their companies and lives at work. People also want to reach beyond themselves and their singular self-interest. At the most primal level, this desire is expressed in their motivations to love, to form and maintain families, and to make some kind of spiritual connection to the world and the cosmos.

Michael Maccoby, in his study of why people work, suggests that there may be something primal about people's motives to work as well.[2] We offer the notion that people work in big enterprises not only out of necessity or security but also to be part of something more significant than themselves. This urge to join in a human community and to contribute to an organized force rests on the belief that, up to a point, greater things can be accomplished collectively than by any single individual. This belief is what validates people's decisions to go to work for one company rather than another and gives meaning to their day-to-day work there.

We have described how cynical companies take advantage of these idealistic expectations and betray people's quest to contribute meaningfully on a significant scale. By contrast, upbeat companies incorporate these ideals into a vision of what the company aims to achieve and manifests them in the way things get done. This vision is most evident in a company's philosophy.

Stated Ideals. In their study of corporate cultures, Terry Deal and Tom Kennedy found that of the eighty companies they surveyed, twenty-five had, in the eyes of their employees, a clearly articulated corporate philosophy.[3] And of these firms, eighteen espoused what the authors call "qualitative values" that bespoke human ideals. They and others make reference to myriad upbeat corporate philosophies. IBM's core values, for example, stress the importance of individuals, service, and excellence; Tandem's emphasize quality, personal initiative, and teamwork; and those at Johnson & Johnson and Mars are quite comprehensive in their commitment to quality in products and services, the work environment, and community relationships.

Statements of philosophy put a company on record as espousing ideals. The most comprehensive statements address, among other subjects, the company's beliefs about people, its attitude toward customers and standards of performance, its style of management, and its expectations of employees. They also define the mission of the enterprise, its attitude toward profits and their distribution, and its ethical standards and responsibilities to the community. These statements let employees, customers, suppliers, and investors know what a company stands for. Upbeat companies are serious about their philosophies and are seen to be serious.

We do not suggest that simply formulating a company credo will capture people's imagination or stir their idealism. Indeed, many companies develop philosophy statements, print them in glossy brochures, and then ignore them in everyday practice. This gap between what companies preach and what they practice can be a sharp spur to cynicism. Nor do we suggest that companies have to articulate their creeds in detail in order to be credible to employees. On the contrary, whether ideals are stated or not, we think it most crucial that companies *live* their corporate ideals.

Ideals are alive and well at many of the most progressive high-tech companies, for example, when they are personalized in stories of the founding and development of the enterprise. It is not uncommon in these companies to hear people tell stories of how Ken Olsen of Digital Equipment did this, how Dave Packard of Hewlitt-Packard did that, how Seymour Cray of Cray Research did something else—always upbeat and always significant—when justifying their own actions or decisions. These stories are not simply paeans to glory days past. On the contrary, they inspire current stratagems and reaffirm company ideals. Such firms actively tell and retell these corporate sagas, reinforcing their guiding character among old hands and inculcating it in new recruits. In this way, employees see management as the keeper of a living culture in which everyone has a stake.

A Different Kind of Business

One need not be part of a big, high-tech company to see ideals in action. Indeed, many smaller outfits and some larger old-line businesses sew idealism into the fabric of the firm. One company we have worked with has done an exemplary job of representing the upbeat outlook in the ways it does business. "Two real guys," Ben Cohen and Jerry Greenfield, head Ben & Jerry's Homemade, Inc., an independent ice-cream producer gaining market share and public approbation against industry competitors Häagen-Dazs (made by Pillsbury), Früsen Gladjé (made by Kraft), and Steve's. The founders run, in their own words, "a different kind of business." Ben's philosophy is simple: "I see business as nothing more than a rich neighbor, and rich neighbors ought to help their neighbors." Jerry adds, "You can run your business with certain ideals and principles and it'll still work, and it will make the world a better place."

Putting Ideals into Action. The story of Ben and Jerry has a romantic, nose-thumbing quality to it that reads like a new-age entrepreneur's dream.[4] The "boys," childhood friends, each dropped out of college in the late 1960s, worked at odd jobs for a time, and together opened a small ice-cream scoop shop in Burlington, Vermont, in 1978, with scant know-how (they learned to make ice cream through a $5 correspondence course) and less capital (they started with $12,000—a third of it borrowed). But they had something else going for them: a combination of old-fashioned values and newfangled ideas.

Neither Ben nor Jerry had any intention of becoming "businessmen." From the start, however, both were committed to making the best ice cream possible and to having fun while doing so. More than this, these "self-styled Vermont hippies," as the press calls them, were committed to the simple notion that business draws from the community and is obliged to give something back. In the early days, this meant giving away ice cream to loyal customers and worthy charities. As the company has grown to sales of over $40 million, Ben & Jerry's has embraced what it calls a "social mission" to improve the quality of life—not only of its employees, but also locally, nationally, and internationally—and to do so in an innovative and upbeat way. Examples:

- The Ben & Jerry's Foundation donates 7.5 percent of pretax company profits to nonprofit organizations and people working for social change. The company also donates tons of ice cream to charitable groups every year, with the expectation that these groups will turn around and host a fair or event such that the ice-cream donation can yield them even more in contributions.
- A portion of the company's advertising budget is devoted to socially responsible marketing. Ben & Jerry's, for exam-

ple, proposed to "adopt" a subway stop in New York City,
cleaning and maintaining it, in lieu of advertising in papers
and on television in the city. When that proposal fell through,
the company took out an advertisement asking for "ideas"
for other socially responsible ways to serve the city. Thousands poured in.

- Ben and Jerry have been working with the "Knowledge
Society" in the Soviet Union on a joint venture to manufacture and sell ice cream in the U.S.S.R. and America. Profits
from the venture will be devoted to cultural exchanges between the two countries. Recently the company introduced
"Peace Pops" as part of the "1% for Peace Campaign."
This effort is aimed at encouraging other businesses to join
a movement urging the government to devote 1 percent of
the defense budget explicitly to peaceful purposes.

Ben and Jerry have been at the edge of innovation since
the company went public. Rather than seeking venture capital
to grow the business, they drew up a stock prospectus on their
own and sold stock to Vermonters door to door. One in every
hundred Vermont families bought in, to the tune of $750,000.
When Häagen-Dazs tried to pressure shopkeepers to keep "Vermont's finest" off their shelves, Ben and Jerry started a grass-
roots campaign against Pillsbury, replete with bumper stickers
("What's the Doughboy Afraid of?") and a one-person picket
line (Jerry) at the Pillsbury headquarters. Calvin Trillin celebrated the campaign in a *New Yorker* article. *Time* magazine
hailed Ben & Jerry's as the "best ice cream in the world."[5]
Ben and Jerry have tried to introduce this same funky
and socially responsible orientation inside the company. The
company's mission and many of its policies and practices (see
Exhibit 2) reflect the upbeat and caring values of the founders.
Yet it became evident to Ben and Jerry, as well as to managers
and employees, that the company's external image—of funk,
fun, and love—was out of sync with the atmosphere inside the
company. The company was always short on ice cream and long
on hours, pressure, and problems. In brief, there were signs
of cynicism cropping up in the firm.

Exhibit 2. Ben & Jerry's Mission and Operating Principles.

Ben & Jerry's, a Vermont-based ice-cream producer, is dedicated to the creation and demonstration of a new corporate concept of linked prosperity. The company has three central missions and several key operating principles.

Three Missions

Product Mission: To make, distribute, and sell the finest-quality all-natural ice cream and related products in a wide variety of innovative flavors made from Vermont dairy products.

Economic Mission: To operate the company on a sound financial basis of profitable growth, increasing value for our shareholders and creating career opportunities and financial rewards for our employees.

Social Mission: To recognize the central role that business plays in the structure of society by seeking innovative ways to improve the quality of life for a broad community—local, national, and international.

Operating Principles

Linked Prosperity: "As the company prospers, the community and our people prosper." 7½ % of pretax profits go to the Ben & Jerry's Foundation for distribution to community groups and charities. 5% of profits are put into a profit-sharing plan. A 5-to-1 salary ratio between top management and entry-level production workers. To raise top pay, raise the bottom up.

Community Development: "Business has the responsibility to give back to the community." Donations of ice cream by request to all Vermont nonprofit organizations. Leveraged assistance, where B&J will help nonprofits stage fund raisers selling Vermont's finest ice cream.

Ownership Perspective: "Everybody is an owner." Employee stock ownership, stock grants, and stock purchase plan. All company "town meetings" monthly.

Integrity: "Two real guys." All-natural products. Commitment to Vermont Dairy Cooperatives. "What you see is what you get." People can speak, act, and dress as they wish.

Work Hard/Have Fun: "Bend over backwards." Pledge to meet orders, satisfy customers, make things right for people. "If it's not fun, why do it?" Company celebrations. Jerry's Joy Committee to spread joy in the workplace.

Human Activism/Social Change: "A model for other businesses." 1% for Peace Campaign. Socially responsible marketing. Joint ventures in Israel and Moscow to spread goodwill.

One of the present authors began to work with Ben & Jerry's to help the board hammer out its mission and begin to empower managers to run the company in a strong, unified, and responsible fashion. There were pragmatic issues to address in this effort to refine the Ben & Jerry's culture: The managers did not see themselves as a team, nor had they worked together to formulate goals and establish roles and responsibilities. There were also matters of principle on the agenda: Many managers had had no prior experience leading a company so dedicated to social responsibility. Several, frankly, did not really accept all the company's socially oriented policies—specifically, the salary ratio of 1 to 5 between the earnings of the lowest paid and the top echelon of the company. To some, the professed mandate of the founders to have fun at work while still achieving record rates of production at superior quality standards was proving to be a lot of hot air.

Clearing the Air. The managers went to an offsite retreat. There, all were blindfolded and roped together in their three work-related clusters and then charged with locating three inner tubes symbolically lashed together, maybe seventy-five yards away. Managers in each cluster shouted out instructions or asked for them, took stabs at leading and then halted in frustration, while the other groups stumbled along vainly searching for the "goal." One group finally located the tubes, then cheered for their own success and chided the other groups. This experience provided a window to examine teamwork, competition, and cooperation throughout the retreat.

Later the managers climbed ropes, worked on problem-solving initiatives, and trekked in the out-of-doors—all in service of finding new ways to work with one another. One evening they talked about their personal lives and values throughout the medium of "mind maps." They all recorded on silhouettes the persons and events that had most shaped their characters, how they wanted to be thought of in the company and by their peers, and what mark they wanted to leave by their lives. Several spoke of their scarring experiences in Vietnam, their poignant efforts to cope with family trials, and the impact that their mothers, their fathers, and now their spouses and children had upon them. Many cried. There were hugs and cheers.

The next evening, the clusters put on skits about their parts of the organization. The manufacturing cluster, drawing from a popular TV game show, dramatized the ''jeopardy'' involved in making high-volume, high-quality foodstuffs. The marketing and sales group selected a member to portray one of the founders and joined him in a song-and-dance routine about the foibles of competing with less socially responsible companies and the ''folly'' of having fun at work.

The search for the inner tubes was repeated at the end of the retreat. But this time, the groups quickly joined forces to analyze the problem, work out a plan, figure out roles and responsibilities, and establish procedures to stay in touch with one another. They reached the goal in one-third of the time. Did this lab make a difference? Certainly managers rate themselves as much more of a team—after spending six weeks defining their goals and responsibilities and examining their work and personal relationships. They also seem far more aligned as a group (and something of a threat to the founders, who are having a little trouble letting go of promised authority).

The management team and founders met recently to examine their differences. Several weeks earlier, the founders had said that management wasn't ''weird enough'' and worried that they couldn't be trusted to keep the fun-loving spirit alive in the company, obsessed as they seemed to be with clarifying goals, roles, and responsibilities. Each member of the management team came to the session wearing a mask bearing the likeness of either Ben or Jerry and a button saying ''We Are Weird.'' They then worked out issues of trust and empowerment with the founders, fleshed out how they would work together, and made a pact that the company would remain committed to high-quality production, good works, and fun.

Realism Alongside Ideals. What's to be learned from this? Ben and Jerry lived their ideals and had the courage to challenge their managers to run their company with these ideals uppermost in their minds. But make no mistake, Ben & Jerry's has rigorous quality standards and insists on top-notch customer service. Lots of time, attention, and training are devoted to ensuring that the company operates with safe, high-volume production and that customers are satisfied by well-tested flavors and attentive service. Those who introduce cost-saving ideas get "Fred Awards" named in honor of the plant manager— another sign that the company is guided by realism alongside its ideals.

Still, Ben and Jerry insist on having fun. The "two real guys" host company outings where Jerry, trained in carnival tricks, uses a sledgehammer to break a cement block on the stomach of the mystical "Habeeni Ben Coheeni." But the founders are also sensitive to the suspicion that they're on an ego trip. It is not uncommon to find Jerry working the third production shift or to see Ben tasting new flavors and reviewing product artwork. These two real guys insist that their external image match perceptions inside the company. The culture at Ben & Jerry's continues to change as the company prospers and grows and as more "corporatelike" systems and practices emerge. That Ben, Jerry, the board, managers, and employees work hard at having fun and ensuring that the upbeat atmosphere in the company is kept alive makes them, in our view, a model of a culture that counters cynicism.

Putting the Work Ethic to Work

Our study has shown that the American work ethic is latent but undernourished in cynical companies. Douglas McGregor's formulations of Theory X versus Theory Y assumptions about human nature provide a sensible demarcation between companies that undermine the work ethic and those that put it to work.[6] Theory X managers and corporate cultures regard employees as lazy, irresponsible, even unmotivatable. Such companies have no appreciation for human capital and potential. On the contrary, employees are treated as "costs," and every effort is made to substitute automation, controls, and procedures for their skills, independence, and intelligence.

Today's employees challenge managers' authority, resent company secrecy, mistrust decisions they have not been involved in, doubt information they can't question, and chafe in organizations that treat them like numbers, robots, or hired hands. Many managers mistake such reactions as signs that their people don't want to work and are only out for themselves. We find these attitudes, of course, among people who do not embrace the work ethic and among the younger Squeezed Cynics and Hard-Bitten types who chafe in unmotivating jobs and calculate what's in it for them to work harder. But Yankelovich comes to quite a different conclusion on the vitality of the work ethic: "The conventional wisdom of a deteriorating work ethic is badly off target; the American work ethic is strong and healthy. . . . The real [problem] lies not with new cultural values or with an erosion of the work ethic, but with the striking failure of managers to support and reinforce the work ethic."[7]

The great majority of Americans believe in the value of hard work and want to do their jobs capably and with care. The problem is that a great many working people also say they lack the information, equipment, and authority they need to do their jobs well.[8] Granted, there is a cynical segment of the work force that is not interested in performing well or in finding better ways to do their jobs. This is particularly true, in our sample, of lazy cynics who will accept shoddy management in exchange for shoddy work. It is true, as well, of cynics with low self-esteem who feel powerless to change things. For many others, upbeat and cynical, the absence of resources and rewards leaves them with the implicit message that management doesn't care about extra effort.

Theory Y managers and companies begin with the assumption that people will work hard and take responsibility. Accordingly, they challenge employees to do their best and hold them to high standards of performance. Most important, they give employees the information, resources, and authority they need to do their jobs well. Our point is that upbeat companies consciously espouse the tenets of Theory Y. They make it plain that management does care about extra effort and they make sure that their employees do too. Moreover, these companies put these ideals into practice in the manufacture of goods and delivery of services.

The Upbeat Production Orientation. Many management writers have provided illustrations of the Theory Y principles in practice. For example, Peters and Waterman's recipes for hands-on, value-driven production, for staying close to the customer, and for building quality in (rather than checking it afterward) all represent credible expressions of realistic corporate idealism.[9] Companies are putting their credibility on the line by designing and, in many instances, redesigning production systems in ways that tap the work ethic.

In his review of new plant design, Edward Lawler refers to a "new plant revolution." Manufacturing facilities, he says, are being participatively designed by teams of experts, managers, and employees to ensure that the technology and work processes fit the needs of the marketplace and employees.[10] Often the production process is run by employees who have the responsibility of building an entire product and inspecting their own work. In one notable case, at a Digital Equipment plant, teams of employees do their own materials receiving, manufacturing, testing, quality control, accounting, and shipping for computer boards. Their rate of productivity far exceeds that of more traditionally designed Digital plants.

Richard Walton cites other instances where practices in older plants have been revamped along these lines.[11] At Ford Motor Company assembly plants, for example, workers can literally shut down production when defects are spotted. We think this has a lot to do with the quality improvements registered by the company.

Fractionation of production and stark division of labor have destroyed product identity in many manufacturing concerns throughout the United States. The creation of massive quality-control departments has communicated to people that they are not really responsible for quality—or, worse, cannot be entrusted with the responsibility. The new message, a rediscovery of ideals, is that craftsmanship counts and that people have the talent and commitment to build it right the first time or fix it on their own initiative.

The Upbeat Service Orientation. Can anything be done about customer service? We have seen how cynical companies treat their customers like jerks. Upbeat companies promulgate the message that, for example, the customer comes first. In one firm we studied, this principle means that the manufacturing complex is "de-fractionated"—people from all over the enterprise come together to analyze customer needs and incorporate them into design, production, and service plans. These meetings become a dynamic "suggestion box" enabling people to understand the priorities and problems of other functions and offer ideas on improving practices company-wide. The company makes it a point to remind people that *everyone* has a customer—including other functions and employees within the firm.

A strong focus on the customer is not only good for business. It also sends a message to employees that what they are doing matters. One engineer we interviewed described himself as a "techno-service" worker. He explained that he regularly meets with customers to ascertain their needs and incorporate them into his designs. Another production worker proudly indicated that he had been sent to a dealership to meet the people who would ultimately buy his products. He had never known exactly what they were looking for when choosing between his company's and a competitor's goods.

Expeditious Fatalism Versus Can-Do Determination

We have seen signs of fatalism in today's work force and find them widely reinforced—in companies that blame workers (or managers) for declining rates of productivity, quality, and innovation, in companies that sacrifice brand building to short-term promotional strategies, in outfits that strip assets and plunder profits for short-term gain. Certainly this sense of fatalism is prominent in efforts to manage the American trade imbalance. Comparatively, the poor quality of, say, American cars and the price of American textiles have led to an outcry for protection from foreign imports, which many Americans see as offering better value for their money. Fatalistic companies rely on the quick-fix or Band-Aid approach, rather than facing up to long-term solutions to America's quality problems.

In our judgment, protectionism is not the long-term answer to competition. It reinforces fatalism and has been misused by cynical companies. U.S. Steel (now USX) was granted protectionist legislation and, instead of reinvesting in steel technology, it purchased an oil company. Some 50,000 laid-off steelworkers are bitter with cynicism about their company and rife with fatalism about their own future. We trace their outlook to a cynical and fatalistic company.

Fatalism also marks the culture of many seemingly successful companies that have obtained a dominant market share and built bloated bureaucracies to ensure that nobody rocks the boat. Such cultures breed caution, conformity, and blind obedience. Risk taking is frowned on, and new ideas are taboo. Bureaucratic companies do not completely drive out people's entrepreneurial spirit. Instead, that spirit is channeled into "creative" forms of self-protection. When problems arise, finger-pointing becomes the operative norm, and people learn to keep their mouths shut and look the other way.

Surely this is the antithesis of American values that encourage entrepreneurism and individuality. The essence of the fatalistic attitude in companies is expressed in their excessive need for control. In an earlier era, this need was met by close supervision and the threat of dismissal. Today, bureaucratic and technocratic controls predominate, both in large corporations and in smaller companies emulating the big shots.

What has this wrought? Surveys show that people are hampered by red tape and fed up with bureaucratic rigmarole.[12] There have also been marked declines in people's perceptions that their companies show respect to employees as individuals. Interestingly, these same surveys indicate that people do not find their supervisors cold and unfeeling. It may well be that supervisors are regarded as powerless given their station in the chain of command and given the myriad rules that tie their hands. Instead, the faceless corporation is the villain.

The Virtues of Small. What can be done to encourage risk taking in these companies and bring back individual initiative? One suggestion is to bring things back to a human scale. Many manufacturers, for instance, have begun to build smaller plants based on the "small is beautiful" ethic. A central tenet of companies such as Kollmorgan, a New England manufacturer, is that economies of scale are offset by inefficiencies of scale. Interestingly, the CEO of Dana Corporation launched an effort to bring work down to a human scale by ceremoniously burning the firm's personnel and policy manuals. In his mind, big-company rules and regulations simply did not fit the requirements of running a lean and close-knit organization.

The emphasis on smallness—and its attendant benefits of product identity and personal autonomy—is evident too in the creation of venture units within companies, such as the one that built IBM's personal computer. We see it as well in the creation and spin-off of smaller product divisions and service functions. All this is part of "intrapreneurism" in organizations. It is easier for working people to gain more freedom, stay closer to the customer and products, and have more say in smaller intrapreneurial units.

Such actions counter people's sense of fatalistic resignation on the job. We also think that companies which embrace this self-determining attitude send a message to their customers, suppliers, and competitors. Quite simply, the message is that the company is master of its destiny—unafraid to compete in a global economy and unwavering in its determination to improve itself through high quality and personal achievement.

Heroism in the Upbeat Company. What has happened to the notion of heroism in corporations? Much as idealism has been forsaken in the corporate atmosphere, so too has the value of heroism. Rigid bureaucracy purges heroic individualism from company life, and technocracy makes the system, rather than people, the driving force in an organization. There is, however, today a renewed emphasis on the business hero.[13]

Would the Chrysler turnaround have been possible without Lee Iacocca? Possibly—but someone else would have had to become the company's hero. Obviously, a measure of heroism is important to the success of any leader who wants to define or redefine a company's culture. But our preferences also run to more everyday heroes and heroines: the man who designs improvements to a product, the woman who makes the unexpected sale, the project manager who gets the work done on time and under budget, the accountant who saves the company money, the recruiter who finds the ideal job candidate.

How can heroism be put in the service of promoting ideals? To an extent, it requires companies to locate heroes whose work is associated with vital corporate values. At Gillette, one such hero is the vice-president of product integrity. More than this, it involves celebrating the initiative and independence of people at all levels whenever their work advances the quality of products and services, the reputation of the company, and the long-term interests of the enterprise.

Cynical companies simply do not entrust their personnel with the authority and responsibility they need to behave heroically. Acts of heroism inevitably violate policies, break rules, and warrant punishment in most firms. A cadre of Administrative Sideliners is in place to ensure that nothing heroic is undertaken. Is it any wonder, then, that we turn to celluloid heroes or the occasional corporate mavericks to become vicarious heroes ourselves?

Plainly, companies cannot invent heroes or create them with press releases. But they can reduce the countless barriers to individual heroism and encourage self-expression in service of both company and personal goals. Nobody can be a hero when everybody operates in the ''protect your ass'' mode in the cynical company. Organizations can breed and reinforce heroism in two ways: by celebrating heroes as role models and by creating organizational structures that liberate rather than constrain people and allow them to put their ideals into practice.

Fighting Cynicism Against the Odds

Cynicism and estrangement go hand in hand in the work force. They also coexist in the cynical company, where management seems to take actions contrary to the well-being of employees or the good of the commonweal. Part of this, we believe, has to do with the ways companies deal with today's economic climate. Short-term expeditiousness is one of the failings of American business practices vis-à-vis our offshore competitors. This shortcoming has been exacerbated in this era of global competition and twenty-four-hour money-market management. It is as though American companies have lost confidence in the future and fear that they're running out of time. Many companies are caught up in the takeover game; large corporations have spent more than $400 billion since 1980 to repurchase their own stock or buy out other firms. As a result, companies have enormous debts, have become preoccupied with short-term earnings, and have undertaken massive divestitures and layoffs—often at the expense of their products, brands, managers, employees, and the communities in which they do business.

Turnover among American executives has been more rapid than ever before—as if they're in revolving doors. The larger implication is that a great many working people conclude that their managers are only in for the short haul and only out for themselves. We see executives becoming even more self-interested in the megamerger boom today. As Paul Hirsch says, "Wall Street's advice to managers searching for excellence has been to tell them to become excellent at searching for new jobs."[14]

The auto giants have reduced their work force by over 25 percent in the past few years. AT&T has laid off over 25,000 workers, and twice as many have lost jobs in USX. The words of one GE employee whose plant was closed are becoming a familiar refrain: "I'm the third generation in my family to work at this plant. My grandfather said it, my father said it, and today I'm saying it: 'You just can't trust General Electric.'" This lad bespeaks the larger point: Whenever times are tough, it seems, people have simply come to expect that management will run scared and operate expeditiously.

Can American companies adopt a longer-term orientation to time and preserve employees' goodwill while managing downturns and pressures? In our studies, we find that many companies that have a long-term view of the future simply create the time necessary for planning and even dreaming. They also make time for celebrating achievements and for undertaking the rituals necessary for humanizing corporate life.

There are exemplars, too, of companies that cope with difficult times in a more evenhanded and upbeat fashion. We have seen how cynical companies facing economic trials will ravage the work force while retaining management posts and perks. But we also find other companies undertaking layoffs and cost reductions according to the principle of equality of sacrifice. At Polaroid, for example, people were given a realistic picture of the economic conditions facing the firm and were actively involved in decisions associated with staff and expense reductions. Everybody ultimately shared the pain by taking pay reductions.

One of the present authors worked on a corporate merger in which the two parties devised realistic-cum-idealistic principles to guide the merger. When cynical companies merge, there is often a bloodbath, with few winners and many losers. In the case of Unisys, however, emphasis was given to the creation of a partnership between people from the Burroughs and Sperry corporations and to meritocracy in restructuring the new corporation.

Creating an Upbeat Culture After a Merger. Wall Street scoffed at the deal. Industry analysts likened it to two male dinosaurs attempting to mate. The merger of Burroughs and Sperry corporations, then the third-largest in U.S. history and the largest hostile one, seemed doomed at the outset. W. Michael Blumenthal, chairman of Burroughs, had attempted to arrange a stock swap with Sperry shareholders in 1986. One year later, he put a "bear hug" on Sperry, incurring massive debt and doubt in the markets. He promised to retain Sperry's mainframe architecture in hopes of retaining customers, but the added costs in product development, service, and sales seemed ominous. Worse, Sperry's top management had resisted the bid and had $62 million in "golden parachutes" on hand as an incentive to jump ship. Prospects were dim for making this merger a success. One reason was that cynicism was at work in both firms.

From the outset, however, Blumenthal had a vision of the combined company. He believed that managers and employees from both sides, as well as investors and customers, would find it bold and credible. He wrote: "Great companies are built by people willing to make bold moves, who take events into their own hands and dare to act on their vision . . . we are in the vanguard of a movement that is sure to redirect the course of the computer industry."[15] Many corporate raiders in the 1980s have been transparent opportunists whose prime motivation has been to take the money and run. Blumenthal had been warned not to make an unfriendly bid because it would tarnish his reputation and send shock waves throughout the computer industry. But Blumenthal didn't see himself as a raider, nor did he believe that top talent would countenance hostile dealings and asset stripping. Thus he made the pitch that the combined company would have sufficient "critical mass" to compete with IBM in the mainframe market, and he promised to draw the best talent from both Burroughs and Sperry to build a new company that would have the product offerings and sales strength to survive the industry shakeout. The day the bid was made, Blumenthal announced that henceforth it would be a "Sperry/Burroughs Partnership."

Often CEOs make high-sounding promises that mergers will draw the best from both companies, and they try to smooth over anxieties by assuring people that nothing will change. Then they withdraw from the action and leave their vice-presidents, comptrollers, and assorted hatchet men to carve up a subsidiary. Studies show that nearly 70 percent of the executives in a target company leave after its takeover. Employees feel aggrieved and abandoned; their loyalty and esprit de corps are lost. Small wonder, then, that so many mergers prove to be financial failures.[16]

Blumenthal put a different scenario into motion. (See Exhibit 3 for a summary.) Right after the merger, he went on the stump, defending the logic behind the deal to customers, industry analysts, and employees throughout Burroughs and Sperry. He didn't soft-soap the bad news: The merger would require the sale of some assets and a reduction in the work force of up to 5 percent. But he did promise that the new company would be built in the spirit of partnership and draw upon the "best people" and "best organizations" from both companies. Then came the action.

Blumenthal formed a merger-coordination council, drawing top executives from both Burroughs and Sperry together, and appointed co-chairs to head task forces studying the ideal structure and operations of the new company. The council and task forces met for over six months, evaluating each company's business systems and talent and choosing the best or, in many instances, proposing new ways of doing things. Blumenthal

Exhibit 3. Success Factors in a "Surprisingly Sexy Computer Marriage."

The successful merger of Burroughs and Sperry corporations into Unisys was accomplished against all odds. Several factors contributed to the retention of top talent and the creation of a new and unifying Unisys culture.

A Rallying Point

Clear Vision: "Our alliance will help reinvigorate the industry's competitive and technological potential." The deal was defined as a "procompetitive merger," with plans to merge functions and operations and maintain distinct lines of computing architectures. People rallied behind the "Power of 2."

Partnership: "No winners and losers." Chairman Michael Blumenthal defined this as a Sperry/Burroughs partnership that would draw from the strengths of both companies. "Best person/Best organization." People were appointed to new posts, and organizational structures were chosen, on the basis of merit.

A New Culture: Blumenthal met with executives throughout the company to explain his beliefs about how the new company should operate and what it should stand for in the marketplace. Several months later, the company issued a statement of its values and guidelines for bringing the new culture to life.

Information and Support

Speechifying: Blumenthal went on the stump in both organizations, explaining the rationale behind the merger and rallying employees to the challenges ahead. He regularly met one-to-one with executives to discuss their concerns and career plans and personally "signed them up" to the new company.

Newsletters: The company issued regular merger updates to report on progress, highlight problems, and suggest ways for people to cope more effectively with merger stresses and strains.

Sensitization Seminars: A team of psychologists conducted seminars for executives so that they could understand and work with the anxiety and insecurity faced by people going through the transition. Other professionals offered individual counseling for employees.

Involvement

Coordination Council: Top executives from both companies joined in a merger-coordination council or participated in task forces to study the best way to put the organizations together and manage changes.

Name the Company: Employees were invited to name the new organization. For a time it was called NEWCO (New Company). The employee who dreamed up Unisys (United Systems) won a handsome cash prize.

Feedback: Employees were surveyed several months after the merger, to evaluate how integration was progressing and determine whether a Unisys way of doing things was emerging.

worked closely with these groups to ensure that the analyses were sound and that politics and horse-trading were kept to a minimum.

Frankly, many Burroughs executives were distressed at his role. As victors, they had anticipated reaping the spoils. Instead, they often found themselves in competition for top jobs with their Sperry counterparts. Sperry executives were initially mistrustful of the merger process. They figured it was just a show and that Blumenthal would ultimately protect his people and his company's way of doing things.

One of the present authors worked closely with Blumenthal and the coordination council to monitor people's reactions to the merger and help them cope with the attendant anxiety and stress. Training sessions were held for executives on managing people through the process, and many managers used the sessions to air their own frustrations and doubts. Gatherings were held where people on all the task forces could come together to report on their progress, compare notes, and openly talk about the problems they were encountering in reaching decisions. Several sessions focused on the differences between the two companies' cultures.

There were both substance and ceremony at these meetings. During one, Blumenthal arrived wearing a red baseball hat bearing the Sperry and Burroughs logos. The executives, all in power suits, were forced to wear these hats when they began to disparage one company or the other. At another meeting, Blumenthal reviewed his own personal background and work experiences. He told of how a falsehood in childhood—lying to his mother about going to the movies—had backfired. The point was that people had better be honest about how things were going in the business. He told of how cliques and petty politics had soured him on one company. The point was that gamesmanship wouldn't be tolerated in the new company. Finally, he launched an attack on the ''half-assed'' bureaucracy and red tape in Burroughs. His people took notice and so did those from Sperry. And when a couple of Administrative Sideliners and Articulate Players lost out on top jobs, the message took on new meaning.

Over the course of months, the Burroughs/Sperry partnership came into being. A *Fortune* article described it as a ''surprisingly sexy computer marriage.''[17] Earnings-per-share targets were met well ahead of schedule. Most Sperry executives traded in their parachutes and, according to insiders, very few top people from either company left for other jobs. The company was christened Unisys—one suggestion among more than ten thousand offered by employees who were invited to name the new company.

How did Blumenthal pull it off? He put his credibility on the line in making the deal and worked hard to make it work. He made hard decisions on divestitures, layoffs, executive appointments, the location of headquarters, and hundreds of other difficult judgment calls. Yet in doing so, he was sending a message to people in both companies about the kind of culture they would find at Unisys. Blumenthal was straightforward on what kind of culture it would be: ''You try to be open and honest and let it all hang out with your colleagues . . . try to have a team consensus . . . talk it out, with give and take, and with a minimum of instruction from on high.''

Countering the Cynics. In this instance, there was a constant risk of incurring the cynical fallout that attends so many mergers where bosses signal that it's all a numbers game and people only look out for themselves. When asked whether he feared losing his own credibility and the loyalty of people, Blumenthal commented on his managerial philosophy:

> I believe that an organization is a social structure that has a continuing life and soul of its own. People want a sense of belonging. The cynical, look out for yourself, approach is uncomfortable for a lot of people. . . . They don't want to apply it, they want to have a flag under which they fly. They want to be loyal to their organization. . . .
>
> There are industries where a bunch of people just come together for a while and, when the grass looks greener, they take off. . . . We have people here that are thirty-, forty-year people; we have an increasing number of people whose parents worked here, and in some cases a third generation of people.

When asked how he would justify the costs of the merger to his son—say, twenty years hence—he continued:

> I hope he's studying economics and understands that in a market economy adjustment to changing circumstances is the best guarantee of a rising standard of living. And that the failure to adjust is the best guarantee of a decline. . . .
>
> It's not just what you do, it's how you do it. You must pay attention to people and figure out a humane way to [make cuts], but you must do what is required because, in the market system, they will be absorbed in another job in which they add something.
>
> When I was an undergraduate in college I was a socialist. I thought government would be much better off making all these decisions and it would all be fair and just and the underdog would be protected. I have learned since that governments don't make those decisions very well and we're better off having bastards like Blumenthal make them if they make them fairly and humanely.

Will a new culture take hold at Unisys? The company is now run by a management board peopled by executives in their late thirties and early forties. Burroughs's style is evident in product development, but Sperry's is to be found in the sales organization. Other parts of the company are taking on a stamp different from that of either company. At an offsite meeting concluding the merger coordination effort, executives saw a slide show narrated by the evening's CAO (chief anthropological officer), telling the history of each of the two companies. Many of them presented mementos from their careers to the new company's archives. The final submission was a book bearing the signatures of each of them—it was their way of signing up to a new venture and committing themselves to a new company culture.

We cannot, however, point to many other optimistic examples that companies are coping effectively with the pressures

of Wall Street and the current wave of corporate restructuring.
The few efforts at regaining private ownership—whether through
leveraged buyouts by existing management or through the sale
of assets to employees—still result in heretofore unimagined corporate debt loads and consequent business perils. We think it
high time, however, that companies tell it like it is when the
outlook is pessimistic. This means that if companies must reduce
costs to compete or improve quality or levels of innovation, they
simply must take their case credibly to employees.

Isn't it hypocritical when executives complain they are
at the mercy of ''short-term Wall Street demands'' and then
fire their pension fund directors for not maximizing short-term
financial returns? Doesn't it seem disingenuous when companies
plead poverty in wage negotiations but won't open their books?
Isn't it selfish for management to cut back on benefits but then
pay eye-popping bonuses to one another, for fear of losing talent?
Doesn't it seem self-serving for companies to undertake layoffs
and plant closings without forewarning—all in the name of the
expedient that early notification would hurt productivity and
upset the work force? Surely there are more straightforward,
less cynical ways to handle hard times and market pressures,
ways that represent realistic idealism and address the upbeat
values of American working people.

11

Regaining Trust
and Restoring
Credibility

By failing to meet expectations and address discontent, companies can breed cynicism in the work force. This happened at Caterpillar Corporation in the late 1970s, when the compact between labor and management—good pay and security in exchange for hard and dedicated work—was broken. The United Auto Workers struck Cat, for the first time in its history, and the conflict centered on what negotiators called "noneconomic" issues. Management could neither define nor respond to the union's complaints over low morale and the loss of dignity felt by its membership. Nor could the union muster much energy to press its case. Less than half the work force bothered to participate in the strike vote, and picket lines were poorly staffed. It seemed as though this was a strike that no one even cared to win.

During this same period, productivity and profits declined in Cat, and Komatsu, a Japanese competitor, began making inroads into foreign and domestic markets. Cat's credit rating

231

dropped, and its premier lines of earthmovers, once the envy of the industry, revealed comparative design flaws and signs of shoddy workmanship.

Personnel managers knew there was a breakdown in the long-standing relationship of trust between employees and the company. At a special year-end meeting, they met and agreed that the "old rules" no longer worked at Caterpillar. Sharp distinctions between managers and nonmanagers were alienating many up-and-comers, who were choosing to leave Cat rather than bide their time for a promotion. Cat could no longer buy loyalty with a healthy paycheck. Blue-collar workers and clericals expected good pay and wanted more challenge on their jobs and more opportunities to express their ideas. They were also fed up with all the rules, orders, and sermons—what was collectively dubbed "all the crap"—that came from management. Instead, they wanted more say in decisions that affected them.

Like many other mature industrial companies, Cat faced the challenge of managing a changing work force. There were many new-breed workers in the company, and many more women and minorities, some seeking to move up into management. People at all levels took for granted their existing benefits and working conditions and were demanding more in the way of self-expression and participation in decisions. Cat's culture, style of leadership, and approach to industrial relations were out of step with these new expectations. Something new was playing in Peoria. We think it was cynicism at work.

Cat executives misread the signals and saw all the unrest as another sign that the work ethic was dead. They complained that they couldn't find "the kind of people they used to" and hoped to wait out the departure of troublemakers and misfits. The personnel representatives had another agenda: Cat needed to rethink its methods of managing people. Their ideas were not positioned as a "people program." On the contrary, they told top management that the company's needs to automate and reduce costs would *require* such a change. A new relationship would have to be forged with the union to meet competitive challenges. They thought they had made a strong "business case" for rebuilding trust in the company. Instead, the person-nel representatives were stigmatized as "choir boys" and, ac-cording to one, their chorus "fell on deaf ears."

In rebuttal, management issued a pamphlet to the public that complained about the lazy and careless workers coming into industry and recommended the use of more laborsaving equip-ment to fight offshore competition. The battle lines were drawn. Top management, out of touch with workers, their union, and even the personnel community, seemed entrenched and un-yielding.

Then a corporate hero stepped into the breach. Roger Kelly, a rock-ribbed Cat man, former official in the Ford admin-istration, and no-nonsense top executive with credibility among his peers, decided to see for himself what troubled Cat people around the world. Kelly toured plants and dealerships, offices and field service sites, talking with managers and workers, clericals and sales representatives, in groups and one-to-one. He got an earful. Reports came from plant managers that the company was building "paper tractors" at the expense of prod-uct innovation. Finance seemed to dominate every decision in the company. Quality control was an afterthought, rather than something that was built in. Top managers were characterized as aristocrats grown smug with unquestioned authority and fat from all the perks of their jobs.

It was one thing for top management to hear hints of this criticism from personnel representatives. To hear it bluntly and boldly from one of their own threw down the gauntlet. Aristo-cratic or not, top management proved to be pragmatic and per-suadable. In light of the company's needs and Kelly's urgings, they gave the go-ahead to formulate a new human resource strategy for the next decade.

Fixing the Machine

Exhibit 4 summarizes Cat's innovative efforts to identify peo-ple's expectations and formulate a new strategy for meeting them.[1] It details, in earthmoving imagery, the phases of a

Exhibit 4. Rebuilding Trust at Caterpillar.

Caterpillar Corporation, a multibillion-dollar manufacturer of earthmoving equipment, undertook a corporate-wide human resource strategy conference in 1980 to understand the changing expectations of its work force and redirect its approach to meeting them. The phases of the program were as follows:

I. The Lay of the Land. A number of factors led Cat management to rethink its approach to managing people, including a strike by the United Auto Workers, rising disaffection in the work force, and pressing business problems.

II. Natural Obstacles. Still, there was resistance to a new human resource emphasis in the company. Personnel representatives' reports that the old rules no longer worked at Caterpillar "fell on deaf ears."

III. Surveying the Terrain. Their words did get the attention of one Cat officer, who met with employees at all levels all over the world. He heard the same message and had the credibility to awaken top management.

IV. The Right Vehicle for the Job. Cat had previously undertaken strategy conferences to plan the modernization of its factories and services. This approach was adopted to study human resource needs and develop strategies of change for the company. The study was organized in six modules.

V. The Straight and Narrow Road. The first five modules focused on traditional human resource issues, including a study of Cat's labor force in the next decade and future requirements for education, training, recruiting, staffing, and placement. Management teams in each module read technical reports, consulted with experts, and developed action plans.

VI. Moving Earth. Module 6 defined the expectations of Cat employees and those of the company, and ways that they could be integrated. Subcommittees interviewed and surveyed diverse groups of people. All told, over five thousand Cat employees were involved in fact-finding in this module.

VII. Backfilling. The study began to outpace the organization's ability to digest it. The roster of recommendations was pared down to specific proposals for improving communication, equal opportunity, and employee involvement in decision making. Position papers were prepared to show how actions in these areas could meet both employee and company needs.

VIII. The New Road. Many of the recommendations were supported by top management and implemented by the line organization. One plant established a two-way communication system to inform employees about new products and developments and gain their input. Another undertook human relations training for supervisors. Still another involved workers in redesign of the production system. Cat traveled a bumpy road the next few years, but the company has regained business momentum and, most important, gone a long way toward regaining the trust and commitment of its once disaffected employees.

worldwide human resource strategy conference whose recommendations are still being implemented today. A task force of line and personnel managers organized the conference, which followed, in the early stages, the straight and narrow road.

The first five modules of the conference focused on the composition of Cat's work force in the next decade, competition in the labor market, and educational trends. Age profiles showed that Cat would have too many older workers and too few younger ones to staff plants adequately. Accordingly, suggestions were proposed for developing early retirement plans and energetically recruiting and training younger workers. Plans for hiring and placing computer technicians, needed in large numbers, were developed. A need for university-based training for managers was also dealt with. All the recommendations from these first modules were sound, supported by extensive data, and linked with distinct organizational needs. They were consistent with Cat's traditional definition of human resource management and were ratified without much debate.

Module 6, by contrast, was aimed, metaphorically, at moving some earth. It was commissioned to delve into the expectations of the work force and to propose strategies for meeting them. Bill Dronan, a corporate personnel executive, took a gamble in designing and leading this module. He knew that a thorough study of people's attitudes would surely put a spotlight on disaffection in the ranks and might put top management on the defensive. Anything less, however, would make the company appear disingenuous. He was also worried that the study would stir up expectations and further erode trust if nothing substantive followed. Nevertheless, he was committed to breaking new ground and co-opted resistant colleagues by making them part of the study.

This module differed from previous ones in several respects. First, subcommittees were formed to study the expectations of blue-collar workers, first-line managers and professionals, computer operators, and people employed at smaller facilities and dealerships. These groups were the most disaffected at Caterpillar. Special studies were undertaken to investigate the needs of women and minorities and those of handicapped employees. Dronan reasoned that this effort would highlight discrepancies between Cat's equal employment policies and the realities that people experienced on the job.

Second, the subcommittees investigated expectations directly by asking employees what they wanted out of a job and what they looked for from the company. Committee members queried over five thousand people throughout the company through interviews, surveys, and focus group discussions. One of the authors worked with these subcommittees to interpret the findings and formulate recommendations.

The overall conclusion was that many unmet expectations could be traced to management's failure to communicate with workers, to offer them sufficient challenge and participation in decisions, and to treat them as individuals. The company was simply not asking enough of its people. This module broadened the scope of the study—increasing its potential and increasing its threat. Top management sent signals that too many people, too much time, and too much hullabaloo were involved. To counter this attitude, the conference organizers explained how meeting people's expectations would serve the interests of employees and the company.

After heated debate, and some enlightenment, Cat's top management approved many of the recommendations and incorporated them into the company's operating plan. Attitude surveys were undertaken to evaluate progress in implementing them. Human relations training was begun, in hopes of improving two-way communication in the offices and on shop floors. A cooperative labor–management program was initiated so that teams of workers and managers could diagnose work-related problems and fix them. Finally, Cat's top management went on record with a statement: They were committed to integrating the needs of people and the organization.

Not everything came up roses. Top management backtracked on the proposal to have broad participation in the new communication and problem-solving efforts. Efforts to increase face-to-face communication and employees' participation in decisions were left to local management. Some plant managers moved ahead vigorously—introducing suggestion programs and holding multilevel meetings, creating teams to plan and implement technological changes, and in other ways involving people more fully in the firm's operations. Other managers, however, made a few cosmetic changes and ran their operations pretty much as usual.

For a time, Cat's profitability continued to decline; again the company was struck by UAW; and massive layoffs, along with more automation, seemed to betray the intent of the human resource conference. "Developing and approving strategies is easier than implementing them," noted one Cat insider. By 1988, however, things were getting back on track at Cat. Productivity and profitability were on the rise, and signs of disaffection and discontent were declining. The compact has been repaired, and trust is being regained.

Managing Expectations—Preventive Medicine

Earlier we saw how the cynical company plays on the expectations of people by inflating their hopes and then preys on their lack of job mobility. To be fair, Caterpillar never systematically oversold the company to employees. It didn't have to: Decades of providing people with rising wages, secure work, generous benefits, and a chance to get ahead made Cat a model employer in Peoria and elsewhere. Nor do we suggest that Cat people were exploited or locked in to otherwise depressing jobs. Our point is that Caterpillar simply did not keep up with the times. Changes sweeping the country ultimately swept into Caterpillar, and management was, in our view, unaware of their implications.

What can be learned from Cat's efforts to regain the trust of its work force? First, management found employees ready and able to talk cogently about their expectations, as well as about the needs of the business. It was initially feared that employees would have a "wish list" completely divorced from the competitive realities facing the firm—or, worse, that employees would expect the company to meet all their needs once they had aired them. Instead, management found that most people had reasonable expectations and appreciated the chance to talk about themselves, their aspirations, and their views of the company.

Second, the way the study was organized lent credence and respect to the diversity in the Cat work force. A widespread concern that focusing on the expectations of subgroups of employees would prove divisive and lead to "interest group" lobbying proved unfounded. Instead, management discovered that employees had a broad common agenda and that, for the most part, the special needs of subgroups did not conflict with common aims.

Third, the way the study was conducted enabled large numbers of people to be involved in a company-wide assessment of expectations and to participate in developing a broad-based action agenda. This made the process visible and credible and made the company's intent clear to its employees. Furthermore, the overall emphasis was on fact finding rather than on flank protection, on understanding rather than on posturing, on open two-way exchange rather than on directives from management.

There is much to learn about follow-through here as well. The case affirms that any company-wide effort to address people's concerns is limited by the vision of key executives, and that recommendations for change must take account of unique cultural factors within a firm. Cat's culture is not free and funky like Ben & Jerry's, and its record of success was as much a bane to massive change as a merger had proved a boon to transformation at Unisys. The case also shows that financially driven and bureaucratically dominated organizations, even when facing performance problems, resist making fundamental changes that threaten to upset the balance of power or go against vested interests. The Cat case really illustrates how tough it is to rebuild trust in a corporation.

Lest we concentrate on the problems of meeting expectations and restoring goodwill in companies, we must point out that many in Cat have a new orientation to people and, more broadly, that the human resource conference mobilized the interest, attention, and energy of a big corporation to the importance of understanding expectations and then meeting them. This kind of mobilization is an antidote to cynicism.

It is, of course, always hard to change existing attitudes and to redefine a long-standing company culture. We believe that companies can take steps to prevent the discontent experienced at Caterpillar by inoculating employees as they enter the work force with what we have termed realistic idealism. This means giving people a realistic picture of what they can and cannot expect of the company and what is expected of them. The most effective way to ensure that people have realistic expectations is to tell them the truth.

Give People a Realistic Job Preview. The development of realistic expectations starts when people are hired. Several studies have shown that there are benefits to giving people a realistic preview of their jobs. In one study, a local telephone company was experiencing low morale and high turnover among operators.[2] Its recruiting pitch included a color film showing operators handling emrgency phone calls, chatting away with interesting and sexy-sounding callers, and using the latest technology. In practice, however, operators were required to turn emergencies over to their supervisors; their calls were monitored and time-limited; and their equipment was cumbersome and dated.

An obvious solution was to redesign the jobs, give operators more discretion, and modernize the equipment—a solution implemented in other parts of the phone company. In this case, however, such efforts were not feasible. So management decided to give recruits a realistic picture of the job—its advantages and disadvantages. Current employees prepared the orientation film, realistically depicting the tedium and pacing of the work, along with its attendant responsibilities and the chance it gave operators to serve the calling public. Information about pay, job security, camaraderie, and working conditions was presented openly, and recruits had the chance to talk with veterans about what life would be like on the job. The phone company discovered that the educational level of new hires dropped in the months that followed. But their performance exceeded expectations, and turnover was reduced significantly. There is little doubt that self-selectivity was operating among job applicants, but we think that's an example of realistic idealism in practice. Realistic job previews let employees know what they can expect. Interviews need not be downbeat, but neither should they misrepresent opportunities and working conditions. Certainly they can enable applicants to select companies that match their interests.

What can be done to keep veteran employees' expectations in line with reality? Studies suggest that most people adjust their expectations in time and develop a more reasonable
picture of their prospects.³ To ensure that they have an informed
picture, several companies we know of regularly post information on rates of promotion and publish statistics on the effectiveness of their job-posting programs. This gives people a clear
picture of opportunities and helps them to formulate realistic
career plans.

   Make People Responsible for Their Work Environment. In
keeping with the theme of informed realism, many companies
are also relegating some of management's day-to-day responsibilities to their employees. In traditional organizations, basic
decisions about pay, benefits, and promotions, not to mention
work hours, job assignments, and performance standards, are
solely the responsibility of management. This sharp division of
responsibility reinforces the old compact that the company provides and the employee works. The truth of the matter is that
companies cannot or will not provide as much today, and working people have the intelligence and interest to take more responsibility for managing their own working conditions.

   As an example, several U.S. manufacturing plants have
initiated "skill-based pay," whereby people are compensated
for learning specific job skills. It's up to employees to regulate
their pay within the confines of an overall plan. As workers acquire more skills in the operations of, say, a factory, their base
pay increases. This in turn ensures companies a more flexible
work force. This new compact gives working people more control over their rewards and the chance to see their training pay
off.

   One corporation with which we have worked has the
motto of obtaining "extraordinary results from ordinary people." Here employees negotiate their personal and professional
goals with supervisors and are given budgets and resources to
reach them as a matter of course. Employees have a say-so in
selecting their supervisors, in designing their jobs, even in making decisions about corporate pay and benefit policies. They are
also offered regular counseling on their career development—

inside the corporation and by external specialists—and are actually encouraged to pursue outside opportunities when those better fit their needs. This company practices realistic idealism at its best. High rates of productivity and low rates of turnover show how these practices pay off.

There is always a risk that delegating such responsibilities will backfire and that people will, in a cynical fashion, take advantage of a company. What can be done to channel ambitious employees' efforts toward mutually valued rather than self-serving ends?

Channel Ambition to Desirable and Ethical Ends. There are so many opportunities for unethical conduct in companies today that special efforts are needed to ensure that all employees, beginners and veterans alike, internalize corporate standards of morality. Kenneth Goodpaster, an instructor at the Harvard Business School, knows the story. He reflects on his own efforts to enlighten managers about the necessities of corporate ethics: "There was a certain cynicism that said, 'What good will philosophy do when everyone knows the bottom line is profit? Why bother putting a veneer over that, when in fact the driving impulse is going to be amoral if not immoral?'"[4] The chairman of Chemical Bank has given the special effort it takes to ensure that his company's commitment to ethics is perceived as more than just veneer. He personally drafted the bank's statement of corporate ethics and met with employees all over the world to reinforce its importance. Surveys at Chemical Bank show that people are today more sensitive to shady practices and that the company means business when it promises to enforce its ethical code.

We want to emphasize, however, that upbeat companies also take steps to teach younger managers and workers the values of corporate citizenship. Kathy Kram has studied several companies where managerial trainees are assigned senior mentors, who not only groom them for advancement but also socialize them in corporate ideals.[5] Her research shows that these role models take seriously their responsibilities to prepare a new generation of ethical and upbeat executives. Furthermore, the management trainees, in the eyes of their peers, seem to emulate their role models. Other companies sponsor training seminars, where managers are challenged to work through case studies and simulations involving ethical dilemmas. The point is this: Companies *can* take steps to inculcate responsible conduct in their people. In this way, the ''driving impulse'' toward profitability is informed by higher ideals.

Modulating expectations, delegating responsibility, and channeling ambition are three ways that companies can manage the expectations of the new work force and leaven its cynical predispositions. The next task is, of course, to deliver on people's realistic expectations and to be *seen* to do so—even by doubting Thomases.

Four Cynical Perceptions and How to Turn Them Around

What is behind the ostensible erosion of the traditional work ethic and the loss of commitment in the American work force? Demographic and value changes are only part of the story. Within seemingly benign corporations, there are many commonplace practices that deeply disillusion working people and breed cynicism. It is clear, for example, that promises of generous benefits, frequent performance reviews, and bright career opportunities, while initially motivating, breed cynicism when these very benefits are reduced by corporate fiat, reviews become perfunctory, and career planning gets pushed off to a more profitable quarter. The sense of disillusionment is increased by unresponsive hierarchies that promote a class system and by nonparticipatory decision making that makes it plain who really counts in a firm.

There are, however, four specific aspects of company life that, according to national surveys, not only disappoint people but also disillusion them. Let us see, then, which company practices convince people that management is taking advantage of them, that business is marked by *mano a mano* conflicts, and that corporations are inherently unfair and unresponsive to human needs. In these practices, we see cynicism starkly at work.

Complaint 1: The Pay System Is Rigged

Polls show there is a widespread belief among working people that hard work and commitment are simply not rewarded by American companies. Some 75 percent of the work force believe that what employees are paid has very little to do with the quality and amount of effort they put into their work.[6] Furthermore, people are not getting anything like the recognition they expect for doing their jobs well, but they hear about it when they perform poorly.

If people's expectations of reward for hard work are being frustrated in industry today, who profits from their efforts? Polls show that nearly 50 percent of the American working population believe that their companies profit from their hard work.[7] For these employees, it's the same old disillusioning story: Management is taking advantage of the workers, whipping up motivation, introducing new equipment, and then hoarding the fruits of success.

Even more striking is the finding from a Gallup poll conducted for the Chamber of Commerce in 1980, which found that only 9 percent of jobholders believed they would be the primary beneficiaries of improvements in their companies' productivity.[8] The rest saw the benefits going to the managers, stockholders, and consumers. It is worth noting that these results stand in sharp contrast to those found in a recent study of Japanese workers. In Japan, 93 percent of the jobholders believed they would benefit from improvements in their employer's profitability.

Solution: Make It Fair and Make It Public. One obvious means of countering employees' perceptions that hard work doesn't pay off is to institute a merit pay plan. Many firms have done so, but with very mixed results. A poll of *Psychology Today* readers, arguably a rather upscale sample, found that almost half expressed suspicion over the secretive and authoritarian ways companies manage their compensation systems.[9]

These and other data show that a substantial segment of the American work force believes that the reward system in companies is rigged: People say that promises of pay increases for good performance are fallacious, that chances for a promotion hinge on politics and the right connections, that wages and salaries are worth less than the value of their output, and that everybody seems to benefit from their hard work but themselves. What feeds cynicism further is that so many of them work in companies that preach meritocracy. It seems hypocritical to them.

Companies that preach they offer rewards on the basis of merit have to practice it. We think it prudent, then, that companies have their merit pay and promotion systems audited in some fashion. We know of companies, for example, that had these systems reviewed by independent consulting firms. These consultants then tell management the extent to which pay and promotion decisions truly reflect meritorious performance. In our own studies, we have surveyed employees on these counts and reported the results throughout the corporation. We have also worked with corporate compensation committees, composed of managers and employees, that regularly review merit pay and promotion practices.

Of course, cynics will suspect that something is being manipulated behind their backs. To counter this belief, management systems have to be open. Edward Lawler proposes, for example, that companies adopt open pay systems—wherein rates, steps, and grades are made public to employees.[10] Interestingly, Lawler finds that people overestimate what their peers are making until the rates are made public. Clearly, then, management has to convince the cynics—through substance, not rhetoric—that the game is fair.

Companies that undercompensate employees buy high turnover, shoddy work and service, and cynicism. Lawler proposes three further solutions to the mismanagement of pay systems he finds so commonplace in corporations today:

1. In addition to publishing pay rates, publish the results of industry and area salary surveys. That way, people can judge for themselves whether their pay is fair in comparison with what other firms pay.

2. Involve employees in setting compensation levels, rates of pay increase, and general pay administration. Certainly in unionized organizations these matters are subject to collective bargaining, but only insofar as the rank and file are concerned. Employees should be involved in setting the compensation rates of both employees and management. A participative process produces a credible and motivating pay system for all concerned.
3. Make public the individual rates of pay, as well as information on all bonuses. Though this idea may not sit well with employees who regard their pay as a private matter, it buys motivation when pay rates are fair.

Furthermore, we see merit in establishing gain-sharing or profit-sharing systems in corporations. The former reward employees according to gains in productivity or cost savings; the latter give them a share of corporate profits. The corporate ideal concerns equality of benefits, as well as equality of sacrifice, on the basis of company performance.

Complaint 2: Management Can't Be Trusted

There is disconcerting evidence that a large proportion of working people simply do not believe what management tells them. We see this as stark evidence of cynicism in the work force and corroborate this trend with our own data on people's attitudes about the evenhandedness and trustworthiness of management.

No doubt, there are cold and callous companies and manipulative and selfish managers. But the general perception that management cannot be trusted, we believe, transcends individual managers and companies. It is a story that has great currency throughout today's work force. To an extent, this defines the cynical national atmosphere and the cynical corporate culture. But the fallout infects basic attitudes and outlooks in an organization, and it feeds the cynical outlook.

The cynical drums beat in a new generation of self-help books and periodicals that counsel people on surviving company takeovers, restructuring efforts, and the threat of layoffs. The keys seem to be personal positioning, posturing, and making the right power play. The guides also counsel to keep your résumé current, maintain contact with headhunters, stay connected to a job network, and, above all, always look out for yourself.

In the teeth of all this received wisdom, can companies regain employees' trust and commitment? Trends are working against them. One million managers were fired or asked to retire early in the 1980s. Today's top CEOs say unremittingly that these practices will increase as global competition gets rougher and expediency becomes even more a way of corporate life.

Solution: Make Hard Truths Testable. Joe Henson, then CEO of Prime Computer, made an error from which few CEOs could ever recover. After Prime's acquisition of ComputerVision through a takeover, Henson stated that staff reductions would be handled through "normal attrition." After a detailed analysis of ComputerVision's operating results, however, he had to face the harsh truth: To make the combination work would require eliminating 5 percent of positions in the company.

Prime had never had a layoff and, frankly, Prime people expected that any work-force reductions would come from ComputerVision. Henson, by contrast, wanted reductions to be based on merit. When he recognized that layoffs were required, he issued a press release and went on the stump in both companies, taking full responsibility for his mistaken promise and insisting that both sides would bear the pain. He and his top managers personally reviewed rosters of proposed staff reductions from both companies to ensure that performance, not politics, was guiding layoff decisions. Several placement centers were established to help find people jobs within Prime or, if necessary, with area employers. A generous severance agreement was formulated, and its terms were published to employees. Job posting and outside hiring were suspended, to ensure that people whose jobs had been eliminated had first crack at any openings.

Two manufacturing vice-presidents, Mel Friedman and Cathy Kote, took the lead in handling layoffs in their areas. Both met with groups of employees to address their concerns and grievances openly. The financial rationale for the layoffs, as well as statistics on the numbers of people and positions affected, was presented to employees. Both managers faced the firing line and refused to delegate the transmission of bad news to their subordinates.

A task force, staffed by employees from throughout the company, was charged with monitoring the progress of the merger and handling staff reductions. One of the present authors worked with this task force, whose reports were circulated in the company and communicated to Henson directly in a briefing. Prime had ''lost its innocence,'' noted one task force member; others said the company could never count on people's loyalty again. A subsequent takeover bid for Prime has shaken trust and confidence even more.

People are skeptical at Prime. But Henson and his successor, Hane, told the truth and told it directly to people. They have published information that will allow all to judge whether the reductions, painful but necessary, are fair. And management continues to take its case to Prime people in the face of trial— when the expedient thing to do is to keep quiet and act ruthlessly.

Complaint 3: The Company Doesn't Care

Many people told us flat out that their companies didn't give a damn about everyday working people or the communities in which they did business. All the layoffs and plant closings—not to mention unhealthy working conditions and environmental pollution—contribute to this perception. But we also believe that this perception about management can be traced squarely to the ways companies have been traditionally managed. The old saw that the business of business is business dominates the mindset of many managers. Human relations and concern for the commonweal are given short shrift or neglected altogether.

We have seen the cynical fallout: Many people in our survey find the business world cold and impersonal today. Harris polls in the 1980s show a sharp decline in people's ratings of business's efforts to keep the environment clean and contribute to the well-being of communities. Ratings of its success in providing steady work for employees have dropped 34 points. And 80 percent of the populace believes that companies do not pay their fair share of taxes.

At the same time, surveys show that most people find their immediate supervisors honest, likable, and concerned about them as individuals.[11] Between the abstraction of the faceless company and the flesh-and-blood presence of a caring boss, however, lies the group known as "management." It is this collective entity that everyday working people deem callous and indifferent. This perception is magnified when management is generally invisible, routinely absorbed in life at the top, and seemingly uninterested in the day-to-day concerns of people in an office or plant. This isolation builds a wall between management and employees and can be devastating to the sense of community in the workplace.

Solution: Bring Community to the Workplace. There are distinct ways that companies can promote a sense of community within the enterprise. More egalitarian practices are one example. Upbeat companies are getting rid of executive parking places, private dining rooms, and limited stock options. Instead, they host company-wide gatherings, provide communal eating facilities, and promote employees' stock ownership.

Such practices put everyone on a common footing. This in turn reinforces upbeat attitudes and helps quiet the cynics, who will have fewer grievances to rail against and must avoid getting too far out of step with their peers. To take a somewhat different approach to building community, such firms as Johnson & Johnson put their corporate ideals into practice through health-improvement programs that include physical exercise and regular paid checkups for employees. Company health facilities are another way of bringing community to the workplace.

Several companies have created community liaison offices to work with leaders of civic and nonprofit groups in planning new facilities or handling plant closings. Ombudsmen regularly hear the complaints of community groups. All this sends a message that the company is responsive to community interests. Bank of America goes so far as to issue a "social audit," describing the company's investments in community, civic, and charitable activities, and evaluates its compliance with environmental and equal employment legislation. Bank of America's branch managers are charged with contributing to community groups in their geographical areas by, say, building and maintaining parks or day-care facilities. Their performance in this respect is evaluated and used in salary and promotion decisions.

Polaroid goes even farther in connecting the company with the community. Teams of workers contribute to decisions about the corporation's charitable giving and, in effect, adopt community groups in overseeing company philanthropy. Often they lend their own technical and managerial expertise to these groups and contribute their own money to them. Interestingly, Polaroid employees regard this as a perk, rather than a burden, and take pride in knowing that their company cares about people.[12]

Complaint 4: Time Is at a Premium

In many company cultures, so-called productive time is an obsession. People are not supposed to have time to talk or socialize with one another or to join in lunchtime or after-work bull sessions. For those living for the moment, digital watches add precision to the management of time, as do day-by-day planning guides, minute-to-minute appointment schedules, and the like. Taking time for people simply takes time away from everyone's busy schedule—and having a "busy schedule" is a mark of success.

In our view, much of this preoccupation with time is a reflection of people's heightened sense of self-interest and self-importance. Many executives use time today, much as they use money, for instrumental purposes. It buys them more analysis and meetings, more contacts and information, more persuading and selling. Even people's leisure time is compressed into more exciting vacations and more action-packed recreation. All this fixation on time limitations has its costs, of course, including personal stress, not to mention feelings of being in a rat race and simply being overwhelmed by the lack of time to get anything done properly.

Can Americans adopt a less obsessive orientation to time? Plainly, our culture discounts the inevitability of aging and slowing down, devalues patience, and, to a degree, undervalues persistence. We see no evidence, then, that Americans will embrace a longer-term outlook without feeling guilty. The live-for-the-moment mentality is here to stay. Even so, within the confines of present time there are ways that companies can put time into the service of corporate ideals.

Solution: Give People More Control over Their Time. Some leading companies—IBM and Xerox, for example—provide executives with time off to pursue worthy volunteer pursuits. Executives on sabbatical can be found teaching at community colleges and providing leadership to charitable organizations. Many more have at least adopted flextime to allow people to formulate their own work schedules. In this way, people can use time to assert their independence, control their own pace, and meet their personal and domestic priorities.

Many companies face the twin challenges of meeting baby boomers' insistent demands for independence and working parents' desires for more flexibility and control over their work schedules. Some younger Americans, for example, are choosing to work at night and to use their days for recreation, playing with their children, or socializing with friends. In the same way, more people are working at home or adopting four-day rather than five-day work schedules. Time has become a medium for self-assertion, and we think that time should become an essential component of the corporate reward system.[13]

The managerial implications of this notion are enormous. Time can be a reward assuming many forms. It opens up the possibility of job sharing for two-career couples with children, of desirable part-time work, and of providing people with longer holidays and shorter work weeks producing temporal instead of financial rewards. Our point is this: Responding to these values in the new work force means changing basic patterns of management but promises a rich payoff for both companies and employees.

Restoring Credibility

Cradle-to-grave employment is gone in most companies. In this era of downsizing, wage givebacks, benefit cutbacks, and general belt tightening, companies cannot and will not provide all that they once did for employees. When seeming entitlements are canceled, cynicism is the result. And many companies compound the problem by losing the confidence of the work force. Graphic Controls, a Buffalo manufacturer with which one of the present authors has worked, was at risk of losing the confidence of its people after a series of unforeseen developments in the business. The company, a thousand-person manufacturing firm, had had a record of success from its founding at the turn of the century through the 1970s. Then its acquisition by a conglomerate and a downturn in the market caused some top executives to leave the company and left its progressive orientation in doubt. How GC won its people back is a lesson in restoring credibility in the climate of current times.

GC's Commitment. From 1920 through 1950, GC was known as a fine and decent employer, nonunionized, whose culture was marked by high-minded paternalism. Employees were regarded as family and frequently joined the founder at his home for summer picnics and seasonal outings. In the 1950s, control of the company was passed to the founder's eldest son, who began to institute many progressive management practices. Employees were given and sold shares of stock and met yearly, in the cafeteria, for a boisterous shareholders' meeting. Benefits were expanded to cover health care and longer vacations—well ahead of the trend in larger corporations. The company became a leader in civic and community affairs, and its employees were enthuasiastic members of a social club.

In the mid 1960s, shortly after the company went public, it experienced a significant business downturn. A new CEO, a younger son of the founder, was appointed, in hopes of renewing the organization. This man, William Clarkson, had been characterized as extremely tough, intellectually aggressive, and personally insensitive as the head of the company's main operating division. As he assumed the top leadership post, however, he saw a need to change his management style.

Clarkson himself participated in sensitivity training in the early 1970s—a T-group for company presidents. He described the training as "hellish" but came away committed to changing his own behavior. Comments from peers had taught him the adverse consequences of his tough, dominating, and insensitive managerial manner. Next he invited a few behavioral scientists to meet with him and other top managers, to educate them about new management philosophies and models. His managers confided personal dreams about the company's future and their own. Subsequently, they decided to operate as a corporate management team oriented to consensus-style decision making. Everyone was encouraged to comment on everyone else's function.

In the late 1970s, a task force of managers and hourly personnel was formed to study problems in the company's compensation system and recommend a new plan. The task force, working with a consultant, prepared a survey on employees' views of their pay and other aspects of work in the firm. The results were used to develop a new compensation package. The data indicated, however, that the company's progressive practices were not reaching the hourly work force. Accordingly, Clarkson and his team composed a statement of its commitment to quality of work life, undertook an audit of work life in the company, and published the results to stockholders and employees (Exhibit 5).

This began what has become a biennial study of work life in the company.[14] The initial study included an attitude survey measuring employee satisfaction, jobs, supervision, work groups, and people's views of management's trustworthiness and fairness, as well as an audit of the firm's personnel records. The results showed that satisfaction with benefits increased from 69 percent to 90 percent following the introduction of a new benefit plan designed by employees. The great majority of GC workers reported satisfaction with their pay, jobs, and working conditions and saw management as fair and committed to people's well-being—and over 90 percent said they were loyal to the organization.

Significantly, nearly all employees participated in the surveys and strongly supported the overall quality-of-work-life program. Comparisons with other surveys showed that GC workers had more satisfaction with their pay, benefits, and

What is the Managerial Task? Peter Drucker says that there are three different kinds of work that the Chief Executive Officer should be sure of doing effectively:

1.   The Operating Task, which produces the results of today's business;
2.   The Innovative Task, which creates the company's tomorrow; and
3.   The Top Management Task, which directs, gives vision, and sets the course for the business of both today and tomorrow.

The first one, the Operating Task, has to do with today and yesterday, and the tangible results of the organization. In Graphic Controls, as in most companies, we measure these results with painstaking accuracy and at high cost. This provides us a clear and accurate historical financial measurement of where the corporation has gone.

Now for the other two, the Innovative and Top Management Tasks . . . these relate to the results of tomorrow and to people. What measuring methods do we have to let us know where we stand and how we are doing on these tasks? On the assumption that we have capable people who want to make a contribution to the organization . . . regular Quality of Work Life Audits provide us an important measurement. They tell us how we are doing with the people in our organization in terms of providing them with the motivation, hygiene, and environmental factors that enable them to work effectively. . . .

Psychological research tells us that a key human need is to know where one stands and how one rates. A good manager has measurements for key areas of the business. A Quality of Work Life Audit provides valid data for one of the cornerstones that makes a business successful—its human resources. It provides data about the organizational climate that lets managers and employees know how they and the organization are performing today and are probably going to be performing in the days ahead.

As with audited financial information, it is important to let others, outside of the organization, know how we are doing. Publishing the results of the Quality of Work Life Audit demonstrates to stockholders, potential employees, customers, and suppliers the credibility of management's frequently used statement that "our people are our most important asset."

These are the reasons we started the audits and continue them. It is of vital importance to know where we stand with the people of our organization.

working conditions than those in other companies. They also had many more chances to participate in decisions, and they found management far more trustworthy and evenhanded. Interestingly, investors too endorsed the idea of auditing the quality of work life. More than 80 percent reported satisfaction with the issuance of a quality-of-work life report, and two-thirds said that other companies should issue them as well.

The survey results were reported to groups of employees, who used them to discuss the data, define problems, and undertake new programs to address them. This feedback process helped to stimulate the formation of quality circles in several areas of the company. One plant converted its traditional work system to a design whereby employees could build the product from its beginning through inspection. All this was stimulated by data showing that many employees lacked challenge in their jobs and involvement in decisions in their work areas.

Surveys also showed there to be misunderstanding and conflict between men and women in the company. Accordingly, an education and consciousness-raising program was developed to promote understanding between the sexes. Data on affirmative action were publicly reported in the organization.

A Challenge to Work Life at GC. In the late 1970s, the firm was acquired by a conglomerate many times its size. The acquirer was characterized as more traditional in its management style and put a stronger emphasis on short-term return on investment. Plainly, there was a clash of cultures between the firms. As so often happens in such acquisitions, Clarkson retired some time after the sale. A new man, an insider, took the helm. This was a time of big change in the company.

Before long, the company issued an "updated" statement of its beliefs and values. The old value statement had been based on the CEO's abiding belief in people and emphasized personal openness and teamwork as keys to the company culture. This new value statement addressed people, but also customers, innovation, products, strategy, the company's profit objectives, and the security of its work force. It read, frankly, like many another declaration of company philosophy in fashion today.

Of course, the key to relevance lies in the style of implementation. Back in the 1960s, the company's original values had been internalized by management in team-building exercises and infused into the organization through participative management. These new values, by contrast, were developed in a series of position papers by top management and a new

CEO. They were then communicated to the work force in a glossy brochure.

The new CEO had a different outlook on managing people and running the business. Through a series of management meetings and videotaped presentations to employees, he criticized the time wasted by excessive participation and argued that a heavy reliance on task forces blurred individual responsibility. Memos were issued: The company had become "lean and mean" in the face of business challenges, and staff reductions were undertaken in line with new strategic directions.

In the months that followed, top management meetings became more crisp and businesslike. There were fewer discussions of company philosophy and managers' own effectiveness. It was left to division heads to develop their own management structures and manage their people in the way they saw fit. Divisions were reorganized to redirect the company away from its emphasis on product toward a market orientation. A special division charged with new-product development was created. All this was consistent with the new company strategy: to defend its position in mature markets and to prospect in new ones.

How did GC workers view the changes? Survey data show that people had less favorable views about work life in the company and were losing confidence in the new leadership. Nearly half the work force reported that participative management was being sacrificed by the new regime and that the human organization was suffering. They found the company to be more interested in profits than in people. It was not practicing what its philosophy statement preached, they said.

No doubt, pressures from the parent company, a more competitive marketplace, and his own preference for no-nonsense management led the new CEO to believe that the company had to become business-directed and results-oriented. He was stunned, however, to learn that people were put off by the new emphasis in the company. Not only that, employees were losing confidence in his leadership and the company's capacities to succeed. Cynicism was creeping into GC.

Turning It Around. The CEO and his team decided on a bold course. They had been chafing under their parent company's control and felt personally aggrieved at losing the support and confidence of so many employees. In a dramatic move, they undertook a leveraged buyout and repurchased their company. To signal that they wanted everyone to be part of the "new" GC, they made generous stock-option grants and instituted a profit-sharing plan for all employees.

By 1987, participatory management was back at GC. Fully 60 percent of the work force formally participate in team decision making or company-wide task forces and, of these, nearly 80 percent believe their time is well spent. Employees report that the work is more stressful, and they've had to take on added responsibilities. Still, they believe that the company has recommitted itself to people's welfare and well-being, and again they find management open and honest to deal with.

There was very little corporate rah-rah in GC following its leveraged buyout. People at all levels met to discuss the deal and digest the added financial burden it placed on the company. Management flatly stated that it could make no promises about whether the company would succeed. Indeed, management could only promise hard months of hard work ahead. Still, managers pledged themselves to share whatever success was achieved and to ensure that sacrifices would also be shared equally.

Up to this point, the company has earned record profits, and everyone has shared through bonuses. As for the human organization, managers bowl with workers, and workers help managers to set company strategy. Everyone feels part of the new GC, and once again the work-life surveys show that GC is a very special place to work.

Forward to the Fundamentals

In this age of cynicism, we believe it is essential for corporations to commit themselves to the concept of employees' rights and to ensure justice in the workplace. Should employees have the right to refuse overtime, relocations, or job assignments, without fear of reprisal? Many people believe so. Should committees be formed to investigate charges of discrimination, sexual harassment, mistreatment, and the like? Many companies have them, and more are forming every day.

We believe that one means of institutionalizing trust is for companies and employees to articulate a bill of rights that defines the rights and responsibilities of employee and employer. In a sense, this is what Caterpillar did with its human resource strategy conference. We also believe that employees should be allowed to judge whether the company has respected their rights and delivered on its responsibilities. This is what quality-of-work-life audits achieve at Graphic Controls.

We do not envision such a bill as either a legal document or an inflexible set of rules. But neither do we see it as a wish list or public relations exercise. Instead, we regard it as a statement of aspirations and an affirmation of mutual commitment. Its particulars would vary in the case of individual employers and employees, and its true implications would be developed as it was implemented in company life.

Second, having employees judge their company's fulfillment of this pledge should not be construed as a democratic referendum. Both unions and management have a right to their own prerogatives and areas of legal authority. Nevertheless, the upbeat companies we have studied truly believe they exist "by the consent of the governed" and give employees a voice in defining the company's purpose. In the most everyday manner, this voice takes the form of participative management, multilevel corporate communication efforts, and credible suggestion programs, along with regular attitude surveys.

In a larger sense, then, we see the most upbeat companies promulgating and putting into practice corporate ideals in this age of cynicism. The U.S. Constitution embodies many of our American ideals. In many corporations, we see efforts to live its moral precepts. In the auto industry, for example, committees of management and labor representatives have established standards for quality of work life and overseen work-life improvement programs. The International Association of Machinists and Aerospace Workers, in conjunction with employers, has defined a bill of rights for employees facing technological change. Each of these constitutional efforts has involved organized labor and management working together. We think them equally applicable to nonorganized industries.

These efforts need not yield fully democratic organizations, employee ownership, or judicial redress within the corporate structure—though all represent the full expression of constitutional ideals and seem to us worthy and worth broad corporate implementation. They must, however, produce credible corporate leadership and give people more voice in the affairs of the firm. They comprise what Huntington Terrel refers to as a move "forward to the fundamentals."[15] The chief aim is to help companies restore trust and manage their way back to credibility in the decades ahead.

12

Communicating Effectively with a Cynical Work Force

Actions do speak louder than words, but company communications can reinforce ideals, reaffirm trust, and reestablish credibility—particularly if they are truthful, informative, intelligently presented, and followed up. For a start, it is essential to understand that the work force, even in upbeat companies, is an obstinate audience.[1] It has its own agenda that may or may not coincide with management's. It surely brings to the listening situation its own needs and interests. This view of the audience as an active organism, rather than a passive body, is not always understood by company communicators. It is just as important to understand what people do to messages as it is to understand what messages do to people.[2]

Recognizing the nature of active psychological resistance to communications is essential for managers trying to reach their people. The popular prescriptions for improving communications usually suggest consideration of who says what, to whom, through what channels, and for what intended result. These are key factors in getting a message across, but the formula is incomplete. An audience may be segmented psychologically by values, life-styles, and interests or demographically by age, sex, and class. Each segment may in turn be more or less receptive to certain communications and more or less prone to discredit others.[3] In our experience, managers do not keep these distinct audience segments in mind when planning their communications. It will come as no surprise, then, that we recommend communicators' taking into account the resistance of cynics in their work forces.

Communicating with a Cynical Work Force

At first glance, the challenge of trying to communicate credibly with an audience made up of a large number of cynics seems unpromising—especially when we remember that much cynicism stems from history, sources, and events outside the actual and psychological boundaries of the workplace. This poses an ostensible dilemma: If endemic cynicism comes partly from sources outside the workplace, how can management deal with it?

The answer begins with expectations. Management must formulate realistic expectations of what employee communications can and cannot do, whether in print, on TV, or face to face.[4] It is useful to think along a hypothetical scale reflecting people's readiness to trust what they hear. This scale might be anchored with misanthropy and cynicism at one end and naiveté, even gullibility, on the other. In between are skepticism and cautious belief. With this scale in mind, management can reasonably expect its communications to neutralize the naysaying of the hard-core cynics and perhaps move a fair number of cynics to skeptical acceptance of the message and good intentions of the messenger.

This is an ambitious undertaking. It requires careful consideration of a number of elements that interact with the cynical mind-set. Managers need to plan and execute their communications with an awareness of:

- The audience's current perception of management
- The audience's future time perspective
- The degree of ambiguity in the work situation
- The goal of management's communication
- The counterarguments
- The degree of organized resistance

The Audience's Current Perception of Management. Our national survey data indicate that only one-third of employees regard management as trustworthy and evenhanded. It is a given that the more a source of communication is trusted, the more trustworthy its message will be. How has management allowed itself to be considered untrustworthy vis-à-vis its employees? Some of the problem likely lies in managers' unwillingness to lay out the true facts behind company problems and explain why change is essential. Another factor is their inability to solicit employees' opinions on a variety of subjects and respond with empathy and understanding to feelings.[5] While 62 percent of our respondents say that management tries to get employees' feedback, we believe this feedback is largely shop talk or survey research concerning work-related problems, not feelings. Cross-level communications, though heralded as a possible cure for too many ills, have not been very well implemented in thousands of organizations.

Still another reason management is perceived as untrustworthy is its failure to live up to its promises. The average tenure on the job for managers in this country is two and a half years. It is hard for people to trust authority figures they don't get to know and who may not be around in the future to honor pledges and deliver on deals. The perception of managers as expeditious, opportunistic, self-serving job-jumpers makes it easy for the work force to mistrust them and what they have to say.

Finally, American managers are seen as working for themselves first, for the shareholders second, for the banks third, for the firm fourth, and for the employees last. Whether this is the result of today's dog-eat-dog economic climate, the malfeasance of cynical types and misdeeds of cynical companies, or simply populist sentiment is hard to know.

In any event, effective communication with employees is heavily influenced by whether they see management as trustworthy and evenhanded—and an overwhelming number of employees do not. Under the circumstances, improving communications really means trying to improve employees' perception of management's intent. Specifically:

- Don't pretend that management's proposals are being made for the exclusive good of the work force. In other words, make it clear that we are all going to gain by what we are recommending.
- Remind people that change will affect management and employees on all levels. Acknowledge that the change will be tough and everybody is involved.
- Apologize, to some extent, for the need to make management decisions swiftly and for the fact that consultation beforehand is often impossible. For example, cite external pressures and the reasons why a decision had to be made without consulting the work force if this is the case.
- Don't emphasize management's past record to a work force. It is generally counterproductive. Almost anybody, let alone cynics, can find some discrepancies between promise and delivery. You must be certain of the legitimacy of a past record before raising it.
- Talk specifically to the different breeds of cynics in your audience—the Hard-Bittens, the Articulate Players, the Obstinate Stoics. The Hard-Bittens need to be reassured that their opinions count, that you would not be addressing the audience if you were not determined to get their opinions and goodwill. In order to have an effect, this message must be honestly felt and honestly communicated. To Articulate Players, who want to know what's in it for them, emphasize the individual's rather than the company's benefit. One way to deal with Obstinate Stoics is to acknowledge that some people work harder than others; they are not always rewarded, but the new system will be responsive to the higher productivity of some.

The Audience's Future Time Perspective. How optimistic or pessimistic an audience is—in its segments and as a whole—influences its receptivity to messages. In the workplace, receptivity is influenced by the success or failure of the firm. If a firm is seen by its employees as a winner, then doubt about trustworthiness will more than likely be compensated for to some extent by the perception of management's competence. But if employees believe they are tied to a firm of losers, their receptivity will be curtailed, no matter how smoothly the message is presented.[6]

The optimistic perspective makes for more generous audiences. In a climate of optimism, the majority of workers (save the cynics) are either securely indifferent or reinforced in their view that management is competent, if not entirely trustworthy. A pessimistic perspective, on the other hand, makes for defensive listening and gloomy response. Pessimism is rich soil for blooming cynics, so great care must be taken to neutralize their potential influence. Since it's usually easier to speak from a position of success than from failure, the management communicator must be aware of the interplay between message and mood, a relationship that is often in flux and calls for truthful and cautious steering. Specifically:

- Don't raise expectations that probably cannot be met. In this respect, it is well to think of long-term consequences, rather than short-term opportunities.

- Explain how the firm does not operate in a vacuum and what it will require to stay competitive. Most work forces tend to think of themselves as shielded from the exigencies of the outside world. Managers exacerbate this innocence by failing to educate them about business realities.

- The tone of the message should not be inspirational or of the locker-room variety. It should be low-key, factual, and firm. Spending a lot of money on slick presentations will be thought wasteful by a work force facing cutbacks and will probably arouse hostility and disbelief. Humorous how-to-do-it films do, however, have their place and can be very useful in specific situations.

The Degree of Ambiguity in the Work Situation. Ambiguity in high-risk situations produces discomfort, even anxiety, to many who experience it firsthand. Ambiguity in the workplace stems from a lack of clarity about or commitment to a course of action and influences people's views of themselves and their job prospects. It arises in conditions of economic decline, changes in company and industry fortunes, changes in management on all levels, changes in organization and work structure, and the introduction of new technology. Moreover, ambiguity increases in proportion to the rumors and prophecies that surround change.

Once again, it is the cynic who stirs the pot more than others. Articulate Players tend to scare their colleagues by openly talking, say, about jumping ship or about their own real or fancied alternatives. Other cynics, the Obstinate Stoics and the Hard-Bittens, tend toward depression and paralysis in their reactions to change-driven ambiguity. While it is true that most people are uncomfortable in highly charged ambiguous situations, cynics make these conditions even less bearable by their rumor-mongering and gothic views of management and the future.

The role of management communications in ambiguous situations is crucial to the ongoing operations of the firm. Clearly this role does not mean responding, say, to each rumor as it surfaces. Rather, it means acknowledging work discomfort, trying to put this discomfort into a specific time frame, and impressing on people that more information will be forthcoming when events have clarified.

Although advertisers often use ambiguity in teaser campaigns and employ incongruity and surprise to foster novelty seeking and brand experimentation, there are two good reasons why it isn't sensible to hype management communications with uncertainties:

- The work situation is one of high risk, whereas most consumer goods are low-involvement purchases, and people in high-risk situations tend to interpret ambiguity as bad news. Thus, applying lessons from brand advertising to management communications is usually inappropriate.

- Ambiguity encourages nonproductive rumormongering and the development of worst-case scenarios.

Hence, the job of managerial communication should be to reduce ambiguity in the workplace as much as possible. We hasten to add, however, that it's better to acknowledge uncertainty than to trivialize fears when threat is present, or to promise boldly that workers will be taken care of whatever happens. The key is to recognize that change leads to ambiguity and awakens fears, which in turn need reassurance. Specifically:

- Empathize with people. Find out what the audience is thinking, feeling, and believing. Acknowledge uncertainty and people's insecurity about change; recognize that everyone has been subjected to rumors and will be in the future; and reaffirm that, above all, everyone has a personal stake in solving company problems and making any new initiatives successful.
- Don't ask to be trusted on faith alone. Spell out plans, timetables, and benchmarks by which progress will be judged. Don't pretend that everyone is on the team. Thinking and acting like a team takes time.
- Clarify any threats to the company and any opportunities up ahead. Ambiguity gives cynics an opportunity to project their own fears, doubts, and pessimism into the communication process. Disarm them with facts, but show respect for their feelings.

The Goal of Management Communication. The goal of management communication is to inform. A more subtle and useful formulation, however, is to determine whether the goal is to persuade and convert or to reinforce existing ideas and behavior. It is, of course, harder to change beliefs and behavior than to reinforce existing ones.

One reason it is so difficult to change beliefs is that perceptual defenses such as selectivity, distortion, and rationalization come into play.[7] These perceptual defenses against receptivity are triggered by the same personal needs that make ideas acceptable in the first place. Beliefs and attitudes serve a function in the personality structures of holders and thus are defended.[8] Cynics, we have seen, believe that other people are selfish and self-interested and can't be trusted, and this notion sustains them in behaving accordingly. It is hard to change such beliefs without understanding how they are triggered by communications. Planning communications to counter this mind-set is more difficult than simply reinforcing existing ideas. Management needs to offset the cynics while reinforcing the more accepting outlook of skeptical and upbeat audience segments.

Why is it important to distinguish between communications that aim to change rather than reinforce attitudes in the work force? Successful reinforcing communications use more repetition, stress the rewards of the status quo, and emphasize predictability and continuity.[9] Company awards, promotional campaigns, celebrations, outings—all reinforce upbeat and positive attitudes. They work for *some* segments of the work force.

By contrast, efforts to persuade or convert need to address heightened self-interest.[10] Successful approaches require management to enlist, one-to-one, the support of some cynics and to depend on peer-group pressure (usually stressing a bandwagon approach) to counter other cynics. Telling it straight is essential to reaching the cynics in the work force, but it is also important not to reinforce their cynical suspicions. This means:

- Whether in group or one-to-one communications, you must be frank in telling people you are out to persuade them and that you are perforce biased.
- In an age of cynicism, don't ask people to change for the sake of the company. An appeal to loyalty is likely to awaken cynicism in many people. Explain instead what's in it for everyone.
- Always give the reasons behind management's position, and let people know the thinking behind it. This helps people rationalize and justify the direction management is taking. Often it helps to provide graphic financial, product, and market information. Though it may be over the heads of some in the audience, it communicates the seriousness of management's commitment to explain its decisions to the work force.

- Don't confine your remarks to the cynics. Direct them to the audience as a whole. Talk largely to the majority, and let them function as a damper to cynical criticism.

The Counterarguments. To what extent, if at all, should management acknowledge and treat alternative positions? We believe it is wise to deal in a dignified and balanced way with counterarguments.[11] To begin with, it preempts the cynics' treatment of the same material and thereby neutralizes them. Moreover, management is seen to have thought out the options—always a point in favor of competence and respect, if not agreement and support. In short, this approach allows management to position the argument. The question is: What do we mean by positioning the argument?

In its simplest sense, positioning means setting up your argument to be seen as unique, desirable, and value for money, in comparison to alternative arguments.[12] One way to do this is to appeal to people's self-interest and include the basic economic motivators. In addition, you have the choice of tone (formal versus informal), appeal (individual versus bandwagon), and stance (rational versus emotional) as well as the choice of communicators, channels (film versus live), and content. Positioning that tries to create an image has further options in the presentation of arguments and their counters. We believe that management's position should come first because it creates a frame of reference by which other arguments are evaluated. The best way to position management communications is to plan strategy and arguments, as well as the alternatives, before choosing such specific tactics as tone or medium.

Communications, along with small-group leadership, are the best tools for implementing management's strategy. Communications should not be an afterthought or be left to executives who don't appreciate their importance as a two-way delivery system. Specifically:

- Put forward the counterarguments (real and potential) to the work force, thereby anticipating possible objections to management's proposals. It's a good idea to use a two-sided

argument—pro-and-anti—when addressing people, particularly when speaking to cynics who are predisposed to
attribute one-sidedness to management.

- Establish points of comparison, so that workers have the same
  frame of reference as management. Since antimanagement
  arguments will serve as a point of departure, be thorough
  and straightforward in presenting the antimanagement case.

- Cynics can be neutralized and their influence on their peers
  reduced, at least to some degree, if you anticipate and address their views on management's position. Communicators
  might say, directly, ''The cynical view of this or that position is thus . . . '' and then explain why such a gothic perception is unwarranted. It is important, in any case, to acknowledge straightaway that there will be complaints, as well
  as suspicion and disparagement of management's plan.

- Cynics believe they are realists. Thus it is important to deal
  with what they feel is concrete, testable, and specific. Use
  analogies that are well within their frames of reference.

- The person who delivers the communication should be credible—not perceived as a company flunky but, rather, suffi-
  ciently senior in managerial rank to have weight.

The Degree of Organized Resistance. No audience is a
pushover—let alone a workplace audience, with its quota of
cynics. The presence of a union must also be considered in planning communications, especially with respect to follow-up meetings. Moreover, even if workers have no organized forum for
reviewing management's messages, they have many spontaneous
outlets for talking things over. The degree to which cynics gain
the edge in these forums determines how work groups will
ultimately respond to management's missives.

The value of following up formal communications through
organized small-group discussions (fewer than twenty people)
is that it allows arguments to be assimilated and supported by
peers.[13] Further, it dampens the role of cynical activists who
might dominate the discussions. One company we have worked
with follows up its management briefings by having teams of
workers meet to raise questions through a representative. That

way, hot questions and hard objections raised in the small group are anonymously aired in front of management. In unionized settings, having an elected moderator of small-group discussion is an ideal way of proceeding—particularly if the cynical arguments have already been exposed in the large meeting. Finally, if for some reason management has failed to communicate or has missed a crucial employee point of view, it can always set up another, better-planned meeting. We think the small-group follow-up is an important part of management's communications.

The six considerations that affect managerial communications point up the difficulties involved in defining the communications situation and deciding how to tackle it. Up to this point, however, we have been dealing mainly with management's side of the street. It is worth looking at the communications situation from the audience's point of view. Specifically:

- It is valuable to institute a formal feedback mechanism, so that people know management is serious about monitoring employees' opinions. Management must be *seen* to take these opinions seriously.
- Always *ask* people to do something—the tone should range from suggestion to strong recommendation, as warranted. Orders seldom lead to results. Let people discover for themselves the value of a given course of action.
- Give people a way out, so to speak, of the new arrangement. Ask them, for example, to try it for a certain period of time. Try not to force people into an unappealing new situation without giving them the hope of redress or revision.
- People will do so anyway, but encourage them nevertheless to meet in small groups and talk things over without management's presence. Group reinforcement of the upbeat elements in the workplace will be at its strongest in small, informal groups. Their approval will also show chronic cynics when they are out of step.
- Consulting with only certain employees on all levels of management can be a source of trouble. Confidences are just too hard to keep. The rumor mill can get started very quickly

and pick up momentum if management's intentions are revealed prematurely and distorted. If consultation is desirable, make it broad.

Delivering the Message to an Obstinate Audience

At the outset of this chapter, we made the point that the audience is not passive, has its own agenda, and is usually obstinate—especially when confronted with messages implying change. Part of the audience's processing of messages turns on the following points:

- Its ability to understand clearly what is being said
- Its comprehension and acceptance of why it is being said
- Its interest in what is being said
- Its mood at the point of communication
- The dissonance between the message and established ideas or behavior
- The situation and the communication context

These factors, logically enough, are crucial in the delivery of the message because effective communication is really transactional: a two-way street. As straightforward and self-explanatory as these points may seem, considering them one by one may help managers to present their cases more effectively.

Clear Understanding. There is no communication without comprehension. Even partial comprehension can lead to ambiguity and distortion of the intended message. The inherent obstinacy of the audience is often manifested in its refusal to understand. An audience that does not entirely understand what is being said to it (either because of the message's threatening content or because it is faulty per se) often ends up disliking the presenter *and* the message.

Active misunderstanding of a message may take many forms. Audiences may find the information too abstract, complicated, or disorganized, complaining "Where's the beef?" Or they may find the presentation too slick, preachy, or condescending and thereby fail to distinguish the intended signal from all the noise. Thus the message itself must offer little opportunity for distortion. It should be simple and straightforward, and its presentation should be lucid and made without talking down. In crucial or sensitive situations, it's wise to pretest communications on a selected audience to ensure comprehensibility—all the while taking pains to avoid premature leakage of the news.

Why the Specific Message Is Being Sent. Explaining *why* a given message is being transmitted is vital to neutralizing cynics in the audience. Cynics doubt the motives behind messages, whereas skeptics may doubt the facts but remain open to proof. Accordingly, management must not only know why it is sending a message but must also communicate the reason clearly and with justification.

In the absence of reasons, cynics have a field day. They are quite willing to create their own explanations of why management has taken so much of *their* time and spent so much money to get a message across. Their interpretations are usually not flattering. All audiences wonder why people say what they do. Having an audience question management's motives during a presentation can distract from comprehension of the whole message.

One of the first hurdles a presentation must get over is the reasons why it is being given in the first place. Many Command Cynics never ask themselves why they are on a podium, before a camera, or preparing letters to be sent to all employees. They construe it as their "right" to communicate at any time and as they wish to the work force. Often this looks like a power trip to employees (and like self-serving rubbish to the cynics).

Interest in Subject Matter. Another hurdle is whether the message is meaningful to its audience. Attention is a matter of selection. Whether to attend to a message or not depends on its inherent interest to the listener. Tuning out is the response of the bored, as many advertisers have found to their cost. Squeezed Cynics in particular habitually tune out the messages of authority figures.

Today people want to know more than they have to know about what's going on in a company. But they also want information that is relevant—particularly about matters that are personally relevant. Material that involves self-interest is always a hit. Content that deals with the firm's origins, history, dynamic culture, and generosity is generally regarded as pompous and self-serving unless it has ongoing continuity for the people involved.

One sure way of promoting tedium is to have too many meetings. Another way is to hype a meeting in advance, raising false expectations about its importance and the revelations to come, and then present very little of consequence to the audience. Still another way of disillusioning a workplace audience is to call a meeting—presumably to air, and even vote on, an ostensibly significant matter—only to have it seem trivial in the eyes of the audience. In short, meetings are opportunities. They should not be squandered by their frequency, triviality, or staleness, nor by repetition of subject matter, by management power trips, or by transparently phony ''democratic'' procedures.

Mood of an Audience. It is no accident that there are audience warm-ups before live performances in politics and entertainment. The mood of an audience can make or break a performance. In the same way, a workplace audience brings its mood to management communications. If times are bad, chances are the audience will be somber; if good news is expected, the audience will be up. Past practices also play into current perceptions. If the audience is accustomed to hearing the same old management line, it will be restive and jaded. The point is this: All audiences start with anticipations, and these must be sensed if the presentation is to be seen as appropriate. Catching the mood of an audience is a big part of being understood.

Who has not seen an audience turn ugly when the presentation is incongruous with its mood? Jeers, catcalls, and mutterings have a momentum of their own. This is a true manifestation of the audience's obstinacy; it defends itself, as it were, against things it does not wish to hear, does not expect to hear, or does not like. The epidemiology of audience discontent is easy to observe in the scoffing of Articulate Players and the derision of Hard-Bitten Cynics. It's harder to find among Administrative Sideliners and Obstinate Stoics who will simply complain that communications take time from other, more valuable parts of the job.

Strength of Dissonance. It's wise to be aware of the conflict that certain management messages may arouse in the work force. Some management messages are treated with indifference, but those dealing with faultfinding or blame often inflame strong feelings of bloody-mindedness or hostility. Complaints about shoddy workmanship can backfire on managerial communicators who cannot defend waste and sloth in their own ranks. Keeping in mind the audience's probable reaction to public criticism helps to reduce dissonance. Not that communicators should take a mealymouthed approach when people are to be taken to task—criticism often signals that management has noticed sloppy work and won't countenance it. It does, however, call for diplomacy.

The more that proposed changes conflict with core values, the more firmly messages about change will be opposed—unless, of course, the change is seen as salutary or as an improvement.[14] We once worked with an organization that tackled directly the problem of deadwood in the ranks by holding meetings with supervisors and employees about expected levels of effort and contribution. At first, this campaign was labeled a "management crackdown," and many, not just the cynics, predicted it would divide a hitherto united work force. It was simply out of character for management to blame the workers for productivity problems.

When management met with groups of employees, however, it appealed to their strong work ethic and made the case that people at all levels would be asked to accomplish more in the months ahead. Management acknowledged that most people wanted to work hard and earn more, and this basic message fit people's self-picture in the company. Management also pointed out that there was as much deadwood in management as in the work force, and every effort would be made to ensure that managers, as well as workers, did their fair share. When management instituted a bonus program that rewarded accomplishment and provided retraining for those whose skills were becoming obsolete, the jeers gave way to cheers.

Management's sensitivity to the mood of its audience gives it a head start on the entire communications program. The obstinate audience throws up its own flak in response to management's bombs, no matter how well aimed they may be. The key is to understand these defenses and appeal to common values and needs.

Different Audiences, Different Situations. Audiences vary by demography, psychological makeup, size, expectations, and mood. They also vary by the nature of their tasks and by the formal power structures in which they operate. All this shapes the context of managerial communication. A football team, for example, has certain characteristics and expects a certain style of communication from its coach. The same can be said of nurses in a metropolitan hospital, advertising executives listening to a market researcher, salespeople at a national sales meeting, and civil servants listening to their political leader—all have distinct expectations and characteristics that define the communication context. Each group also has its quota of cynics, with more or less representation of the six types we have discussed.

This means that the effective communicator must tailor his or her approach to a uniquely obstinate audience.[15] We trust our points on communicating effectively can be helpful. But it's up to the communicator to configure the elements of the process in the most effective way to meet the needs of the firm and the audience, whether it is a sports, health care, advertising, sales, or administrative group.

In this regard, it is worth listening to William Bailey, onetime managing director of the top British double-glazing company, which has a sales crew making cold calls:

> Salesmen are cynics and sentimentalists at the same time. They don't believe anything I tell them . . . they put down everything with derision. On the other hand, when I'm with them on a sales call, they sell as if they believe everything they have been told about the product. Maybe it's because they've such a low opinion of the buyer, as if they're "Johns" spending on a whore. So how do I talk to them in sales meetings? With hard-boiled humor, as one salesman to another. I tell them things like I'm out to get them, they're lazy boozers, and that every-

thing I am telling them is a lie. It's the old axiom
that salesmen love to be sold. Well, cynics love to
be treated cynically. It works, up to a point, with
that lot. It's like that American play, *Glengarry Glen
Ross*.

Granted that double-glazing salespeople are one kind of
sales audience, and that a football team is another altogether;
there are elements of similarity between the two. As William
Himstreet, former faculty adviser to college championship football teams, observed:

One time these kids would play their hearts out for
the school; you know, win-one-for-the-Gipper stuff.
Now, motivating them has little to do with school
spirit, tradition, or glory. It has to do with individual self-interest, money, and a future with the
pros. They'll play for the newspaper write-ups and
the pro scouts. The coach tells me the only way to
get them up is to tell them the scouts are out watching or to arrange individual publicity. School spirit
is a joke to these guys.

It is of more than passing interest to note how styles of
sports motivation change with coaching and managerial changes.
Holdouts are not uncommon, regardless of the effects on a team.
Insofar as selfish materialism is one manifestation of cynicism,
the sports scene is instructive with its plethora of Articulate
Players. So is the world of advertising. Lester A. Delano, executive director of Lowe Howard-Spink and Bell, PLC, a major advertising global network, comments:

One thing that I find unacceptable everywhere and
anywhere are advertising executives who think that
either the client or the consumer is dumb. More
misguided and wasteful advertising is created within
that framework that [in] any others. We do not need
to tolerate cynics of that style in this business or,
for that matter, any other.

But the distinctive flavor of cynicism would not be complete unless the Administrative Sideliners were included, representing the corresponding bureaucratic component of industry, civil servants, the military, and the utilities. A small excerpt from the brilliant British TV series and book *Yes Minister* captures the essential cynicism of the consummate bureaucrat as two senior government officials talk about their boss, a member of the cabinet whom they presumably serve:

> "He'll be house-trained in no time. All we have to do is head him off the Open Government nonsense, I remarked to Bernard. Bernard said that we were in favor of Open Government. I hope I have not overpromoted young Bernard. He still has an awful lot to learn."
>
> "I explained that we are calling the White Paper 'Open Government' because you always dispose of the difficult bit in the title. It does less harm there than on the statute books."
>
> "It is the law of Inverse Relevance: The less you intend to do about something, the more you have to keep talking about it. Bernard asked us, 'What's wrong with Open Government?' I could hardly believe my ears. . . . Sometimes I wonder if Bernard is really a flyer, or whether we shouldn't send him off to a career at the War Graves Commission."
>
> "Arnold pointed out, with great clarity, that Open Government was a contradiction in terms. You can be open, or you can have government. Bernard claims that the citizens of a democracy have a right to know. We explained that, in fact, they have a right to be ignorant. Knowledge only means complicity and guilt. Ignorance has a certain dignity. . . . Arnold rightly added that if people don't know what you're doing, they don't know what you're doing wrong."[16]

This excerpt, like the others, is not representative. But it does highlight the influence of a cynical outlook on the communication process of today's workplace, regardless of its character. It strikes us as valuable, too, because it reflects the diversity of the world of work and the problems of talking meaningfully to its members.

Throughout this chapter, we've emphasized that the effective use and durable effects of the communication process must be built on the recognition that workplace realities affect everyone and no communication "techniques" can mitigate poor working conditions, unresponsive organizations, or hollow managers. In short, trust in management is a long-term proposition, hard-won and worth it, although winning it takes place in constantly changing conditions to which management must be ever alert.[17]

An Honest Dialogue About Cynicism

Experience convinces us that the best way to communicate effectively with a cynical audience—the law of inverse relevance notwithstanding—is to open up a dialogue directly about the subject. We have promoted, in small groups and in training seminars, no-holds-barred discussions of the signs of cynicism within firms, the presence and impact of the cynical types, what companies are doing to reinforce and counter cynicism, and, finally, both pragmatic and philosophical discussions of whether people can really be trusted. Among the issues that executives and managers, sales and service personnel, blue-collar workers and clericals have addressed are these:

- What values about people are expressed in the ways their organizations operate? Do they detect any lasting vision of the company? Do people believe in company ideals, take pride in their products and services, and think their contributions are valued by management? If not, why not?
- How is management perceived by working people? Is management open, honest, fair-minded, and respectful of employees, or otherwise? Is management available to people at all levels, and does it care about their financial and psychological needs?
- How are workers perceived by management? Are workers seen as responsible, motivatible, competent, and interested

in doing a good job, or otherwise? Are workers responsive to management's direction? Do they care about the company's financial health and reputation?

- How is cynicism expressed in the company? What are the obvious signs of cynicism? Does the company include Command Cynics, Sideliners, and Articulate Players? How about Squeezed Cynics, Stoics, and Hard-Bitten types?
- Which company practices feed the cynical outlook? Which ones bring forth more upbeat ideals? What do people say— about their pay, working conditions, influence and say-so, about their relationships with peers, supervisors, and subordinates, about communications in the company—that suggests cynicism is at work?
- What should the company stand for, and what can be reasonably done to rebuild trust and restore credibility? And, most important, are people willing to earn trust and credibility, and are they willing to work with others to make sure their efforts are genuine and effective?

We close this chaper by urging readers to consider seriously the option of confronting cynicism at work directly. Certainly surveys of employees' attitudes can be useful in detecting the signs of cynicism; the systematic feedback of findings to workers can prove an opening to removing its causes. Intimate small-group meetings, focused specifically on the problems wrought by cynicism, have a strong cathartic value and give people a direct opportunity to say their piece and take a stand. Communicating effectively requires time and two-way dialogue. It takes human interaction, not just technique, to address cynicism at work.

Epilogue:
A Basis
for Optimism

It was over fifteen years ago that Alistair Cooke, keen-eyed observer of American culture for over fifty years, made a statement regarding what he saw as the race in the United States between decadence and vitality:

> I can only recall the saying of a wise Frenchman that 'liberty is the luxury of self-discipline.' Historically, those people that did not discipline themselves had discipline thrust upon them from the outside. That is why the normal cycle in the life and death of great nations has been first a powerful tyranny broken by revolt, the enjoyment of liberty, the abuse of liberty—and back to tyranny again. As I see it, in this country—a land of the most persistent idealism and the blandest cynicism—the race is on between its decadence and its vitality.[1]

279

There are signs—persistent and troubling—that decline is winning. On the grand geopolitical scale, Paul Kennedy argues, America has reached beyond its grasp, much like England a century ago and France and Spain before that.[2] His conclusion is that the American empire is bound for collapse. Certainly there are signs of political and economic failure in this country: We see indications of the emerging characterological consequences in what we've termed the Europeanization of America.

In the sociocultural realm, Peter Sloterdijk observes that postmodern society is in a state of melancholy—keeping up appearances—but suffering from defeated idealism and unable to sustain a reconstructive dialogue.[3] Meanwhile, epidemiological studies confirm that the rate of depression over the last two generations has increased nearly tenfold.[4] Ties to country and ideals, to family and community, that sustain people in jeopardy are no longer available to many. The threat is here, but the time-honored supports, including moral leadership and collective commitment, are not. And this, we feel, is the thin edge of cynicism's wedge.

But this is not the first time the country has been challenged from without and within, nor will it be the last. And, although there is some justification in looking toward the Pacific Basin as the next source of world economic leadership and in looking back toward Europe to see how Americans may cope with decline, we feel this turns a blind eye to our nation's historical record of rising to great challenges, as well as a jaundiced eye to the possibilities of turning around what may seem irreversible trends.

New leadership in the Soviet Union, heralding *glasnost* and *perestroika,* portends fundamental changes in the U.S.S.R. and Eastern Bloc countries, with profound implications for East/West relations, nuclear arsenals, and, ultimately, the prospects of world peace. Europe, about to become a truly common market, shows signs of revival in economy and spirit. Developing countries continue to evolve toward more democratic and, in the best cases, less stratified social structures. And new leadership in our own country, facing economic ills and promising a kinder social outlook, may lead us away from an economic and moral abyss and toward a less contrived and more practical international and domestic policy. No one can foretell whether these progressive directions will be sustained. But, in the near term at least, hopes are held out.

In everyday American life, there are also indications that 1980s-style self-seeking may give way to more generous impulses in the next decade. This may be partly a function of cyclical forces: Historian Arthur Schlesinger makes the case that generational priorities change every thirty years or so, and he posits that a new outlook will emerge among the generation coming of age in the 1990s: "This is equivalent to about 1928 or 1958. There's a lot of pent-up idealism. That will increase, and in the 1990s we'll enter a phase that will be much like the 1930s and the 1960s."[5] Whether that idealism will arise from the grayness of an economic depression (as in the 1930s) or from a rebellion against complacency (as in the 1960s) remains to be seen. One looks forward to the clarion call of national leadership—as from Roosevelt in the 1930s and Kennedy in the 1960s—to give this idealism its voice.

Already there is modest testimony to Schlesinger's thesis: More and better students are seeking out careers in education and social work; volunteerism and community service are on the increase; and the affluent, coked-up, cooled-out life-style seems to hold less appeal today. On the pop-culture front, it is also worth noting that the popularity of "Dallas" has waned and that more family-oriented programming, like "Cosby," is preferred. Popular music has been given a socially oriented direction by bands like U-2 and a peace-giving purpose by Sir Bob Geldof.

On a human scale, there are many new exemplars of personal courage and public outreach that are in sharp relief from the cynical menagerie. While charlatans continue to peddle the power of positive thinking, Norman Cousins has affirmed its true potential for overcoming life-threatening illness. In an essay "The Case for Optimism," he writes: "The capacity for hope is the most significant fact of life. It gives human beings a sense of destination and the energy to get started."[6] In the same fashion, as televangelists continue to spew out threats and rake in funds, Scott Peck has formed the Foundation for Community Improvement, which seeks to create connections for the estranged and offer recognition to the depersonalized. Indeed, there are many who see a resurrection of community as the primary antidote to the narcissism and melancholy afflicting postmodern society. Salutary examples of community leadership and action are legion today.

The Possibilities of Organization

Still, we live in an organizational society. To a degree, the sources and problems of cynicism are individualized, but the modern organization also contributes to the malaise, and the costs of people's self-estrangement and self-serving dealings with others, however personally palpable, also have implications for the GNP. Hence, cynicism is an organizational problem, too, and a matter of concern to any society in which organizations dictate how the society functions and how people live.

Our point is twofold. First, a cynical citizenry and work force cannot be as cohesive or productive as a trusting one. A cynical work force is not as competitive as it could be, because it is focused more on injustice and threats than on the work at hand. Second, reducing cynicism in the work force means reorienting the values in society at large by emphasizing priorities that enhance community and the quality of life and by alleviating sources of mistrust and dispirit.

Corporate America is one place to start. An economic revival is clearly under way in industry. We also think that a social revival is in the offing, or should be. There have been countless prescriptions for revitalizing American industry and reinventing the corporation. The economic success of society and its members is incumbent on the establishment of a new social order in the world of work.

There are also plenty of examples today of thoroughly American companies meeting competitive challenges in partnership with their people. These companies cultivate an upbeat atmosphere, build on the work ethic and people's self-determination, instill realistic expectations, and breed optimism. They are the American success stories—fresh and innovative in practice, but in intent and character curiously based on old-fashioned American ideals.

We have speculated that a prime contributor to national pride and productivity in this country is Americans' desire to be part of something larger than themselves. Robert Bellah and his colleagues make the point that individualism and utilitarianism predominate over collectivism and duty in the American character. But this understates the transcendent ideals most Americans hold and their willingness, when called to duty, to respond with collective and affirmative resolve.

Can companies become a force for community and help to leaven the cynicism that stands in the way of personal commitment and, in our view, competitive potential? Up to this point, traditional American ideals have not been particularly cultivated in the cultures of most companies. On the contrary, we see in the cynical company a cleavage between the interests of the corporation and those of the commonweal and, more broadly, between self-interest and the common good. But there are possibilities—as the cases we have cited suggest.

Mary Parker Follett, a utopian management theorist of the early 1900s, dreamed of a time when organizational life would be positive rather than negative; and Oliver Sheldon, offering a creed to fellow managers, proposed that industry be dedicated to communal well-being.[7] Their conceptions of the human and ethical organization were undone by competing images and harsh realities—Social Darwinism, bureaucracy, technocracy, and other frustrating forces in the organized society. What will happen to the positive images of today? Optimism rests on the perception that the glass is half full rather than half empty.

David Cooperrider offers the thesis that the fundamental forces of organizing are "heliotropic"—moving toward the light rather than the dark—toward whatever and wherever is the source of greatest germinal possibility.[8] Lest this seem like another "new age" chimera, complementary points are made by Norman Cousins and Scott Peck (with reference to the body and the soul), by Nobel laureate Roger Sperry (with reference to consciousness and the mind), and by Kenneth Boulding (with reference to social and economic systems).[9] The morality play that pits light against dark and good against evil was staged in classical Greek theater and was interpreted afresh in George Lucas's *Star Wars* film trilogy. It is the crux of the drama in organizations today.

While cynical companies, managers, and workers act out the dark side of the drama, upbeat companies enlighten and embolden people through a more affirming saga—people know what their companies stand for, and they gain a larger image of their own roles and their own worth. Upbeat companies celebrate rather than manufacture real heroes. And upbeat companies validate people—in their individualistic and collective sense.

Turning It Around, American Style

All countries and societies face crises of strength and spirit. It is how they face these crises—in form, style, and energy—that distinguishes those who act humanely and well from those who resort to tyranny and reap chaos. Those that are successful draw on their traditional strengths, both in resources and national character: the Japanese, on hierarchy and consensus; the British, on humor and grit; the Germans, on effort and organization. America has its own strengths to build on; they are unique and capable of extension into society and the workplace.

The crucible is before us. Whether we succeed or fail lies in our willingness and ability as a nation to acknowledge and act on key elements of our own saga. This means reawakening our increasingly latent dreams of what an American worker is, does, and should be. The themes of America's uniqueness and values have been articulated by Tocqueville and Benjamin Franklin, among others. In an evocative essay, Alex Inkles takes note of these themes and their failure to stir the contemporary American.[10] In this book, we have commented on the same failure. But we believe these cultural imperatives are not too deeply buried to be retrieved, for the fight against cynicism generally and in the workplace specifically.

These cultural themes are implicitly embedded in our distinctions between the cynical and the upbeat company. Drawing from Inkles, we can restate their tenets as follows:

- The intrinsic value of meaningful and satisfying work, as opposed to mind-numbing and ego-deflating toil
- The quality of can-do determination, in contrast to fatalism and handwringing in the face of hard times
- The qualities of innovation and flexibility in work design, in contrast to rigidity and "rule by the rules"
- The belief that honest work brings honest rewards and that honest rewards yield honest work
- The belief in individuality and self-reliance, in contrast to stifling conformity or self-indulgence
- The belief in egalitarianism and equal opportunity, rather than in status-laden and class-preserving management practices
- A persisting belief that American values are superior and will win, rather than the copying of Japanese practices or a succumbing to old-style Europeanization
- A wish for personal recognition based on achievement and hard work, rather than on political connections and opportunism
- Optimism regarding personal upward socioeconomic mobility, rather than pessimism regarding social and material progress
- A willingness to band together with peers and to renounce cutthroat competition and false friendships

Corporate leaders, elected union officials, and politicians—three of the parties most responsible for the future of work in this country—need to face squarely the problems wrought by cynicism in today's work force and workplace. To be competitive in a global economy, we need an involved, committed work force, not a cynical one. It is wrong to blame all our competitive problems on economic forces, trade barriers, or the exchange rate. The problem starts with product and service quality. And this quality will not be fixed until we call on our reserves of pride, hard work, innovation, know-how, and risk taking. We simply need to approach cynicism at work in a less cynical fashion.

What we are proposing is the development of a new social and corporate atmosphere, the fashioning of a basic and fair compact between working people and their organizations, and the development of honest dialogue between leaders and followers in government, society, and the workplace. In terms of managing cynicism at work, we hope we have provided a blueprint.

Appendix A

Composition of Survey Sample

Sex
48% Male
52% Female

Race
87% White
13% Nonwhite

Marital Status
62% Married
23% Single
15% Widowed or divorced

Education
 9% Some high school
35% High school grad
23% Some college or trade school
33% College grad or more

Income
36% Under $19,900
25% $20,000–$29,999
39% Over $30,000

Age
33% 24 and under
30% 25–34
37% Over 35

Appendix B

Measures of Life Attitudes

Question	Reliability (α)
Cynicism People pretend to care more than they do Most will tell lies if they gain by it Unselfish person is taken advantage of Most not honest by nature No ethical standards if money at stake Most dislike putting out for others Most just out for themselves	0.78
Depersonalization I do not count for much I am just a face in the crowd Most people have little control in life Never understand feelings of others	0.58
Estrangement Harder and harder to make true friends Growing loss of basic trust and faith Most people feel alone Not fair to bring child into bleak future	0.68

Appendix B: Measures of Life Attitudes, Cont'd.

Question	Reliability (α)
Work Ethic Work makes me feel good about self Work is good regardless how hard/boring Others think better of me if working Must do work whether want to or not	0.51
Internal Locus of Control Average person is master of fate Most people think for themselves If try hard, can reach goals in life	0.43
Future Ambition Want to be more than a face in the crowd I think about my future a lot	0.37

Appendix C

Measures
of Work-Related
Attitudes

Question	Reliability (α)
Management Style	
Organization I work for is well managed	
Satisfactory information from management	
Management makes effort to get opinions of workers	0.83
People at top are aware of problems at my level	
Immediate boss is doing a good job	
I receive recognition for doing job well	
Lack of Trust in Management	
Often doubt the truth of management	0.42
Management takes advantage if chance	
Work-Group Cooperation and Trust	
Mutual trust in work group	0.76
Workers cooperate to get job done	
Fairness of Rewards	
Concerns about pay dealt with fairly	0.43
Fair chance for advancement	
View of the Job	
I like the kind of work I do	0.68
Employer considers my job important	
View of the Organization	
Overall satisfied with my organization	

Appendix D

Cynicism in the U.S. Population

	Strongly Agree (%)	Slightly Agree (%)	Slightly Disagree (%)	Strongly Disagree (%)
Most people will tell a lie if they can gain by it.	29	31	27	13
People claim to have ethical standards, but few stick to them when money is at stake.	25	37	27	11
People pretend to care more about one another than they really do.	23	35	28	14
Unselfish person is taken advantage of in today's world.	30	23	20	26
Most people are just out for themselves.	19	27	35	19
People inwardly dislike putting themselves out to help other people.	14	32	34	20

Appendix D: Cynicism in the U.S. Population, Cont'd.

	Strongly Agree (%)	Slightly Agree (%)	Slightly Disagree (%)	Strongly Disagree (%)
Most people are not really honest by nature	11	23	34	32

<table>
<tr><td></td><td>High
Cynicism</td><td>Medium
Cynicism</td><td>Low
Cynicism</td></tr>
<tr><td></td><td>43%</td><td>16%</td><td>41%</td></tr>
<tr><td></td><td>THE
CYNICS</td><td>THE
WARY</td><td>THE
UPBEAT</td></tr>
</table>

Appendix E

Cynics' Profile

Variable	The Cynics	The Wary	The Upbeat
Cynicism and Age			
% age 24 or under	51	18	31
% age 25–34	46	14	40
% age 35 or older	39	15	46
Cynicism and Age Group			
% age 24 and under	51	18	31
% age 25–29	44	18	38
% age 30–34	48	10	42
% age 35–39	40	18	42
% age 40–44	28	18	54
% age 45–49	32	9	59
% age 50–54	44	19	37
% age 55–59	45	10	45
% age 60–64	52	24	24
% age 65 and older	55	18	27

293

Appendix E: Cynics' Profile, Cont'd.

Variable	The Cynics	The Wary	The Upbeat
Cynicism and Gender			
% of males	47	14	39
% of females	39	18	43
Cynicism and Race			
% of whites	40	17	43
% of minorities	61	12	27
Cynicism and Education			
% lacking high school degree	58	17	25
% high school graduates	52	12	36
% some college/trade school	44	15	41
% college grad/grad school	29	20	51
Cynicism and Income			
% earning under $19,999	51	16	33
% earning $20,000–$29,999	49	12	39
% earning over $30,000	32	18	50
Cynicism and Marital Status			
% married	41	16	43
% single	43	14	43
% divorced	51	18	31
% widowed	67	17	16
Cynicism and Home Ownership/Locale			
% who own house	40	16	44
% who rent	49	14	37
% rural	50	14	36
% urban	45	13	42
% suburban	38	18	44

Appendix F

Cynics in the Work Force

Variable	The Cynics	The Wary	The Upbeat
Cynicism and Collar			
% blue collar	54	15	31
% white collar	40	18	42
Cynicism and Union Membership			
% who are union members	51	17	32
% who are not union members	41	16	43
Cynicism and Employment Sector			
% in government	50	14	36
% in manufacturing/construction	47	15	39
% in wholesale/retail trade	43	24	33
% in service industries	41	16	43
Cynicism and Organization Size			
% in firms fewer than 20 people	44	18	38
% in firms 21–200 people	44	18	38
% in firms 201–1,500 people	41	12	47
% in firms 1,501–5,000 people	42	17	41
% in firms 5,001–15,000 people	56	7	37
% in firms over 15,000 people	41	15	44

Appendix G

Cynics' Attitudes Toward Work

Variable	The Cynics %	The Upbeat %
Trust in Management		
I often doubt the truth of what management tells us.	40	25
Management will take advantage of you if you give them a chance.	40	25
Trust in Co-Workers		
Members in my work group have trust and confidence in each other.	62	74
The people I work with cooperate to get the job done.	71	79
Fairness of Rewards		
If I have concerns about pay, I know they will be dealt with fairly.	55	64

Appendix G: Cynics' Attitudes Toward Work, Cont'd.

Variable	The Cynics %	The Upbeat %
If there is an opportunity for advancement in my organization, I feel I'll have a fair chance at it.	61	72
Management Style		
In my judgment, the organization I work for is well managed.	59	63
The information I receive from management about what's going on in the organization is quite satisfactory.	51	55
Sufficient effort is made to get the opinions and thinking of people who work in my organization.	44	55
People at the top of this organization are aware of the problems at my level in the organization.	53	55
Overall, my immediate supervisor or boss is doing a good job.	69	74
The amount of recognition I receive from doing my job is sufficient.	60	68
View of the Job		
I like the kind of work I do.	81	89
I think my job is considered important by my employer.	82	92
View of the Organization		
Overall, I am satisfied with the organization I work for at the present time.	67	76

Appendix H

Predictors
of Attitudes
Toward Work

Variable	Predictors (% Agreement)
Trust in Management (Do Not)	
1. Cynicism $(0.28)^a$	
Cynical	40
Upbeat	25
2. Estrangement (0.18)	
Estranged	41
Connected	17
3. Education Level (0.18)	
Less than high school	31
High school degree	36
Some college	37
College grad or more	24
4. Locus of Control (0.16)	
Inner-directed	18
Fatalistic	36

Appendix H: Predictors of Attitudes Toward Work, Cont'd.

Variable	Predictors (% Agreement)
Trust in Co-workers	
1. Cynicism (0.17)	
Cynical	64
Upbeat	73
2. Locus of Control (0.17)	
Inner-directed	72
Fatalistic	61
3. Work Ethic (0.14)	
Hardworking	70
Lazy	65
Fairness of Rewards	
1. Locus of Control (0.21)	
Inner-directed	70
Fatalistic	45
2. Depersonalization (0.19)	
Self-respecting	60
Faceless	43
Management Style	
1. Age (0.18)	
Younger worker	57
Baby boomer	62
Older worker	66
2. Locus of Control (0.22)	
Inner-directed	71
Fatalistic	45
3. Ambition (0.15)	
Ambitious	60
Complacent	65
4. Cynicism (0.15)	
Cynical	59
Upbeat	64
View of the Job	
1. Age (0.28)	
Younger worker	80
Baby boomer	82
Older worker	89

Appendix H: Predictors of Attitudes Toward Work, Cont'd.

Variable	Predictors (% Agreement)
2. Work Ethic (0.16)	
Hardworking	89
Lazy	80
3. Cynicism (0.13)	
Cynical	80
Upbeat	90
View of the Organization	
1. Income (0.25)	
Lower income	63
Middle income	73
Higher income	79
2. Locus of Control (0.25)	
Inner-directed	73
Fatalistic	63
3. Race (0.20)	
White	72
Minority	61
4. Depersonalization (0.16)	
Self-Respecting	74
Faceless	54

[a]b coefficients in regression equations. All are statistically significant ($p < 0.05$).

Notes

Introduction

1. Skepticism and cynicism are not, by any means, interchangeable concepts. Skepticism is healthy, probing, and often creative and is of value to an organization and a society if only to prevent inertia in the first case and demagoguery in the second. Skeptics doubt the substance of communications; cynics not only doubt what is said but the motives for saying it. Cynics project their own suspicions of human nature onto authority figures and other people. Skeptics are basically empiricists—people who may doubt words but are open to reason and willing to be convinced by deeds.
2. J. P. Kotter, in *Power and Influence* (New York: Free Press, 1985, p. 17), writes: "[The cynic] believes that the essence of human nature is dark, competitive, self-centered and fundamentally immoral. The cynic, much like the naive (ironically), attributes organizational outcomes to forces inside individuals. The cynic assumes evil forces are usually at work, the naive assumes good forces are the norm. At the same time both are almost blind to the social milieu surrounding people in organizations and how that milieu can shape behavior, systematically create conflicts among people, and set the stage for power struggles."
3. G. C. Vaillant, in *Adaptation to Life* (Boston: Little, Brown, 1977), posits that the human personality is defined by a hierarchy of coping mechanisms. Mature

301

ego mechanisms include suppression, altruism, and anticipation, as well as a healthy sense of humor. To this we might add sensible skepticism. Less mature mechanisms, common to all of us, include rationalization, dissociation, and compartmentalization. Finally, Vaillant identifies immature modes of adjustment, including fantasy, projection, paranoia, passive-aggressive behavior, and acting out. These mechanisms are in the cynic's arsenal, consciously or not, and, as Vaillant notes, are not so easily amenable to management or even to treatment. We are *not* saying that cynics have personality disorders (though some surely do). Rather, we believe that cynicism—as a disposition to think about and behave toward other people and the world in a suspicious, contemptuous, and wholly self-interested fashion—is an immature mode of adaptation and, in many respects, an unhealthy one. See also K. Horney, *The Neurotic Personality of Our Time* (New York: Norton, 1937).

4. Statistics cited come from *The Yankelovich Monitor,* 1978; *The Harris Survey,* conducted by Louis Harris and Associates, 1966; September 13–25, 1973; January 3–7, 1986; November 26–December 2, 1986; *The ABC Harris Survey,* April 26–30, 1980; *A Survey of the Reactions of the American People and Top Business Executives to the Report on Public Education by the Task Force on Teaching as Profession of the Carnegie Forum on Education and the Economy,* June 30–July 25, 1986; and *Consumer Attitudes and Buying Plans,* NFO Research for Consumer Research Center of the Conference Board, December 1986.

5. D. Goleman, ''The Tax Cheats—Selfish to the Bottom Line,'' *New York Times,* April 11, 1988. See also D. Alters, ''Why Americans Don't Vote,'' *Boston Globe,* July 17, 1988.

6. L. Wrightsman, ''Measurement of Philosophies of Human Nature,'' *Psychological Reports* 14 (1964): 743–751, and *Assumptions About Human Nature: A Social Psychological Approach* (Monterey: Brooks/Cole, 1974); M. Rosenberg, *Occupations and Values* (Glencoe, Ill.: Free Press, 1957).

7. From *The Devil's Dictionary* (New York: Dover, 1958); originally published in 1911.

8. From *The House by the Side of the Road* (Boston: North End Union, 1900).

9. A. Brinkley, ''America Is Back,'' *London Review of Books,* November 1–4, 1984, and Lipsett cited in ''The Talk of the Town,'' *New Yorker,* February 2, 1987.

10. L. Harris, *Inside America* (New York: Vintage, 1987).

11. A. Toffler, *Future Shock* (New York: Bantam, 1981).

12. Harris, *Inside America,* pp. 3–6, 119.

13. M. McLuhan, *Understanding Media: The Extensions of Man* (New York: McGraw-Hill, 1964).

14. G. Wills, *Reagan's America: Innocents at Home* (Garden City: Doubleday, 1987).

15. J. Snider, ''The Power of Positive Cynicism,'' *Utne Reader* (November–December 1987): 106–110, and N. Foy, ''Ambivalence Is Human. Hypocrisy Is in the Eye of the Beholder. Cynicism Can Be Healthy,'' *New Management* (Spring 1985): 49–53.

16. From *Friends* (1970).

17. From *The Critic as Artist* (Girard, Kansas: Haldeman-Julius, Co., 1925).

18. A. Jay, *Management and Machiavelli* (Baltimore: Penguin Books, 1976).

19. L. Jones, *Great Expectations: America and the Baby Boom Generation* (New York: Ballantine, 1986).

20. D. Yankelovich, ''New Rules in American Life: Searching for Self-Fulfillment in a World Turned Upside Down,'' *Psychology Today* (April 1981): 43.

21. G. Hofestede, *Culture's Consequences* (Newbury Park: Sage, 1980). Our own survey data show some significant differences in levels and types of cynicism in U.S. versus European samples. See "New Study Finds High Level of Cynicism Among U.S. and European Workforces," *International Management Europe,* October 1985.
22. T. Hobbes, *Leviathan* (New York: Dutton, 1947).
23. N. Machiavelli, *The Prince* (New York: Dutton, 1974); originally published in 1513.
24. C. W. Ashcraft, "The Relationship Between Conceptions of Human Nature and Judgments of Specific Persons" (unpublished doctoral dissertation, George Peabody College for Teachers, 1963), provides an interesting analysis of how different types of people judge others.

Chapter 1

1. See M. Maccoby, *The Gamesman* (New York: Simon & Schuster, 1976), for a thorough analysis of different organizational "personality" types. See also E. E. Jennings, *An Anatomy of Leadership: Princes, Heroes, and Supermen* (New York: McGraw-Hill, 1960), for characterizations of Commanders.
2. R. K. Merton, "Bureaucratic Structure and Personality," in C. Kluckhohn and H. Murray (eds.), *Personality in Nature, Society, and Culture* (New York: Knopf, 1948), provides a primer on the Administrative Sideliner. See also C. W. Mills, *White Collar* (New York: Oxford University Press, 1951).
3. S. A. Culbert and J. J. McDonough, *The Invisible War: Pursuing Self-Interests at Work* (New York: Wiley, 1980), detail stratagems of players in organizations today.
4. N. West, *Miss Lonelyhearts* (New York: New Directions, 1933), and C. Lasch, *The Culture of Narcissism: American Life in an Age of Diminishing Expectations* (New York: Norton, 1978).
5. R. Whitehead, *The New Collar Voter* (Amherst: University of Massachusetts, 1984–1985). Survey by the Gallup Organization and Yankelovich Clancy Schulman for *Time* magazine describes many of the attitudes of today's Squeezed Cynics. See "The New Collar Class," *U.S. News & World Report,* September 16, 1985; G. F. Will, " 'New Collars,' New Values," *Newsweek,* November 24, 1986; and R. Whitehead, "Courting the Baby-Boom Vote," *Boston Globe,* January 4, 1987.
6. T. Veblen, *Theory of the Leisure Class* (New York: Macmillan, 1899).
7. D. Reisman, *The Lonely Crowd: A Study of the Changing American Character* (New Haven: Yale University Press, 1950), describes some of the characteristics of Stoics.
8. R. Blauner, *Alienation and Freedom: The Factory Worker and His Industry* (Chicago: University of Chicago Press, 1964), delineates the factors shaping the Hard-Bitten Cynic.
9. Our analysis is cognitive and functional. J. Hunt, *Managing People at Work* (New York: McGraw-Hill, 1979), provides an illustration of this method of analyzing adaptation in work situations. Others, such as Harry Levinson, see more value in depth psychology; see his *Psychological Man* (Cambridge, Mass.: Levinson Institute, 1976). See also J. Shklar, *Ordinary Vices* (Cambridge, Mass.: Belknap Press of Harvard University, 1984), on the functional versus dysfunctional coping styles and R. B. Williams, "Type A Behavior and Coronary Heart Disease, Something Old and Something New," paper presented at the annual meeting of the Society of Behavioral Medicine, 1984, on the components of hostility in cynicism.

10. F. W. Taylor, *The Principles of Scientific Management* (New York: Norton, 1947); originally published in 1911.
11. A. G. Marquis, *Hopes and Ashes* (New York: Free Press, 1986).
12. C. F. Forman, "A Generation of Cynics," *Princeton Alumni Weekly* (June 14, 1982): 10-11.
13. D. J. Cherrington, *The Work Ethic: Working Values and Values That Work* (New York: AMACOM, 1980).
14. Statistics from R. Reich, *The Next American Frontier* (New York: Penguin, 1983).

Chapter 2

1. A.J.M. Sykes and I. Lindsay, "Expectations and Attitudes: An Industrial Comparison," *Employee Relations* 5 (1), (1983): 22-26.
2. D. Yankelovich and J. Immerwahr, *Putting the Work Ethic to Work,* Public Agenda Report on Restoring America's Competitive Vitality (New York: Public Agenda Foundation, 1983).
3. D. L. Kanter, "Cynical Marketers at Work," *Journal of Advertising Research* (January 1989): 28-34.
4. "How Working Stiffs Get the Short End," letter to Ann Landers in *Boston Globe,* January 18, 1987.
5. The most manifest aspects of a company's culture are to be found in its structure and practices—the so-called formal organization and all the systems that regulate corporate conduct. Beneath this surface lie the informal organization, the pattern of how things *really* get done in a company, as well as company norms, the principles people follow as they go about their daily business. Deeper still, at the core of the culture, are beliefs and values, the convictions people have about their work and their co-workers. By focusing on the corporate embodiments of people's outlooks, we can explore the core beliefs and values of a company and, in turn, see how they are expressed in the informal and formal aspects of corporate life. See E. Schein, *Organizational Culture and Leadership* (San Francisco: Jossey-Bass, 1985).

   We see value in thinking of companies (or units within companies) as being, for example, optimistic, trustworthy, and people-oriented, in contrast to being pessimistic, cynical, and depersonalizing. One department might be described as being hardworking (high work ethic), entrepreneurial (high sense of internal control), and collegial (the world is not seen as getting colder), while another department could be described as lackadaisical (low work ethic), passive (low sense of internal control), and inhospitable (the world is seen as getting colder). We would expect to see these outlooks manifest in the norms and everyday behavior of people and in the structure and practices of the enterprise.

   Images of corporate culture track prevailing assumptions about human nature. There is a parallel, for example, between the mechanical models of organization prominent in the early part of this century and machinelike conceptions of human nature and between the team management structures of corporate bureaucracies in the 1950s and the then current conceptions of the social needs of working people. Contemporary analyses treat corporate culture as based, in some fashion, upon information-age assumptions about working people. See P. H. Mirvis, *Work in the 20th Century* (Cambridge, Mass.: Revision/Rudi Press, 1984–1985).

6. R. J. Samuelson, "Bureaucracy as Life," *Newsweek,* January 12, 1987, p. 43.

7. Reich, in *The Next American Frontier,* goes on to write: "Paper shuffling has its correlates in people shuffling. All this rearranging of industrial assets and people has made it more difficult for American enterprise to undertake basic change. It has enforced short-term thinking, discouraged genuine innovation, and consumed the careers of some of our most talented citizens. It also has transformed many American companies into fearful and demoralized places characterized by cynical indifference and opportunism" (p. 171).

8. Statistics from Yankelovich and Immerwahr, *Putting the Work Ethic to Work.*

9. P. F. Drucker, "Hysteria over the Work Ethic," *Psychology Today* (November 1973): 87–92; R. A. Katzell, "Changing Attitudes Toward Work," in C. Kerr and J. M. Rosow (eds.), *Work in America: The Decade Ahead* (New York: Van Nostrand, 1979).

10. See T. Levitt, "The Globalization of Markets," *Harvard Business Review* 61 (1983): 92–102, and J. Quelch and J. Hoffe, "Customizing Global Marketing," *Harvard Business Review* 64 (1986): 59–68.

11. D. L. Kanter, "Creating Confidence in Companies," paper presented at the Marketing Science Institute conference on corporate communications, Cambridge, Mass., 1981.

12. M. R. Cooper and others, "Changing Employee Values: Deepening Discontent?" *Harvard Business Review* 57 (1979): 117–125.

13. M. M. Lombardo and M. W. McCall, "The Intolerable Boss," *Psychology Today* (January 1984): 45–48.

14. Opinion Research Corporation, *Changing Worker Values: Myth or Reality?* (Princeton, N.J.: Opinion Research Corporation, 1977).

15. "How to Get a Job," *Esquire,* July 1977; article cited in *Changing Worker Values.*

Chapter 3

1. A. Bierce, *The Devil's Dictionary* (New York: Dover, 1958), and J. Green, *The Cynic's Lexicon* (New York: St. Martin's Press, 1984). Unreferenced quotations on cynicism in this book come from Green's compendium.

2. S. Sarason, *Work, Aging and Social Change* (New York: Free Press, 1977), p. 25.

3. S. Wilson, *Man in the Gray Flannel Suit* (New York: Simon & Schuster, 1955).

4. W. H. Whyte, *The Organization Man* (Garden City: Doubleday, 1956).

5. R. Rovere, *Senator Joe McCarthy* (New York: Harcourt Brace Jovanovich, 1959).

6. D. Yankelovich, *The New Morality: A Profile of American Youth in the 70's* (New York: McGraw-Hill, 1974).

7. G. Melly, *Revolt into Style* (London: Allen Lawe, 1970).

8. T. Palmer, *All You Need Is Love—The Story of Popular Music* (London: Futura Publications, 1976).

9. E. Epstein, *The Warren Commission and Establishment of the Truth* (New York: Viking Press, 1966).

10. M. E. Gettleman and contributors, *Vietnam and America* (New York: Grove Press, 1985).

11. P. B. Kurland, *Watergate and the Constitution* (Chicago: University of Chicago Press, 1978).

12. See Higher Education Research Institute, University of California, Los Angeles, 1967 through 1987, for these statistics and data on the attitudes of young people.

13. R. N. Bellah and colleagues, *Habits of the Heart: Individualism and Commitment in American Life* (Berkeley: University of California Press, 1985); C. H. Cooley, *Social Organization* (New York: Scribner's, 1909).

14. T. P. O'Neill, *Man of the House* (New York: Random House, 1987).

15. W. Watts, "Americans' Hopes and Fears: The Future Can Fend for Itself," *Psychology Today* (September 1981): 36–48.

16. D. Stockman, *The Triumph of Politics* (New York: Harper & Row, 1986).

17. P. Slater, *The Pursuit of Loneliness: American Culture at the Breaking Point* (Boston: Beacon Press, 1970), provides a sharp analysis of disillusioning "facts" that continue to shape the American character.

18. B. Barol, "The Eighties Are Over," *Newsweek* (January 4, 1988): 40–48.

19. Sarason, *Work, Aging and Social Change.*

20. Concept and phrase developed by George Fabian. See D. L. Kanter, "The Europeanizing of America," in H. Thorelli and H. Becker (eds.), *International Marketing Strategy* (New York: Pergamon Press, 1980); R. M. Kidder, "Ethics Awash: Is Europeanized America Sliding into Cynicism?" *Christian Science Monitor,* February 25, 1982, p. B6.

21. See D. Thomas, "Facing the Future—With a Shaky Faith in Human Nature," *Europe 82* 11 (November 7, 1982); W. E. Blundell, "In Europe, the Sullen Eighties?" *Wall Street Journal,* March 11, 1980.

22. Statistics from Watts, "Hopes and Fears," pp. 36–40. See also C. Lasch, *Haven in a Heartless World: The Family Besieged* (New York: Basic Books, 1977).

23. D. L. Kanter, "Student Perceptions of Advertising's Role in Drug Usage and Attitudes," in R. Ostman (ed.), *Communications Research and Drug Education* (Newbury Park: Sage, 1976).

Chapter 4

1. A. de Tocqueville, *Democracy in America* (Garden City: Anchor Books, 1969).

2. H. Gutman, *Work, Culture, and Society in Industrializing America* (New York: Vintage, 1976), reviews early industrialization and the Moral Reform movement.

3. C. Perrow, *Complex Organizations: A Critical Essay* (New York: Random House, 1986), reviews the industrial revolution and the New Thought movement.

4. R. Hofstadter, *Social Darwinism in American Thought, 1860–1915* (Philadelphia: University of Pennsylvania Press, 1945).

5. M. Maccoby, "Leadership Needs for the 1980's," *Current Issues in Higher Education* 2 (1979): 17–23, reviews the characteristics of the leader as "empire builder."

6. T. Veblen, *Theory of the Leisure Class.*

7. E. Hubbard, *A Message to García,* edited by R.W.G. Vail (New York: New York Public Library, 1930), p. 14; originally published in 1899.

8. See E. Mayo, *The Social Problems of an Industrial Civilization* (Boston: Graduate School of Business Administration, Harvard University, 1945), on the "rabble hypothesis."

9. Cited in R. Bendix, *Work and Authority in Industry* (New York: Wiley, 1956).
10. U. Sinclair, *The Jungle* (New York: Harper & Row, 1957); originally published in 1906.
11. S. Gompers, *Labor and the Common Welfare* (New York: Dutton, 1919).
12. Bendix, *Work and Authority*, reviews managerial ideologies and tactics in the industrial revolution.
13. Taylor, *Scientific Management;* E. H. Schein, *Organizational Psychology* (Englewood Cliffs, N.J.: Prentice-Hall, 1980), discusses assumptions of human nature underlying organizational practices.
14. J. K. Galbraith, *The Great Crash* (Boston: Houghton Mifflin, 1979).
15. F. J. Roethlisberger, *Management and Morale* (Cambridge: Harvard University Press, 1943), provides an introduction to the human relations movement. See also F. J. Roethlisberger and W. J. Dickson, *Management and the Worker* (Cambridge: Harvard University Press, 1939), on the Hawthorne studies.
16. Quotes from Bendix, *Work and Authority*, p. 311; Mayo, *Social Problems*, pp. 40–44.
17. D. Carnegie, *How to Win Friends and Influence People* (New York: Simon & Schuster, 1982); from a 1926 tract entitled "Public Speaking and Influencing Men in Business," then retitled and published in 1936.
18. Quote from Bendix, *Work and Authority*, p. 290.
19. W. H. Whyte, Jr., *Is Anybody Listening?* (New York: Simon & Schuster, 1952).
20. E. Fromm, *The Sane Society* (New York: Holt, Rinehart & Winston, 1955); "Man Is Not a Thing," *Saturday Review*, March 16, 1957.
21. Whyte, *Is Anybody Listening?*
22. Jennings, *Anatomy of Leadership*, pp. 190–191.
23. M. Weber, *Economy and Society*, translated by G. Roth and C. Wittach (Berkeley: University of California Press, 1968).
24. Mills, *White Collar*.
25. Ibid., p. 80.
26. M. Dalton, *Men Who Manage* (New York: Wiley, 1959).
27. F. Kafka, *The Castle* (New York: Knopf, 1941).
28. Mills, *White Collar*, p. 110.
29. GE company handbook, cited in Bendix, *Work and Authority*, p. 321.

Chapter 5

1. R. P. Quinn and G. L. Staines, *The 1977 Quality of Employment Survey: Descriptive Statistics with Comparison Data from the 1969–70 and the 1972–73 Surveys* (Ann Arbor: Survey Research Center, Institute for Social Research, University of Michigan, 1979).
2. *Worker Alienation, 1972,* hearings before the Subcommittee on Employment, Manpower, and Poverty of the Committee on Labor and Public Welfare, U.S. Senate (Washington: U.S. Government Printing Office, 1972).
3. *Fortune*, September 1970, on blue-collar blues.
4. White-collar woes are documented in U.S. Department of Labor, *Job Satisfaction: Is There a Trend?* (Washington: U.S. Government Printing Office, 1974). See also Quinn and Staines, *Survey*.
5. Opinion Research Corporation, *Changing Worker Values*, pp. 2–3.
6. E. Ginzberg, "The Changing American Economy and Labor Force," in J. Rosow (ed.), *The Worker and the Job* (Englewood Cliffs, N.J.: Prentice-Hall, 1974).

7. J. O'Toole, *Work, Learning, and the American Future* (San Francisco: Jossey-Bass, 1977), reviews trends in education and work.

8. M. S. Gordon, "Women and Work: Priorities for the Future," in C. Kerr and J. M. Rosow (eds.), *Work in America: The Decade Ahead* (New York: Van Nostrand, 1979).

9. C. A. Reich, *The Greening of America* (New York: Random House, 1970).

10. D. Yankelovich, "Work, Values and the New Breed," in C. Kerr and J. M. Rosow (eds.), *Work in America: The Decade Ahead* (New York: Van Nostrand, 1979).

11. U.S. Department of Health, Education, and Welfare, *Work in America* (Cambridge: MIT Press, 1973), p. xv.

12. D. E. Ewing, *Freedom Inside the Organization* (New York: Dutton, 1978).

13. *Work in America,* pp. xvi–xvii.

14. S. M. Lipset and W. Schneider, *The Confidence Gap: Business, Labor and Government in the Public Mind* (New York: Free Press, 1983).

15. Reich, *Greening of America,* pp. 236–240.

16. D. McGregor, *The Human Side of Enterprise* (New York: McGraw-Hill, 1960).

17. C. Argyris, *Personality and Organization* (New York: Harper & Row, 1957), and *Integrating the Individual and the Organization* (New York: Wiley, 1964).

18. A. Marrow, *Behind the Executive Mask* (New York: American Management Association, 1964), describes T-groups for executives in this era.

19. R. Likert, *New Patterns of Management* (New York: McGraw-Hill, 1961).

20. S. E. Seashore and others, *Assessing Organizational Change* (New York: Wiley-Interscience, 1983), and P. H. Mirvis and B. A. Macy, "Accounting for Costs and Benefits of Human Resource Development Programs," *Organizations, Accounting and Society* 1 (1976): 179–194.

21. New York Stock Exchange, Office of Economic Research, *People and Productivity* (New York: New York Stock Exchange, 1982).

22. J. P. Campbell and M. D. Dunnette, "Effectiveness of T-group Experiences in Managerial Training and Development," *Psychological Bulletin* 70 (1968): 73–104, and P. H. Mirvis and D. N. Berg, *Failures in Organization Development and Change* (New York: Wiley-Interscience, 1977).

23. L. J. Peter and R. Hull, *The Peter Principle—Why Things Always Go Wrong* (New York: Bantam, 1969).

24. J. Gall, *Systemantics—How Systems Work and Especially How They Fail* (New York: Quandrangle, 1975).

25. D. Halberstam, *The Reckoning* (New York: Morrow, 1986), traces this trend in Ford Motor Company.

26. Statistics from Reich, *The Next American Frontier,* p. 142.

27. R. Likert, *The Human Organization: Its Management and Value* (New York: McGraw-Hill, 1967); E. F. Schumacher, *Small Is Beautiful* (New York: Harper & Row, 1973); T. Mills, "Human Resources—Why the New Concern," *Harvard Business Review* (March–April 1975): 120–134.

28. R. Cole, "Diffusion of Participatory Work Structures in Japan, Sweden, and the United States," in P. S. Goodman (ed.), *Change in Organizations* (San Francisco: Jossey-Bass, 1982).

29. B. Kaufman, *Up the Down Staircase* (Englewood Cliffs, N.J.: Prentice-Hall, 1964), and R. Townsend, *Up the Organization* (New York: Knopf, 1970).

30. Maccoby, *The Gamesman.*

31. T. Kidder, *The Soul of a New Machine* (New York: Avon, 1981).

Chapter 6

1. T. J. Peters and R. H. Waterman, Jr., *In Search of Excellence* (New York: Harper & Row, 1982); R. Conwell, *Acres of Diamonds* (Kansas City: Hallmark, 1968).
2. R. Zager and M. P. Rosow, *The Innovative Organization* (New York: Pergamon Press, 1982), present illustrative examples of corporate change programs in the 1980s. See also D. Q. Mills, "Human Resources in the 1980's," *Harvard Business Review* (July–August 1979): 154–162.
3. R. M. Kanter, *The Change Masters* (New York: Simon & Schuster, 1983); H. Leavitt, *Corporate Pathfinders* (Homewood, Ill.: Dow Jones/Irwin, 1986); N. M. Tichy and M. A. Devanna, *The Transformational Leader* (New York: Wiley, 1986); D. Q. Mills, *The New Competitors* (New York: Wiley, 1985).
4. Evidence reported in N. N. Wardell, "The Corporation," *Daedalus* (Winter 1978): 97–110.
5. *Business Week,* May 11, 1981, on the "New Industrial Relations."
6. W. G. Ouchi, *Theory Z* (Reading, Mass.: Addison-Wesley, 1981).
7. J. Naisbitt, *Megatrends* (New York: Warner Books, 1982).
8. R. Harrison, "Strategies for a New Age," *Human Resource Management* 22 (1983): 209–235, discusses alignment and attunement in organizations.
9. See *Time,* January 13, 1986, on Donald Burr and People Express.
10. B. Uttal, "The Corporate Culture Vultures," *Fortune,* October 17, 1983.
11. "Corporate Mind Control," *Newsweek,* May 4, 1987.
12. B. Kuttner, "When Workers Are the Victims of Corporate-Takeover Fever," *Boston Globe,* January 5, 1987.
13. D. J. Bell, "Notes on the Post-Industrial Society (I & II)," *Public Interest* (Spring 1967), and J. D. Rockefeller III *The Second American Revolution* (New York: Harper & Row, 1973).
14. B. Bluestone and B. Harrison, *The Deindustrialization of America* (New York: Basic Books, 1982).
15. E. Ginsberg and G. Vojta, "The Service Sector of the U.S. Economy," *Scientific American* (March 1981): 48–55.
16. Whitehead, *Boston Globe,* January 4, 1987.
17. Reich, *The Next American Frontier,* p. 166.
18. P. Hirsch, *Pack Your Own Parachute* (Reading, Mass.: Addison-Wesley, 1987).
19. R. M. Kanter, "Work in a New America," *Daedalus* (Winter 1978): 47–78, for one, predicted that younger Americans would scale down their expectations about work in the 1980s. D. Yankelovich, *The New Rules,* and *General Social Surveys 1972–1986* (National Opinion Research Center, 1984–1986), show that expectations of work have continued to rise.
20. A. H. Maslow, "A Theory of Motivation," *Psychological Review* 50 (1943): 370–396.

Chapter 7

1. C. Gilligan, *In a Different Voice: Psychological Theory and Women's Development* (Cambridge: Harvard University Press, 1982), describes this line of research on male and female differences.
2. See L. D. Johnston, J. G. Bachman, and P. M. O'Malley, *Monitoring the Future: Questionnaire Responses from the Nation's High School Seniors* (Ann Arbor:

Institute for Social Research, University of Michigan, 1979–), and "Annual Survey of Entering Freshmen," Higher Education Research Institute, for data on the attitudes of today's young people.

3. From H. Broun, *Pieces of Hate* (New York: George H. Duran, 1922).
4. From Reich, *The Next American Frontier;* see also R. Reich and I. C. Majaziner, *Minding America's Business: The Decline and Rise of the American Economy* (New York: Harcourt Brace Jovanovich, 1982).
5. D. Leavitt, "The New Lost Generation," *Esquire,* May 1985, p. 94.
6. Ibid., p. 93.
7. Jones, *Great Expectations.*
8. Whitehead, *New Collar Voter.*
9. H. H. Munro (Saki), "Reginald at the Carlton," *Short Stories of Saki* (New York: Modern Library, 1958).
10. *The Future of Older Workers in America* (Scarsdale, N.Y.: Work in America Institute, 1980) summarizes research on the capabilities of older Americans at work.
11. Gilligan, *Different Voice,* and R. B. Williams, Jr., "The Health Consequences of Hostility," in *Anger, Hostility, and Behavioral Medicine* (New York: Hemisphere/McGraw-Hill, 1984), present contrasting female and male coping patterns.
12. P. Gurin and E. Epps, *Black Consciousness, Identity, and Achievement* (New York: Wiley, 1975), review blacks' attitudes and societal experiences.
13. Anatole France quoted in J. R. Solly, *A Cynic's Breviary* (London: J. Lane, 1925).
14. See C. Jencks, *Who Gets Ahead?—The Determinants of Economic Success in America* (New York: Basic Books, 1979), on the importance of education to later success.
15. See Quinn and Staines, *Survey,* for data on education level and ratings of the importance of job facets.
16. From *Work in America,* pp. 121–134.
17. From Reich, *The Next American Frontier.*
18. A. Campbell, *The Quality of American Life: Perceptions, Evaluations, and Satisfactions* (Newbury Park: Sage, 1972), and C. Rubenstein, "Money, Self-Esteem, Relationships, Secrecy, Envy, Satisfaction," *Psychology Today* (May 1981): 29–44.
19. *The Wasey Report: The Divorcynic* (London: Wasey-Campbell-Ewald, 1982).
20. See C. Rubenstein, "Regional States of the Mind," *Psychology Today* (February 1982): 22–30, for an illustrative study of the psychological outlooks of people in different regions of the United States.

Chapter 8

1. For interesting research on the relationship between work and personality see M. Kohn and C. Schooler, "Job Conditions and Personality: A Longitudinal Assessment of Their Reciprocal Effects," *American Journal of Sociology* 87 (1982): 1257–1286, and J. Mortimer and J. Lorence, "Work Experience and Occupational Value Socialization: A Longitudinal Study," *American Journal of Sociology* 84 (1979): 1361–1385. For accounts of the development of cynicism in uniform service jobs, see R. M. Regoli, E. D. Poole, and J. L. Schrink, "Occupational Socialization and Career Development:

A Look at Cynicism Among Correctional Workers," *Human Organization* 38 (Summer 1979): 183–187, and H. Holzman and B. J. O'Connell, "Organizational and Professional Cynicism Among Police," paper presented at annual meeting of the American Sociological Association, 1981.

2.   L. Harris, *Inside America,* pp. 232–238.

3.   For a more encompassing understanding of such "compartmentalization" of attitudes among professionals and managers, see Sarason, *Work, Aging and Social Change;* A. K. Korman, U. Wittig-Berman, and D. Lang, "Career Success and Personal Failure: Alienation in Professionals and Managers," *Academy of Management Journal* 24 (2) (June 1981): 342–360; and H. McClosky and J. Schaar, "Psychological Dimensions of Anomie," *American Sociological Review* 30 (1965): 14–40.

4.   T. Kochan, "How American Workers View Labor Unions," *Monthly Labor Review* (April 1979): 23–31.

5.   P. H. Mirvis and E. J. Hackett, "Work and Workforce Characteristics in the Nonprofit Sector," *Monthly Labor Review* (April 1983): 3–12, examine differences in people's job attitudes in the private, governmental, and nonprofit sectors.

6.   A survey of *Industry Week* readers shows a more positive trend: 27 percent of *IW* readers "almost always" trust management. See S. Modic, "Cultivating Trust," *Industry Week,* August 1, 1988. J. W. Driscoll, "Trust and Participation in Organizational Decision Making as Predictors of Satisfaction," *Academy of Management Journal* 21 (March 1978): 44–56, reports on how trust influences other work attitudes.

7.   G. W. Allport, *The Nature of Prejudice* (Reading, Mass.: Addison-Wesley, 1954), presented the first review of research on prejudice and personal contact. His classic contributed significantly to prescriptions to desegregate schools.

8.   D. Roy, "Banana Time: Job Satisfaction and Informal Interaction," *Human Organization* 18 (1960): 158–169, describes mechanisms for gaining peer acceptance.

9.   Cooper and others, "Changing Employee Values," and follow-up study by W. A. Schiemann and B. S. Morgan, "Managing Human Resources— Employee Discontent and Declining Productivity," Opinion Research Corporation, 1982.

10.   E. E. Lawler, *Motivation in Work Organizations* (Monterey: Brooks/Cole, 1973), makes the point that satisfaction sometimes reflects the attitudes of "contented cows."

Chapter 9

1.   R. H. Tawney, *Religion and the Rise of Capitalism: A Historical Study* (Gloucester, Mass.: Peter Smith, 1962), has outlined the factors essential to economic development in an earlier age. See also D. McClelland, *The Achieving Society* (New York: Free Press, 1961). A. Etzioni, "Work in the American Future: Reindustrialization or Quality of Life," in C. Kerr and J. M. Rosow (eds.), *Work in America: The Decade Ahead* (New York: Van Nostrand, 1979), argues that investments in the quality of life will have to be sacrificed, in the short run, if America is to regain its competitive strength. We have seen some of the cynical fallout in our depiction of the rise of cynicism

in the 1980s and would caution that callous indifference to human concerns by country and companies could increase people's sense of estrangement and depersonalization and undermine the strength of traditional values—with all the attendant costs. See P. H. Mirvis and E. E. Lawler, "Measuring Financial Impact of Employee Attitudes," *Journal of Applied Psychology* 62 (1977): 1–8.

2. M. Seeman, "On the Meaning of Alienation," *American Sociological Review* 24 (1959): 783–791, distinguishes between alienation from the material versus social environment. Karl Marx drew this distinction between alienation from the processes of production and one's fellow workers; see *Karl Marx: Early Writings,* edited by T. B. Bottemore (New York: McGraw-Hill, 1963).

3. B. Bettelheim, *The Empty Fortress* (New York: Free Press, 1967), addresses the link between personal efficacy and self-esteem in child development. W. Ryan, *Blaming the Victim* (New York: Vintage, 1971), shows how estrangement and depersonalization are cause and consequence of feelings of powerlessness. P. Zimbardo, "The Human Choice: Individuation, Reason, and Order Versus Deindividuation, Impulse, and Chaos," in W. J. Arnold and D. Levine (eds.), *Nebraska Symposium on Motivation, 1969* (Lincoln: University of Nebraska Press, 1970), pp. 237–307, provides another analysis of the sources and possible consequences of depersonalization.

4. Yankelovich, *The New Rules.* See D. Yankelovich, "The Meaning of Work," in J. Rosow (ed.), *The Worker and the Job* (Englewood Cliffs, N.J.: Prentice-Hall, 1974), for a more thorough discussion of the work ethic.

5. J. B. Rotter, *Social Learning and Clinical Psychology* (Englewood Cliffs, N.J.: Prentice-Hall, 1954), and E. J. Phares, *Locus of Control in Personality* (Morristown, N.J.: General Learning Press, 1976).

6. H. M. Lefcourt, *Research with the Locus of Control Construct,* vol. 1 (New York: Academic Press, 1981), shows a relationship between locus of control and attitudes about authority.

7. There is always an element of self-fulfilling prophecy in social relationships. C. Argyris, *Reasoning, Learning, and Action* (San Francisco: Jossey-Bass, 1982), explicates self-reinforcing patterns of behavior in organizations.

8. T. R. Mitchell, C. M. Smyser, and S. E. Weed, "Locus of Control: Supervision and Work Satisfaction," *Academy of Management Journal* (September 1975): 623–631, show related consequences for people with high versus low loci of control.

9. How group members' behavior is regulated has long been an area of study; see Roethlisberger, *Management and Morale.* For a description of current research see J. R. Hackman, "Self-Management," in M. S. Pallak and R. O. Perloff (eds.), *Psychology and Work* (Washington: American Psychological Association, 1986).

10. See W. A. Schiemann and B. S. Morgan, "Managing Human Resources—Employee Discontent and Declining Productivity," Opinion Research Corporation, 1982, on attitudes toward fairness.

11. See J. Raelin, "The 60s Kids in the Corporation: More than Just 'Daydream Believers,'" *Academy of Management Executive* (February 1987): 21–29, and W. G. Dyer and J. H. Dyer, "The M*A*S*H Generation: Implications for Future Organizational Values," *Organizational Dynamics* (Summer 1984): 66–79, on age-related attitudes about organization life.

12. S. E. Seashore and J. T. Barnowe, "Collar Color Doesn't Count," *Psychology Today* (August 1972): 53–54, 80–82, show that collar color per se is not a significant predictor of job satisfaction.

13. Campbell, *Quality of American Life.*

14. B. E. Anderson, "Minorities and Work: The Challenge for the Next Decade," in C. Kerr and J. M. Rosow (eds.), *Work in America: The Decade Ahead* (New York: Van Nostrand, 1979), reviews minorities' attitudes about work.

15. B. Baxter, *Alienation and Authenticity: Some Consequences for Organized Work* (London: Tavistock, 1982).

16. See R. N. Kanungo, *Work Alienation: An Integrative Approach* (New York: Praeger, 1982), on the intermingling of different forms of alienation in personality and the consequences for work attitudes.

Chapter 10

1. See A. H. Maslow, *Motivation and Personality* (New York: Harper & Row, 1964), and C. P. Alderfer, *Existence, Relatedness, and Growth: Human Needs in Organizational Settings* (New York: Free Press, 1972), for basic research on why people work.

2. M. Maccoby, *Why Work—Leading the New Generation* (New York: Simon & Schuster, 1988).

3. T. Deal and A. A. Kennedy, *Corporate Cultures* (Reading, Mass.: Addison-Wesley, 1982).

4. J. Adolph and F. Graves, "How Two Vermont Hippies Are Redistributing Wealth by Selling Millions of Dollars Worth of All-Natural Ice Cream," *New Age Journal* (March/April 1988): 33–37, 72–77, and E. Larson, "Forever Young," *INC Magazine*, July 1988, describe Ben & Jerry's. Some of the descriptions of the company in this book come from these sources.

5. C. Trillin, "American Chronicles—Competitors," *New Yorker*, July 8, 1985; *Time*, August 10, 1981.

6. McGregor, *Human Side of Enterprise.*

7. Yankelovich and Immerwahr, *Putting the Work Ethic to Work*, pp. 19–24.

8. G. L. Staines and R. P. Quinn, "American Workers Evaluate the Quality of Their Jobs," *Monthly Labor Review* (January 1979): 3–12.

9. Peters and Waterman, *In Search of Excellence.*

10. E. E. Lawler, "The New Plant Revolution," *Organizational Dynamics* (Winter 1978): 3–12, and *High Involvement Management* (San Francisco: Jossey-Bass, 1986).

11. R. E. Walton, "Work Innovations in the United States," *Harvard Business Review* 57 (1979): 88–98, and "From Control to Commitment in the Workplace," *Harvard Business Review* 63 (1985): 76–84.

12. Mirvis and Hackett, "Work and Workforce Characteristics."

13. W. Bennis and B. Nanus, *Leaders: The Strategies for Taking Charge* (New York: Harper & Row, 1985).

14. P. Hirsch, "So Much for Managers' Loyalty," *New York Times,* February 27, 1987.

15. Personal interview of P. Mirvis with Michael Blumenthal.

16. Lamalie Associates, 1985. For a review of postmerger dynamics see M. L. Marks and P. H. Mirvis, "The Merger Syndrome," *Psychology Today* (October 1986): 36–45.

17. B. Uttal, "A Surprisingly Sexy Computer Marriage," *Fortune* (November 24, 1986): 46–55, and *Information Week,* June 8, 1987, describe the process and results of the Burroughs and Sperry merger forming Unisys. Quotes from Mirvis interview with Blumenthal.

Chapter 11

1. See P. H. Mirvis, "Formulating and Implementing Human Resource Strategy: A Model of How to Do It, Two Examples of How It's Done," *Human Resource Management* 24 (1985): 385–412, for a description of this work with Caterpillar Tractor.
2. J. P. Wanous, "Effects of a Realistic Job Preview on Job Acceptance, Job Attitudes and Job Survival," *Journal of Applied Psychology* 58 (1973): 327–332.
3. R. T. Mowday, L. W. Porter, and R. M. Steers, *Employee–Organization Linkages: The Psychology of Commitment, Absenteeism, and Turnover* (New York: Academic Press, 1982).
4. Goodpaster quoted in *Time,* May 25, 1987, p. 29.
5. K. Kram, *Mentoring at Work* (Glenview, Ill.: Scott, Foresman, 1985).
6. Yankelovich and Immerwahr, *Putting the Work Ethic to Work,* pp. 36–45.
7. Ibid., pp. 36–45.
8. R. H. Clark and J. R. Morris, *Workers' Attitudes Toward Productivity* (New York: Chamber of Commerce of the United States, 1980), p. i.
9. P. A. Renwick and E. E. Lawler, "What You Really Want from Your Job," *Psychology Today* (May 1978): 53–65, 118.
10. E. E. Lawler, *Pay and Organization Development* (Reading, Mass.: Addison-Wesley, 1981), summarizes Lawler's recommendations on pay.
11. *ABC News/Harris Survey,* conducted by Louis Harris and Associates, April 26–30, 1980, and *The Harris Survey,* conducted by Louis Harris and Associates, January 3–7, 1986.
12. See M. Useem, "Market and Institutional Factors in Corporate Contributions," *California Management Review* 30 (1988): 77–88, for a description of Polaroid's program.
13. M. Melbin, *Night as Frontier* (New York: Free Press, 1987).
14. E. E. Lawler and others, "Measuring the Quality of Work Life: How Graphic Controls Assesses the Human Side of the Corporation," *Management Review* (October 1981): 54–63.
15. Terrel cited in *Time,* May 25, 1987, p. 29.

Chapter 12

1. R. Bauer, "The Obstinate Audience: The Influence Process from the Point of View of Social Communication," *American Psychologist* 19 (1964): 319–328.
2. R. A. Bauer and others, *Advertising in America: The Consumer View* (Boston: Harvard Graduate School of Business Administration, 1968).
3. D. L. Kanter, "Communications Theory and Advertising Decisions," *Journal of Advertising Research* (December 1970): 3–8, and "It Could Be: Ad Trends Flowing from Europe to U.S.," *Advertising Age* (February 9, 1981): 49–52.
4. See R. Haley, *Developing Effective Communication Strategy* (New York: Wiley, 1985), for an authoritative review.

5. M. K. Kogay, "Workers Want Employers to Listen to Them, Survey Shows," *New York Times,* June 14, 1988.
6. G. Katona, B. Strumpel, and E. Zahn, *Aspirations and Affluence* (New York: McGraw-Hill, 1971).
7. J. R. Kirk and G. D. Talbot, "The Distortion of Information," in A. G. Smith (ed.), *Communication and Culture: Readings in the Codes of Human Interaction* (New York: Holt, Rinehart & Winston, 1959).
8. D. J. Bem, *Beliefs, Attitudes, and Human Affairs* (Monterey: Brooks/Cole, 1970).
9. J. Koehler, K. Anatol, and R. Appelbaum, *Organizational Communication and Behavioral Perspectives* (New York: Holt, Rinehart & Winston, 1976), and J. T. Klapper, *The Effects of Mass Communication* (New York: Free Press, 1960).
10. H. I. Abelson and M. Karlins, *Persuasion: How Opinions Are Formed and Attitudes Are Changed* (New York: Springer, 1970).
11. See C. I. Hovland, I. L. Janis, and H. H. Kelley, *Communication and Persuasion* (New Haven: Yale University Press, 1953), for the first research on this subject.
12. See J. Lannon and P. Cooper, "Humanistic Advertising—A Holistic Cultural Perspective," *International Journal of Advertising—Quarterly Review of Marketing Communications* (July–September 1983): 195–213; D. Lloyd and K. Clancy, "A Study of the Effects of Television Program Involvement on Advertising Response," paper presented at the Annual Copy Research Conference, New York, May 3, 1988; M. Thompson-Noel, "Europe's Advertising Is Boring, Trivial and Uninformative," *Financial Times* (London), January 25, 1979.
13. See K. Lewin, "Group Decision Making and Social Change," in T. Newcomb and E. Hartley (eds.), *Readings in Social Psychology* (New York: Holt, Rinehart & Winston, 1947), for the first research on this subject.
14. P. G. Zimbardo, E. B. Ebbesen, and C. Maslach, *Influencing Attitudes and Changing Behavior* (Reading, Mass.: Addison-Wesley, 1977).
15. J. P. Hatfield and R. C. Huseman, "Perceptual Congruence About Communication as Related to Satisfaction," *Academy of Management Journal* 25 (1982): 349–358.
16. J. Lynn and A. Jay (eds.), *The Complete Yes Minister* (London: BBC, 1984).
17. F. H. Goldner, R. Ritti, and T. P. Ference, "The Production of Cynical Knowledge in Organizations," *American Sociological Review* 42 (4) (August 1977): 539–551, offer a roster of considerations for communicators.

Epilogue

1. A. Cooke, *Alistair Cooke's America* (New York: Knopf, 1973), p. 388.
2. P. Kennedy, *Rise and Fall of Great Nations: Economic Change and Military Conflict* (New York: Random House, 1987).
3. P. Sloterdijk, *Critique of Cynical Reason* (Minneapolis: University of Minnesota Press, 1987).
4. M. Seligman, "Boomer Blues," *Psychology Today* (October 1988): 50–55.
5. A. Schlesinger, *The Cycles of American History* (New York: Houghton Mifflin, 1987); quoted in *Newsweek,* January 4, 1988, p. 48.
6. N. Cousins, *An Anatomy of an Illness as Perceived by the Patient* (New York: Norton, 1979); essay from *Outward Bound.*

7.   M. P. Follett, *Freedom and Coordination* (London: Pitman, 1949), from lec-
      tures given in London in 1933; O. Sheldon, *The Philosophy of Management*
      (London: Pitman, 1923).
8.   D. Cooperrider, ''Positive Image, Positive Action: The Affirming Basis
      of Organizing.'' In S. Srivastva and Associates, *Executive Appreciation* (San
      Francisco: Jossey-Bass, forthcoming).
9.   N. Cousins, *An Anatomy of an Illness;* M. Scott Peck, *The Different Drum* (New
      York: Simon & Schuster, 1987); R. Sperry, *Science and Moral Priority* (New
      York: Praeger, 1984); K. Boulding, *The World as a Total System* (Newbury
      Park: Sage, 1985).
10.   A. Inkles, ''Continuity and Change in the American National Character,''
      paper presented to the American Sociological Association, Chicago, 1977.

Name Index

Olsen, K., 210
O'Malley, P. M., 309 n.2
O'Neill, T. P., 85, 306 n.14
O'Toole, J., 308 n.7
Ouchi, W. G., 132, 309 n.6

P

Packard, D., 210
Pallak, M. S., 312 n.9
Palmer, T., 305 n.8
Parton, D., 155
Paycheck, J., 39–40
Peck, M. S., 316 n.9
Peck, S., 282, 283
Perloff, R. O., 312 n.9
Perrot, R., 138
Perrow, C., 306 n.3
Peter, L. J., 122, 308 n.23
Peters, T. J., 129, 133, 217, 309 n.1, 313 n.9
Phares, E. J., 312 n.5
Pickens, T. B., 128, 142
Poole, E. D., 310 n.1
Porter, L. W., 314 n.3

Q

Quelch, J., 305 n.10
Quinn, R. P., 307 nn.1, 4; 310 n.15; 313 n.8

R

Raelin, J., 312 n.11
Raft, G., 40
Reagan, R., 11, 16–17, 84, 86, 128, 133, 142
Regan, D., 87
Regoli, R. M., 310 n.1
Reich, C. A., 115; 308 nn.9, 15, 26; 309 n.17; 310 nn.4, 17
Reich, R., 63, 118, 140–141, 304 n.14, 305 n.7
Reisman, D., 34, 38, 303 n.7
Renoir, 28
Renwick, P. A., 314 n.9
Ritti, R., 315 n.17
Rivers, J., 32
Rockefeller, J. D., III, 309 n.13

Roethlisberger, F. J., 104, 111, 307 n.15, 312 n.9
Roosevelt, F. D., 28, 104, 281
Rosenberg, M., 7, 302 n.6
Rosow, J., 307 n.6, 312 n.4
Rosow, J. M., 305 n.9; 308 nn.8, 10; 311 n.1; 313 n.14
Rosow, M. P., 309 n.2
Rotter, J. B., 312 n.5
Rovere, R., 76, 305 n.5
Roy, D., 311 n.8
Rubenstein, C., 310 nn.18, 20
Ruth, B., 71
Ryan, W., 312 n.3

S

Sacco, N., 71
Samuelson, R. J., 63, 305 n.6
Sarason, S., 72, 89, 305 n.2, 306 n.19, 311 n.3
Schaar, J., 311 n.3
Schein, E., 304 n.5
Schiemann, W. A., 311 n.9, 312 n.10
Schlesinger, A., 281, 315 n.5
Schneider, W., 118, 308 n.14
Schooler, C., 310 n.1
Schrink, J. L., 310 n.1
Schumacher, E. F., 124, 308 n.27
Seashore, S. E., 308 n.20, 312 n.12
Seeman, M., 312 n.2
Seligman, M., 315 n.4
Shakespeare, W., 18
Sheldon, O., 283, 316 n.7
Shklar, J., 303 n.9
Silkwood, K., 155
Sinclair, U., 100, 307 n.10
Slater, P., 306 n.17
Sloterdijk, P., 280, 315 n.3
Smith, A., 18
Smith, A. G., 315 n.7
Smith, B., 19
Smyser, C. M., 312 n.8
Snider, J., 302 n.15
Solly, J. R., 310 n.13
Speakes, L., 87
Sperry, R., 284, 316 n.9
Srivastva, S., 316 n.8
Staines, G. L., 307 nn.1, 4; 310 n.15; 313 n.8

Subject Index

A

Action for Children's Television, 17

Administrative Sideliners, 27, 30–32; attitude of, 168; and authority, 175; and bureaucracy, 108, 276; communication with, 272; as cynical realists, 187; functions of cynicism for, 43–44; and heroism, 222; and hypocrisy, 110, 111; as managers, 67; in technocracies, 126; work ethic of, 200

Advertising, 4, 17–18, 275; Articulate Players in, 275; by Ben & Jerry's, 211–212; of cynical companies, 67

Age: and cynicism, 148–154, 293; in survey sample, 287

Alienation, 6

Allstate Insurance, 76

Ambiguity, in work situation, 264–265

Ambition, 289; channelling, 241–242; unbridled, 56–58; versus complacency, 191, 202–203

America: cynical society of, 71–88; Europeanizing of, 90–94; human relations movement in, 103–111; industrial revolution in, 97–100; optimism about, 279–282; outlook on life in, 184–191; regions of, and cynicism, 164–166; roots of cynicism in, 88–90; signs of cynicism in, 5–7; strengths of, 284–286; unions in, 100–103; work in preindustrial, 95–97; worker attitudes in, 50–51

Apple Computer, 29, 128

Articulate Players, 27, 32–35, 145; and ambition, 57, 202; attitude of, 168; and authority, 175; communication with, 262, 264, 272; as cynical realists, 187; as cynical strivers, 201,

323